LINUX and UNIX
Programming
Tools

A PRIMER
for Software Developers

SYED MANSOOR SARWAR
Lahore University of Management Sciences (LUMS)

KHALED AL-SAQABI
Kuwait University

Addison
Wesley

D0074518

Boston San Francisco New York
London Toronto Sydney Tokyo Singapore Madrid
Mexico City Munich Paris Cape Town Hong Kong Montreal

Senior Acquisitions Editor	Maite Suarez-Rivas
Executive Editor	Susan Hartman Sullivan
Executive Marketing Manager	Michael Hirsch
Editorial Assistant	Maria Campo
Production Supervisor	Marilyn Lloyd
Project Management	Keith Henry/Dartmouth Publishing, Inc.
Composition and Art	Dartmouth Publishing, Inc.
Cover Design	Joyce Cosentino Wells
Design Manager	Gina Hagen Kolenda
Prepress and Manufacturing	Caroline Fell

Access the latest information about Addison-Wesley titles from our World Wide Web site:
http://www.aw.com/cs

Library of Congress Cataloging-in-Publication Data

Sarwar, Syed Mansoor.
    LINUX and UNIX programming tools : a primer for software developers/
    Syed Mansoor Sarwar, Khaled H. Al-Saqabi.
       p. cm.
    Includes bibliographical references and index
    ISBN 0-201-77345-7
       1. Linux. 2. UNIX (Computer file) 3. Operating systems (Computers)
I. Al-Saqabi, Khaled H. II. Title.

QA76.76.O63 S35542 2002
005.4'469—dc21   2002038616

1 2 3 4 5 6 7 8 9 10-MA-06050403

DEDICATIONS

To my children, sisters, and brothers.

To my parents.

S.M.S.

K.S.

PREFACE

WHY WE WROTE THIS BOOK

This concise programming companion prepares students for programming in the LINUX/UNIX environment. Together we have more than 28 years of practical teaching experience at the university level. During these years, we have taught a wide range of courses in programming, data structures, operating systems, and software engineering on UNIX and LINUX platforms. Our desire to write this book came out of our frustration for at not finding a decent and current textbook that describes systematically the LINUX and UNIX programming tools and utilities for compiling multi-module programs, debugging, dealing with libraries, software profiling, and version control. We believe that a book that describes these tools in a detailed and orderly manner and includes pedagogy incorporating in-chapter exercises and useful end of chapter problems and questions was long overdue. *Although almost all of the commands and tools discussed in the book can be used on both LINUX and UNIX, all of our shell sessions were captured under Mandrake and RedHat LINUX systems.*

THE PURPOSES OF THIS BOOK

The book is divided into two parts:—Part I,: "Using LINUX and UNIX Effectively" and Part II, : "Program Development on a UNIX or LINUX Platform." Each part has seven chapters. Part I describes systematically the LINUX and UNIX commands and tools for file, process, and printer control, in addition to describing the logon and logoff procedures, file security, and file system backup and restoration. These commands and tools allow the reader to use his or her LINUX/UNIX system in an orderly, efficient, and secure fashion. The primary purpose of this textbook is to describe some important LINUX and UNIX software engineering tools for developers of C/C++ software; coverage of Java is sometimes included, too. Software engineering tools are described in detail in Part II. The tools covered in Part II include `gcc`, `make`, `ar`, `gdb`, `gprof`, `nm`, `size`, `rcs`, and `cvs`. In writing this textbook we assumed the reader had no previous knowledge of LINUX/UNIX or programming. Because of the breadth and depth of coverage of programming tools, both a novice and experienced programmers can benefit from the book.

OUR INTENDED AUDIENCE

This book is designed to be used as a companion to the main text in introductory programming and data structures courses on a LINUX or UNIX platform or as a supplementary text in advanced programming, introduction to software engineering, and operating systems courses.

THE PRESENTATION FORMAT

The book is laced with diagrams and tables, hundreds of in-chapter interactive shell sessions, in-chapter exercises, and end-of-chapter questions and problems. A syntax box for every command, tool, and application covered in detail describes the syntax of the command, its purpose, its output and its useful options and features. Most chapters contain a table of useful Web resources. In addition, every chapter contains a summary of the material covered in the chapter. A glossary of terms appears at the end of the book.

PATHWAYS THROUGH THE TEXT

If this book is used as a companion to the main text for CSI and CSII courses on LINUX/UNIX, all the chapters except 13 and 14 should be covered. In a data structures course, relevant chapters in Part I should be covered, as well as Chapters 8–12. If the book is to be used as a companion to the main text in a software engineering course, Part II should be covered completely. For use in an operating systems course, chapters 1, 2, 3, 5, and 6 in Part I and Chapters 8, 9, 11, and 13 will be of most help to students.

THE DESIGN AND FONTS

The following typefaces have been used in this book to identify various types of text items.

Typeface	Text Type
Boldface Roman	Keywords
Boldface Monospace	Any character or string typed at the keyboard (commands, shell variables, key presses, and user input)
Monospace	Commands, tools, library functions, system calls, applications, and their options in the text and output of commands, error messages, and the shell prompt
Monospace Italic	A shell or program variable
Italic	A word being used as a word and text being emphasized
Roman	Everything else, including file pathnames

Keyboard presses are enclosed in angle brackets (e.g., <Enter> and <Ctrl-D>). The instruction "press <Ctrl-D>" means to hold the <Ctrl> key down while pressing the <D> key. This instruction is also denoted ^D or <Ctrl-D>.

SUPPLEMENTS

A comprehensive and informational Web site containing solutions to the In-Chapter Exercises, source code, and further references and links to other LINUX and UNIX sites can be found at the Addison Wesley Web Site at www.aw.com/cssupport.

In addition, solutions to the problems at the end of each chapter are available exclusively to professors using this book to teach a course. Please contact your local Addison-Wesley sales representative.

We take full responsibility for any errors in this textbook. We appreciate error reports and comments; please send them to msarwar@lums.edu.pk. We will incorporate your feedback and fix any errors in subsequent editions.

A c k n o w l e d g e m e n t s

We thank everyone at Addison-Wesley who was involved in this project. First and foremost, we convey our sincere thanks to our editor, Maite Suarez-Rivas, who supported our idea of the need for a textbook on LINUX and UNIX programming tools and gave invaluable advice for its timely completion. She gathered a great team to work on the project and we thank every member of the team: Marilyn Lloyd, Regina Hagen Kolenda, Karen Schmitt, and Maria Campo. Special thanks to Keith Henry and the crew at Dartmouth Publishing, Inc. for their excellent work and patience during the production phase of this book.

We sincerely thank the following reviewers who provided valuable feedback and many accurate comments. Their contribution greatly enhanced the quality of the final product.

Yang Wang, Southwest Missouri State University

Adair Dingle, Seattle University

Jozo Dujmovic, San Francisco State University

Charles P. Wright, State University of New York, Stony Brook

George Williams, Union University

Mark Hutchenreuther, P.E., Cal Poly State University

PERSONAL ACKNOWLEDGEMENTS

Syed Mansoor Sarwar This is my third book in as many years and I could not have written it without the support, love, and encouragement of my wonderful family: my beloved parents, my loving wife, my wonderful children—Hassaan, Maham, and Ibraheem—my awesome sisters—Rizwana and Farhana—and my brothers (also my great friends)—Masood, Nadeem, Aqeel, and Nabeel. They all have inspired me in many ways and made a difference in my life. The unending love, affection, inspiration, and guidance of my parents led me to a meaningful life. The love, support, and understanding of my wife and children have been out of this world! They let me work long days and long nights to complete the book. Thank you guys for tolerating me for the past three years! Special thanks to my youngest son, Ibraheem, the "snug-bug" who was born on September 12, 2001, for giving us all love and happiness at some of the most difficult times in our lives. My sisters and brothers have all been extremely generous to me all my life and are my best friends. Thanks for everything!

I also thank the teachers, colleagues, and friends who encouraged and inspired me over the years: Art Pohm and Jim Davis at the Iowa State University; Sabah Al-Fidaghi and Mansoor Jaragh at Kuwait University; Tom Nelson, Robert Albright, Aziz Inan, Peter Osterberg, Bob Koretsky, Matthew Kuhn, Larry Simmons, Zia Yamayee, Kent Thompson, Dales Frakes, Debbie Speer, Kitty Tilton, and Jamie Strohecker at the University of Portland; Ashraf Iqbal, Haroon Babri, Mohammad Ali Maud, and Syed Zahoor Hassan at the Lahore University of Management Sciences (LUMS); and my dear friend Arif Kareem at the Radisys Corporation (who never thought that I could do more than make a rock wall). I also thank my coauther, Khaled Al-Saqabi, for his friendship and love.

viii Acknowledgements

Finally, I want to convey my very special thanks to four very special individuals. First, I am grateful to my uncle Syed Shabbir Hussain ("Shahjee"), an accomplished journalist and writer, for his inspiration as he continues his brave fight with Parkinson's disease. Second, I thank my uncle Syed Nazir Hussain, who supported my father during his studies, and for his love of our whole family. Third, I thank my late grandmother "Bayjee" for being the source of special light to her whole family and for her unending love for my father. Finally, I express my gratitude to my late grandmother "Ammanjee" for her special love for our whole family and for teaching me some of the most important values in my life.

Khaled H. Al-Saqabi I thank my dear parents who didn't spare any effort in bringing me up. I express my sincere thanks to my family for their support over many years and for providing me a convenient atmosphere during my work. I also thank my good friend and the first author of this book, Syed Mansoor Sarwar, for his support and encouragement.

TABLE OF CONTENTS

Chapter 7 File System Backup and Restoration   **139**

Part II: Program Development on a LINUX or UNIX Platform

Chapter 8 Program Development Process   **149**

Chapter 9 Program Generation Tools   **159**

Getting Started

OBJECTIVES

- To describe briefly the history of LINUX and UNIX
- To describe the procedure for logging on and off in LINUX and UNIX
- To explain what a LINUX and UNIX shell is
- To describe briefly some commonly used shells
- To describe briefly the system and shell startup files
- To describe briefly important system setups
- To discuss some useful general-purpose commands for the beginner
- To discuss briefly the shell metacharacters
- To list important Web resources for LINUX and UNIX
- Commands and primitives covered: `!`, `$`, `*`, `[]`, `?`, `~`, `cal`, `cat`, `cd`, `chsh`, `date`, `echo`, `export`, `help`, `lpr`, `ls`, `man`, `mkdir`, `more`, `passwd`, `ps`, `pwd`, `rmdir`, `set`, `tcsh`, `uptime`

1.1   INTRODUCTION

UNIX and LINUX are time-sharing systems. A **time-sharing system** is an interactive system that allows multiple users to use the system simultaneously and each user can run multiple programs. (A running program is known as a process.) UNIX was born in 1969 at Bell Labs and LINUX in 1991 at the University of Helsinki, Finland. Today, millions of users around the world use these systems on their office and home computers. In order to use a LINUX- or UNIX-based computer system, you must have an account on it. Once you log on, the system will run a **command interpreter** called a **shell** that allows you to use the system by typing commands and hitting `<Enter>`. Your work environment is set up for effective, efficient, easy, and secure use of the system and you can change many of the system setups according to your taste. In this chapter, we give a brief history of LINUX and UNIX, describe the logon and logoff procedures, discuss the various LINUX and UNIX shells and important system setups, illustrate the use of some important general-purpose commands for the beginner, discuss the shell metacharacters, and list useful LINUX- and UNIX-related Web sites.

1.2   A BRIEF HISTORY OF THE UNIX AND LINUX OPERATING SYSTEMS

UNIX was written by Ken Thompson and Dennis Ritchie at the Bell Labs in 1969. It was written in the C programming language and had many features of the MULTICS operating system, also developed at the Bell Labs. The development of UNIX continued at the Bell Labs and as a result different editions came out. The sixth edition became quite popular among the academic community because it was available with source code, which allowed development of many practical courses in operating systems and made UNIX the most popular operating system in the academic world during the 1980s. Figure 1.1 describes the three main branches of UNIX systems as they were developed from 1969 to the present.

In response to the changing business environment in the early 1980s, Bell Labs/AT&T licensed further releases of UNIX as System III and finally as System V, starting in 1983. This main branch of UNIX continued to be developed, as shown in Figure 1.1, through System V, Release 4, when it again diverged and evolved to survive as SCO UNIX in the mid to late 1990s. Note that UNIX Support Group (USG), UNIX Software Development Laboratory (USDL), and UNIX System Laboratories (USL) were commercial spin-offs of AT&T. The UNIX Programmer's Work Bench (PWB) was distributed initially through USG.

The University of California Berkeley initiated and maintained the development of UNIX along its second main branch throughout the 1980s and into the 1990s. Contractual agreements made the operating system freely available to universities, so these releases contributed in large part to the further popularization of UNIX. These versions were released as Berkeley Software Distribution, 3BSD and 4BSD-4.4BSD. Most recently, BSD UNIX survives as FreeBSD and NetBSD. One of the most popular commercial UNIX operating systems during the 1990s, Sun Microsystems's Solaris, is based on 4BSD.

LINUX is a child of the Internet. In October 1991, Linus Torvalds, a 21-year-old student at the University of Helsinki, Finland, posted the following message on the comp.os.minix newsgroup:

> I'm doing a (free) operating system (just a hobby, won't be big and professional like GNU) for 386(486) AT clones.

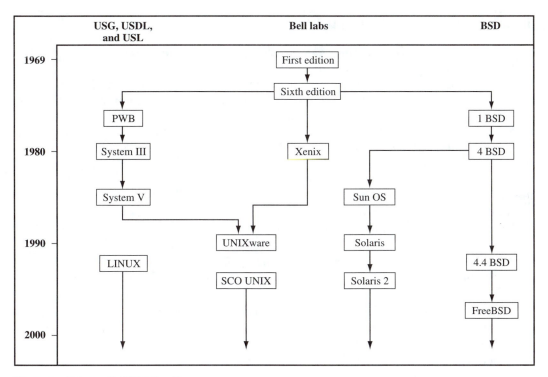

Figure 1.1 Schematic UNIX timeline

Torvalds' "hobby" eventually became what is known as the LINUX operating system. Although LINUX, a UNIX look-alike, is about 12 years old, it has revolutionized the PC and Internet world. Millions of users around the world use LINUX on their home PCs and office workstations.

Initially designed and written for PCs based on Intel CPUs, LINUX now runs on a wide range of hardware platforms, including Alpha, Amiga, Atari, Macintosh, and Sun SPARC. Operating systems for many personal digital assistants (PDAs) use the LINUX kernel as their base. As of this writing, there are more than 250 varieties of LINUX, used on a wide spectrum of hardware platforms, from large 64-bit processor architectures and Internet servers to tiny embedded processors, PDAs, and wristwatches. Some of the major LINUX distributions are Caldera, Mandrake, Red Hat, Slackware, and SuSE. The two popular graphical environments for LINUX are KDE and GNOME. The source codes for the LINUX kernel and many tools developed for it are available from various Web sites free of charge.

LINUX is the most talked about operating system on the Internet. The search for the keyword "LINUX" on the Google search engine (www.google.com) resulted in 55.5 million hits compared to the combined hit total of less than 18 million for all Windows operating systems (3.1, 95, 98, NT, 2000, ME, and XP) combined! It is estimated that about 20 million people around the world use LINUX. This user community is growing rapidly and is presently spread over 200 countries, from Greenland to Antarctica and Mauritania to Japan. Browse the counter.li.org Web site for more information on the worldwide use of LINUX.

1.3 LOGON AND LOGOFF PROCEDURES

The LINUX and UNIX systems are multiprocess, multiuser, and interactive computing environments. *Multiprocess* means that a user can start and run several computational processes or programs at once. *Multiuser* means many users can be using the same system at the same time; logging on and logging off are necessary, because each individual user must identify and differentiate him- or herself on the system when he or she enters and leaves. LINUX/UNIX can be run on a standalone computer, such as a PC, or on a PC that is part of a network, but identification of the individual user via logon is mandatory, because of the access privileges the user is given at logon. For example, certain users need administrative privileges to maintain system integrity and performance, and other users need only to be able to run applications and store files on the standalone computer.

There are two approaches to logging on and logging off a LINUX or UNIX system: a text-based (i.e., commandline) interface or a graphical user interface (GUI). Since this books deals with the commandline interface, we explain the methods of logging on and logging off using a text-based interface. GUI-based methods for logging on and logging off are not any different except that the prompt appears in a window.

A text-based interface logon uses one of three basic methods, or a combination of two or more of them. Variations are affected by the system setup of any single component. The basic methods are as follows.

1. Standalone connection: In the standalone method a computer is dedicated to a single user who logs on to use LINUX or UNIX on that hardware platform only. In fact, the methods 1 and 2, when used with a text-based interface, eventually look and feel exactly like a LINUX or UNIX interaction using this method.

2. Local area network (LAN) connection: In any LAN system the terminal has little or no compute power—it acts as a dumb graphical server—and the computer can serve many such terminals. The terminal is connected via a high-speed communications link to a single computer or to multiple computers that are all interconnected with a LAN, and the terminal is the user's interface to the operating system running on the single or multiple computers. This method could also be called intranet login. A variation of this method involves using a LINUX or UNIX workstation with compute power to log in to a LINUX/UNIX server.

3. Internet connection: The Internet method is similar to LAN login. In its simplest form, a remote, standalone computer, via software such as Windows Telnet for the PC or NCSA Telnet for Macintosh, connects to a LINUX/UNIX system over a high-speed telecommunications link. The telnet software then becomes the graphical server, allowing the user to log in and use a remote computer or system that is running LINUX or UNIX. This method could also be called Internet login. A variation of this method involves using the LINUX/UNIX `telnet` command to establish a connection between a LINUX/UNIX machine acting as a telnet client and a LINUX/UNIX machine acting as a telnet server. For example, if you want to log on to the LINUX/UNIX machine whose **fully qualified domain name** is linux1.someschool.edu, type the command `telnet linux1.someschool.edu.` You will be prompted for login name as if you are using a standalone LINUX/UNIX computer. You can use the **IP address** of the machine in **dotted decimal notation** instead of its domain name, as in `telnet 201.25.10.29`. A variation on this method not covered in this textbook is the use of SLIP or PPP to dial in to a host computer over a telecommunications line.

A combination of the three methods could work as follows: The user sits at a standalone computer that is networked to other computers via a LAN, boots up, and sees the LINUX/UNIX login prompt. The user logs in to this standalone machine, then enables the LAN connection on this standalone computer. The user then types in the LINUX/UNIX `telnet` command to log in to a remote host on the intranet, which is also running LINUX/UNIX, and works with the operating system there. Finally, the user "telnets" from the LAN to a remote site on the Internet and logs in to a computer in a remote location—perhaps even in another country—and works with LINUX/UNIX on that computer. All of these computers are running LINUX/UNIX.

When using any of the three methods or a combination of them to connect to a LINUX/UNIX system, identifying yourself to the system is your first task. Doing so involves typing in a valid username, or login name, consisting of a string of valid characters, associated with a userid given to you by your system administrator. For our purposes, we use the terms *username, login name,* and *userid* interchangeably. You then must type in a valid password for that username. If your username and password check out fine, a shell program starts running. The shell program that runs when you log on, known as your **login shell,** gives you a prompt and waits for your commands. When you type a command and hit **<Enter>**, the shell tries to execute the command. The prompt (a character or a string of characters) depends on what your system administrator has set it to. You can change your default prompt and set it to something that suits your taste.

In the following session, we show a sample logon session on a computer running Mandrake. The password is not displayed in an actual session; we have shown ************** to indicate that you enter your password when the system prompts you for it. The **shell prompt** is **$** in the following session. Depending on the flavor of LINUX/UNIX on your computer system, your login shell, and your system setup, your login message and prompt may be different. The directory that the system places you in after you log on is known as your **login/home directory.** It is denoted by **~** or **$HOME** (**$home** in the TC shell).

```
Linux Mandrake release 6.1 (Helios)
Kernel 2.2.13-4mdksmp on an i686
login: sarwar
Password: **********
Last login: Mon Feb 11 19:32:33 from up
You have mail.

$
```

Your login shell waits for your commands now. Once you have used the system and are ready to call it a day, you should log out. The standard way to log out is to press **<Ctrl-D>** on a new line. The **exit** and **logout** commands also let you log out. When you log out, the system displays the **login:** prompt again, informing you that it is ready to accept another login.

```
$ <Ctrl-D>

login:
```

The following In-Chapter Exercise asks you to practice logon and logoff procedures on your LINUX/UNIX system.

IN-CHAPTER EXERCISES

1.1   Get a user account on your LINUX/UNIX system and practice logon and logoff procedures a few times. Try the various methods to log off. Do they all work? If not, which ones don't? Write down the logon message that appears on your system.

1.4 LINUX/UNIX SHELLS

When you log on, the LINUX/UNIX system starts running a program that acts as an interface between you and the LINUX/UNIX kernel. This program, called the LINUX/UNIX shell, executes the commands that you have typed in via the keyboard. When a shell starts running, it gives you a prompt and waits for your commands. When you type a command and press **<Enter>**, the shell interprets your command and executes it. If you type a nonexistent command, the shell informs you, redisplays the prompt, and waits for you to type the next command. Because the primary purpose of the shell is to interpret your commands, it is also known as the LINUX/UNIX command interpreter. When you get a new account on a LINUX/UNIX system, your default login shell is chosen by the system administrator but you can use the shell of your liking by running an appropriate command as discussed at the end of this section. The Bourne Again shell (Bash), TC shell (Teesh), and Z shell (Zsh) are the most popular LINUX shells. The most popular UNIX shells are Bourne, Bourne Again, Korn, and C shells. We focus on Bash and Teesh in this book. The shell sessions shown in the book were captured under Bash, unless stated otherwise.

A shell command can be internal (built-in) or external. The code to execute an internal command is part of the shell process, but the code to process an external command resides in a file in the form of a binary executable program file or a shell script. Because the shell executes commands entered from the keyboard, it terminates when it finds out that it cannot read anything else from the keyboard. You can so inform your shell by pressing **<Ctrl-D>** at the beginning of a new line. As soon as the shell receives **<Ctrl-D>**, it terminates and logs you off the system. The system then displays the **login**: prompt again, informing you that you need to log on again in order to use it.

The shell interprets your commands by assuming that the first word in a command line is the name of the command that you want to execute. It assumes that any of the remaining words starting with a hyphen (–) are options and that the rest of them are the command arguments. After reading your command line, the shell determines whether the command is an internal or external command. It processes all internal commands by using the corresponding code segments that are within its own code.

1.4.1 SEARCH PATH FOR A SHELL

To execute an external command, your shell searches several directories in the file system structure (see Chapter 2), looking for a file that has the name of the command. It then assumes that the file contains the code to be executed and runs the code. The names of the directories that a shell searches to find the file corresponding to an external command are stored in the shell variable *PATH* (or path in the TC shell). Directory names are separated by colons in the Bash shell and by spaces in the TC shell. The directory names stored in the variable form what is known as the search path for the shell. You can view the search path for your variable by using the *echo $PATH* command in Bash and the *echo $path* command in the TC shell. The following is a sample run of this command under the Bourne Again and TC shells, respectively. Note that in the Bourne Again shell the search path contains the directory names separated by colons and that in the TC shell the directory names are separated by spaces.

```
$ echo $PATH
/usr/sbin:/usr/X11/include/X11:.:/home/faculty/sarwar/bin:/usr/ucb_:/bin:/
usr/bin:/usr/include:/usr/X11/lib:/usr/lib:/etc:/usr/etc:/usr_/local/bin:/
usr/local/lib:/usr/local/games:/usr/X11/bin
$
% echo $path
/usr/sbin /usr/X11/include/X11 . /home/faculty/sarwar/bin /usr/ucb /bin
/usr/bin /usr/include /usr/X11/lib /usr/lib /etc /usr/etc /usr_/local/bin
/usr/local/lib /usr/local/games /usr/X11/bin

%
```

The *PATH* (or *path*) variable is defined in a hidden file (also known as a dot file) called .profile or .login in your home directory. If you can't find this variable in one of those files, it is in the startup file (also a dot file) specific to the shell that you're using. You can change the search path for your shell by changing the value of this variable. To change the search path temporarily for your current session only, you can change the value of *PATH* at the command line and use the **export PATH** command to make the new value of the *PATH* variable available wherever it is accessed in future. For a permanent change, you need to change the value of this variable in the corresponding dot file. In the following example, the search path has been augmented by two directories, ~/bin and . (current directory). Moreover, the search starts with ~/bin and ends with the current directory.

```
$ PATH=~/bin:$PATH:.
$ export PATH
$
```

1.4.2 LOCATIONS OF VARIOUS SHELLS

You can use the **chsh -l** or **cat /etc/shells** command to determine the locations (as absolute pathnames—see Chapter 2) of the shells that are available on your system, as shown in the following session. Both commands produce identical output.

```
$ chsh -l
/bin/sh
/bin/bash
/bin/bash2
/bin/ash
```

```
/bin/bsh
/bin/tcsh
/bin/csh
$
```

The **whereis** command allows you to display the location of a command and other relevant information about it, such as its manual page entry (see Section 1.5). In the following session, we use this command to display the locations of the executable programs (i.e., commands) for Bash and TC shells and their manual pages.

```
$ whereis bash tcsh
bash: /bin/bash /usr/man/man1/bash.1.bz2
tcsh: /bin/tcsh /usr/man/man1/tcsh.1.bz2
$
```

You can determine the name of your login shell by using the **echo $SHELL** command. In this command, *SHELL* is a **shell variable,** a placeholder that is used to store the location of the shell program. In the following session, the login shell is Bash.

```
$ echo $SHELL
/bin/bash
$
```

The following In-Chapter Exercises ask you to identify your login shell and its search path and the locations of all the shells available on your system.

IN-CHAPTER EXERCISES

1.2   What is the name of your login shell? Display the search path for it. If the search path does not include the current directory and /sbin directories, include them in your search path. Write down the set of commands that you used for performing the above tasks.

1.3   Display the locations of all the shells available on your system. What command did you use to perform this task? Write down another command to perform the same task.

1.4.3 WHICH SHELL SUITS YOUR NEEDS?

Most shells perform very similar functions, and knowing the exact details of how they do so is important in deciding which shell to use for a particular task. These functions are interactive command use, the control of command input and output, and programming. Also, some shells are better in shell programming than others. Thus choosing a shell is a matter of preference and need. Whereas Bash and

TC shells have similar features, Bash has more advanced programming features than the TC shell, and both are equally powerful in their interactive use. Bash and C (or TC) shells are the most popular shells on LINUX and UNIX based systems.

1.4.4 VARIOUS WAYS TO CHANGE YOUR SHELL

You can change your shell in one of three ways: (1) by changing to a new default for every subsequent login session on your system; (2) by creating additional shell sessions running on top of, or concurrent with, the default shell; and (3) by changing your shell for only the current login session. The premise of all three methods is that you have confirmed that the shell you want to change to is available on your system. Whether these shells are indeed available for execution is determined by the system administrator on your system.

To change your default shell, after you have logged on type **chsh** and press **<Enter>**. Depending on your system, you will be asked for your login password and be prompted for the name of the shell you want to change to. Type the complete path to the shell you want to change to; for example, **/bin/tcsh** to change to the TC shell. You can use this method only if you are the system administrator, in other words, if you are logged in as the user called root. To create or run additional shells on top of your default shell, simply type the name of the shell program on the command line whenever you want to run that shell. The following session illustrates this method. In this session, your default shell is Bash, which uses **$** as the shell prompt. Your objective is to change to the TC shell, which shows **%** as the shell prompt.

```
$ echo $SHELL
/bin/bash
$ tcsh
% ps
  PID TTY        TIME    CMD
12911  pts/0  00:00:00    bash
12949  pts/0  00:00:00    tcsh
14954  pts/0  00:00:00    ps
%
```

The first command line in this session allows you to determine what your default shell is. The system shows you that this default is set at Bash. The second command line allows you to run the TC shell at the same time as Bash. The fourth line shows that you have been successful, because the **ps** command has listed your current processes, or programs that you are running as **bash**, **tcsh**, and the **ps** command itself. If the TC shell were not available on your system, or were inaccessible to you, you would get an error message after line 3. If your search path does not include **/bin**, you either have to type **/bin/tcsh** in place of tcsh or include **/bin** in your shell's search path and then use the **tcsh** command.

In order to terminate or leave this new, temporary shell and return to your default login shell, press **<Ctrl-D>** on a blank line. If this way of terminating the new shell does not work, type **exit** on the command line and press **<Enter>**. This exits the new shell, and the default shell prompt will appear on the display.

You can also change your shell by using the exec command. For example, if you have determined that your current shell is Bash and you want to change to the TC shell, simply type exec /bin/tcsh on the command line, and you will be running the TC shell instead of Bash. With this method, you cannot go back to your previous shell.

The following In-Chapter Exercise asks you to practice these commands.

IN-CHAPTER EXERCISES

1.4   Practice the shell session described in this section on your system. If your login shell is the TC shell, then use the **bash** (or **/bin/bash**) command to run Bash on top of your login shell.

1.4.5 SHELL STARTUP FILES AND ENVIRONMENT VARIABLES

The actions of each shell, the mechanics of how it executes commands and programs, how it handles command and program input and output (I/O), and how it is programmed are affected by the setting of certain environment variables. Each LINUX/UNIX system has an initial system startup file, usually /etc/profile. This file contains the initial settings of important environment variables for the shell and some other utilities. In addition, there are hidden files, or dot files, for specific shells, which are executed when you start a particular shell. These, also known as shell startup files, are found in a user's home directory (signified by a ~) as ~/.profile, or in a particular shell's profile or login file in each user's home directory. For example, Bash profile and login files are usually named ~/.bash_profile or ~/.bash_login. These hidden files are initially configured by the system administrator for secure use by all users. Table 1.1 lists some important environment variables common to Bash and TC shells; if the TC shell variable name that performs the same function is different, it follows the Bash name.

Table 1.1	Shell Environment Variables
Environment Variable	**What It Affects**
CDPATH	The alias name for directories accessed with the cd command
EDITOR	The default editor you use in programs such as the e-mail program pine
ENV	The path along which LINUX or UNIX looks to find configuration files
HOME	The name of the user's home directory, when the user first logs in
MAIL	The name of the user's system mailbox file
PATH	The directories that a shell searches to find a command or program
PS1, prompt	The shell prompt that appears on the command line; prompt is for TC shell
PWD, cwd	The name of the current working directory; cwd is for TC shell
TERM	The type of console terminal the user is using

When you log on and your login shell is Bash, Bash first executes commands in the **/etc/profile** file, if this file exists. It then searches for the ~/.bash_profile, ~/.bash_login, or ~/.profile file, in this order, and executes commands in the first of these that is found and is readable. When a login Bash exits, it executes commands in the ~/.bash_logout file.

When you start an interactive Bash shell, it executes commands in the ~/.bashrc file, if this file exists and is readable. When started noninteractively to run a shell script, Bash looks for the environment variable **BASH_ENV** to find out the name of the file to be executed.

If your shell is a TC shell, it executes commands in the /etc/csh.cshrc or /etc/.cshrc file, if it exists and is readable. A login shell then executes commands in the /etc/csh.login file, if it exists. Every shell (login or non-login) then executes commands in the ~/.tcshrc file (or the ~/.cshrc file if ~/.tcshrc does not exist), followed by reading the ~/.history file. A login shell then executes commands in the ~/.login and ~/.cshdirs files. When a login TC shell exits, it executes commands in the /etc/csh.logout and ~/.logout files, if they exist and are readable. Table 1.2 shows the names of some important startup files and when they are executed.

The following In-Chapter Exercises allow you to view the settings of your environment variables. They assume you are initially running Bash. If you aren't, change to that shell as shown in Section 1.3.4 before doing the exercises.

IN-CHAPTER EXERCISES

1.5   At the shell prompt, type **set**, then press **<Enter>**. What do you see on your screen display? Identify and list the settings for all the environment variables shown.

1.6   At the shell prompt, type **exec/bin/tsch** and press **<Enter>**. Then type **setenv** and press **<Enter>**. Identify and list the settings for all the environment variables shown.

Table 1.2	Shell Startup Files for Bash and TC Shells
File	**What It Does**
/etc/profile	Executes automatically at login
~/.bash_profile, ~/.bash_login, ~/.profile	Executes automatically at login
~/.bashrc	Executes automatically at shell login
~/.bash_logout	Executes automatically at logout
~/.bash_history	Records last session's commands
/etc/passwd	Source of home directories for ~name abbreviations
~/.cshrc or ~/.tcshrc	Executes at each shell startup
~/.login	Executed by login shell after ~/.cshrc (or ~/.cshrc) at login
~/.cshdirs	Executes after ~/tcsh.login
~/.logout	Executes at logout from C or TC shell

In addition to the shells, several other programs have their own hidden files. These files are used to set up and configure the operating environment within which these programs execute. They are called **hidden files** because when the names of files contained in the user's home directory are listed—for example, with the `ls -l` command and option (see Chapter 2)—these files do not appear on the list. The hidden file names always start with a dot (`.`), as in .profile.

1.5 SOME IMPORTANT SYSTEM SETUPS

For effective, efficient, easy, and secure use of the system, the system administrator sets up your work environment with various system setups. You can change most of the setups to your taste. Some of the setups are your login shell, your **home directory** (also known as your **login directory**), your terminal type, and your user group. You can display the values of all system setups by using the `set` command and the values of specific setups by using the `echo` command. The setups are stored in shell variables. For example, the variable *TERM* contains the type of your terminal. In the following session we use the `set` command to display the values of all system setups and the `echo` command to display the values of the home directory and terminal type, respectively.

```
$ set
BASH=/bin/bash
BASH_VERSINFO=([0]="2" [1]="03" [2]="16" [3]="1" [4]="release" [5]="i586-
   mandrake-linux-gnu")
BASH_VERSION='2.03.16(1)-release'
EDITOR=vi
EUID=121
EXINIT='set redraw'
GROUP=faculty
HISTFILE=/home/faculty/sarwar/.bash_history
HISTFILESIZE=500
HISTSIZE=500
HOME=/home/faculty/sarwar
IFS='
'
KDEDIR=/usr
LANG=C
LD_LIBRARY_PATH=/usr/X11/lib:/usr/lib:/usr/local/lib
LINES=24
LOGNAME=sarwar
MAIL=/var/spool/mail/sarwar
```

```
MAILCHECK=60
MAILER='comp -e vi'
MANPATH=/usr/X11/man:/usr/local/man:/usr/man
OSTYPE=linux-gnu
PATH=/usr/sbin:/usr/X11/include/X11:.:/usr1.d/sarwar/bin:/usr/ucb:/bin:/us
r/bin:/usr/include:/usr/X11/lib:/usr/lib:/etc:/usr/etc:/usr/local/bin:/usr
/local/lib:/usr/local/games:/usr/X11/bin:/usr1.d/sarwar/bin
PS1='$ '
PS2='> '
PS4='+ '
PWD=/home/faculty/sarwar
SHELL=/bin/bash
SIGNATURE=sarwar@egr.up.edu
TERM=vt100
UID=121
USER=sarwar
VISUAL=pico
WWW_HOME=http://www.egr.up.edu/
inbox=/home/faculty/sarwar/Mail/inbox
$
$ echo $HOME
/home/faculty/sarwar
$ echo $TERM
vt100

$
```

You can change your terminal type, login shell, and home directory by setting the shell variables that contain the values of these parameters. In the following session, we change the type of our terminal to ansi. Note that there is no space before or after the equal sign. The **export** command is used to make the new value of the *TERM* variable available wherever it is accessed in future.

```
$ TERM=ansi
$ export TERM
$ echo $TERM
ansi

$
```

The following In-Chapter Exercise asks you to display, identify, and change the names and values of the environment variables on your system.

IN-CHAPTER EXERCISES

1.7   Use the **set** command on your system to display the environment variables on your system. Write down the values of the environment variables listed in Table 1.1. Set your terminal type to ansi. If it is already **ansi**, set it to vt100. Write down the sequence of commands that you used for performing this task.

1.6 USEFUL GENERAL-PURPOSE COMMANDS FOR BEGINNERS

In this section, we discuss briefly a few useful general-purpose commands for the beginner. In order to highlight the purpose of each command, each command is described in a separate section with at least one example.

1.6.1 DISPLAYING THE CURRENT TIME AND DATE

You can use the **date** command to display today's date and current time as shown in the following example.

```
$ date
Tue Feb 12 02:02:12 PST 2002

$
```

1.6.2 DISPLAYING A TEXT FILE

You can use the **cat**, **more**, or **less** command to display the contents of one or more text files. Whereas the **cat** command displays the whole file, the **more** and **less** commands display the file one screen at a time. We discuss these commands in detail in Chapter 2 but show the use of **more** with an example. The more command below is used to display a system setup file in your home directory, called .profile, a screenful at a time. You must hit **<Spacebar>** to display the next page and **<B>** to display the previous page. You need to press **<Q>** to terminate the **more** command gracefully.

```
$ more ~/.profile
LANG=C export LANG       #!@ Do not edit this line !@

#! /bin/sh
PATH=/etc:/usr/etc:/bin:/usr/bin:/sbin:/usr/sbin:/usr/lbin:/usr/local/bin:
  .:$HOME/bin
export PATH

...

$
```

The following In-Chapter Exercise asks you to practice using the **date** and **more** commands.

IN-CHAPTER EXERCISES

1.8 Use the **date** and **more** commands as used in sections 1.6.1 and 1.6.2. What are the contents of your **~/.profile** file? If this file doesn't exist, use the **more** command to display the contents of the **/etc/profile** file.

1.6.3 CREATING A DIRECTORY

You can use the **mkdir** command to create a directory. We discuss this command in detail in Chapter 2 but show a simple use of the command so you can create a directory for your coursework. If you execute the following command on your system without changing your home directory, it creates the courses directory in your home directory. You can create the same directory regardless of the directory you are in by running the **mkdir ~/courses** command.

```
$ mkdir courses
$
```

You can create multiple directories in one command line. The **mkdir personal taxes** command will create the directories personal and taxes in your current directory (see Chapter 2).

1.6.4 DISPLAYING A DIRECTORY

You can use the **ls** command to display the contents of a directory (i.e., the names of files and directories in it). We discuss this command in detail in Chapter 2 but show a simple use of the command so you can get going with your work. The following command displays the contents of your home directory, in other words, the names of all the files and directories in it, including the hidden file. Without the **-a** option, the hidden files are not displayed. Note that **.** (pronounced as "dot") stands for your current directory and **..** (pronounced as "dotdot") stands for the parent of your current directory. We have used **...** to indicate that only partial output has been shown.

```
$ ls -a ~
.                   ..              .addressbook        .addressbook.lu
.bash_history       .bash_logout .screenrc             .bash_profile
courses             ...
...
$
```

You can create multiple directories in one command line, as in **ls ~ /etc** to list the contents of your home directory and the /etc directory. You can use the **ls** command with the **-C** option to display output in multicolumn sorted order and with the **-1** option to display long listings of directory contents (we discuss this option in detail in chapters 2 and 5).

1.6.5 Displaying the Name of Your Current Directory or a Home Directory

You can use the **pwd** command to display the location (absolute pathname—see Chapter 2) of your current working directory. The output the following **pwd** command shows that your current working directory is /home/faculty/sarwar.

```
$ pwd
/home/faculty/sarwar
$
```

You can use the **echo** command to display the location of anybody's home directory by passing it ~username as argument, where username is the login name of the user. The output of the following command shows that the location of kuhn's home directory is /home/faculty/kuhn.

```
$ echo ~kuhn
/home/faculty/kuhn
$
```

In the following In-Chapter Exercises you are asked to use the mkdir, pwd, and ls −a commands to appreciate how they work.

IN-CHAPTER EXERCISES

1.9   Use the mkdir command to create the courses directory in your home directory. What command did you use?

1.10   Display names of all the files in your home directory, including hidden files. Write down the command that you used for this purpose and its output.

1.11   Use the pwd command to display the location of your current directory. What is it?

1.6.6 Changing Directories

You can use the **cd** command to jump from one directory to another. In other words, the command allows you to make a directory your current/working directory. Again, we discuss this command in detail in Chapter 2 but show a simple use of the command so you can move around among your directories. The first **cd** command in the following session makes the ~/course directory your current directory. The first **pwd** command displays that you are presently in the /home/faculty/sarwar/courses directory. The second **cd** command places you in the /etc directory (i.e., makes it your current working directory). The second **pwd** command shows that /home is your current directory at this time. The **ls −C** command is used to display the contents of the /home directory, i.e., your current directory at this time.

```
$ cd ~/courses
$ pwd
/home/faculty/sarwar/courses
$ cd /home
$ pwd
/home
$ ls -C
admin    faculty lost+found        students
$
```

When you run the **cd** command without any argument, it makes your home directory your current directory.

1.6.7 REMOVING DIRECTORIES

You can use the **rmdir** command to remove one or more empty directories. We discuss this command in detail in Chapter 2 but show a simple use of the command so you could remove a directory that you may have created by mistake. The following command will remove the empty courses directory in your home directory.

```
$ rmdir ~/courses
$
```

We discuss the removal of non-empty directories in Chapter 2; discussing it at this juncture may be too dangerous for you!

In the following In-Chapter Exercises you are asked to use the **cd**, **pwd**, and **rmdir** commands to appreciate how they work.

IN-CHAPTER EXERCISES

1.12 Use the **cd** command to make the ~/courses directory your current directory. Use the **pwd** command to display the location of the current directory. Now use the **mkdir** command to create the CS161, CS213, and memos directories in it. What command did you use for performing this task?

1.13 Use the **cd** command to make your home directory your current directory and use the **rmdir** command to remove the memos directory that you created in Exercise 1.11. What command did you use for removing the directory?

1.6.8 Printing Files

We discuss commands related to printing and printer control in detail in Chapter 4 but briefly describe here the commands needed to print files. You can print files by using the lpr command. In the following session the first command line is used to print the lab1 file on the hp2left printer. Note that with the **lpr** command, you need to use the -P option to specify the printer to print on and the -n option to specify the number of copies to print. The second command prints three copies of the UsefulLinux-Commands file on the same printer. Ask your instructor the name of the printer that you can send your files to for printing

```
$ lpr -P hp2left lab1
$ lpr -P spr -n 3 UsefulLinuxCommands
$
```

1.6.9 Getting Help

To get help in using all the LINUX/UNIX commands and their options, go to the LINUX/UNIX Reference Manual Pages. The pages themselves are organized into eight sections according to the topic described and the topics that are applicable to the particular system. Most users find the pages they need in Section 1. Software developers mostly use system and library calls and thus find the pages they need in Sections 2 and 3, respectively. Users who work on document preparation get the most help from Section 7. Administrators mostly need to refer to pages in Sections 1, 4, 5, and 8.

The manual pages comprise multipage, specially formatted, descriptive documentation for every command, system call, and library call in LINUX/UNIX. This format consists of seven general parts: name, synopsis, description, list of files, related information, errors/warnings, and known bugs. You can use the **man** command to view the manual page for a command. Because of the name of this command, the manual pages are normally referred to as LINUX man pages. When you display a manual page on the screen, the top-left corner of the page has the command name with the section it belongs to in parentheses, as in **ls (1)**.

The **man ls** command can be used to display the manual page for the ls command, as shown below.

```
$ man ls

LS(1)                           FSF                           LS(1)


NAME

      ls - list directory contents


SYNOPSIS

      ls [OPTION]... [FILE]...
```

```
DESCRIPTION
        List information about the FILEs (the current directory by
        default).  Sort entries alphabetically if none of -cftuSUX
        nor —sort.

        -a, —all
              do not hide entries starting with .
        -A, —almost-all
              do not list implied . and ..
        -b, —escape
              print octal escapes for nongraphic characters
...
$
```

Because the manual pages are multipage text documents, the manual pages for each topic take more than one screenful of text to display their entire contents. To see one screenful of the manual page at a time, press the space bar on the keyboard. To quit viewing the manual page, press the <Q> key.

If more than one section of the man pages has information on the same word and you are interested in the man page for a particular section, you can use the -S option. The following command line therefore displays the man page for the **read** system call and not the man page for the shell command **read**.

```
$ man —S2 read
[ manual page for the read system call ]
$
```

You can specify the section number without the **—S** option. On such systems, **man 2 read** displays the manual page for the **read** system call. The following command displays the manual pages of the three C library calls, **fopen**, **fread**, and **strcmp**, one by one.

```
$ man —S3 fopen fread strcmp
[manual pages for the fopen, fread, and strcmp C library calls]
$
```

Another example of using the **man** command includes typing the command with the **—k** option, thereby specifying a keyword that limits the search. The search then yields man page headers from all the man pages that contain just the keyword reference. This option is very useful when you don't remember the name of the command you need information about but know the topic that the command deals with. For example, typing `man -k passwd` yields the following onscreen output on our system. (Output on your system may be a bit different.)

```
$ man -k passwd
chpasswd(8)   -      update password file in batch
gpasswd(1)    -      administrate the /etc/group file
mkpasswd(8)   -      update passwd and group database files
nwpasswd(8)   -      change password for a Netware user
passwd(5)     -      password file
yppasswd(1)   -      NIS password update clients
$
```

You can use the `info` command to display the information similar to the `man` command, as in `info mkdir` to display information about the `mkdir` command.

If you want to display information about a built-in (internal) command, you need to use the `help` command. In the following session, we use the `help cd` command to display information about the `cd` command.

```
$ help cd
cd: cd [-PL] [dir]
    Change the current directory to DIR.  The variable $HOME is the
    default DIR.  The variable CDPATH defines the search path for
    ...
$
```

The following In-Chapter Exercise asks you to use the `man` and `help` commands and to note their characteristics.

IN-CHAPTER EXERCISES

1.14 Practice using the commands discussed in the above section to appreciate what the `man` and `help` commands do.

1.6.10 CHANGING YOUR PASSWORD

To maintain the general security of your system and, in particular, to keep your files secure on the system, you should change your initial password. Then perform a password change regularly to ensure that no unauthorized person can gain access to your system. Limit your password by making it easy to remember, not a word in any dictionary in any language, at least six characters long, and a mix of uppercase and lowercase letters, numbers, and punctuation marks.

To change your password, use the **passwd** command, as shown, where your_username is your login name.

```
$ passwd
Changing password for your_username
old password: YourCurrentPassword
new password: YourNewPassword
retype new password: YourNewPassword
Changing password for your_username.
$
```

You now have a new password. If you are running LINUX/UNIX over a network, you may have to use the **yppasswd** or **nispasswd** command instead of the **passwd** command to change your password on all the computers to which you have access on the network.

The following In-Chapter Exercise asks you to use the **passwd** command to change your password.

IN-CHAPTER EXERCISES

1.15 Change your password with the **passwd** command, log out, and log in again with the new password. On some systems you won't be able to use the **passwd** command. If yours is such a system, ask your instructor or system adminstrator why the **passwd** command is disabled.

1.6.11 THE COMMAND HISTORY

The commands (also called events) that you type at your terminal are saved in a history list. The environment variable HISTSIZE can be set to a number to specify the number of commands to save in the history list. The default value is 500.

You can manipulate the history list by using the built-in command history, as shown in the following session. The command output shows four commands or events in the history list.

```
$ history
    1   10:40   ps
    2   10:41   gcc -o lab1 lab1.c -lm
    3   10:43   more /etc/profile
    4   10:51   gcc -o lab1 lab5.c -lpthreads
    5   11:01   echo ~kuhn
    6   11:01   history
$
```

You can invoke any event from the history list by using the **history expansion** feature of the Bash and TC shells. The ! character allows you to specify an event designator for the command to be invoked from the history list. Table 1.3 describes the three most commonly used event designators. With the history list shown above, typing !! will execute the `history` command. Typing `!gcc` and hitting `<Enter>` will invoke the `gcc -o lab1 lab5.c -lpthreads` command. You can invoke the first `gcc` command by typing `!2` and hitting `<Enter>`.

1.6.12 DISPLAYING A CALENDER

The command to display a calendar for a year or a month is `cal`. A brief description of the command follows. The optional parameter month can be between 1 and 12, and year can be from 0 to 9999. If no argument is specified, the command displays the calendar for the current month of the current year. If only one parameter is specified, it is taken as the year. Thus the `cal 3 2003` command displays the calendar for March 2003. Note that the `cal 3` command displays the calendar for year 3 and not for March of the current year. The command `cal 1991` displays the calendar for the year 1991, the year the LINUX operating system was born.

1.6.13 DISPLAYING SYSTEM UP TIME

You can use the `uptime` command to display system up time (the duration of time the system hs been running since it was last booted) and some other useful statistics, such as the number of users currently logged onto the system. The command doesn't require any parameters. The following example shows the output of the command.

```
$ uptime
2:30pm  up 37 day(s),  5:51,  3 users,  load average: 0.09, 0.10, 0.24
$
```

A recent study involving more than 2,400 LINUX machines (http://counter.li.org/reports/uptimes-tats.php) has shown that the average up time for a LINUX machine is more than 38 days. The same study found one LINUX-based machine that had been running for more than three years without crashing! We encourage you to browse the counter.li.com Web site for many interesting statistics on the use of LINUX.

Table 1.3	Commonly Used Event Designators for History Expansion	
Event Designator	**Meaning**	**Example**
`!N`	Reinvoke the event is the `!4` command at line N in the history list	The command at line 4 in the history list
`!!`	Reinvoke the event in the previous `!!` command	The last command that you executed
`!string`	Reinvoke the event in the most recent `!more` command starting with "string" "more"	The most recent command starting with the string (most likely the last more command)

The following In-Chapter Exercises ask you to use the `history`, `cal`, and uptime commands to appreciate their working.

IN-CHAPTER EXERCISES

1.16 Use the `history` command to display your command history and then use the various event designators from Table 1.3 to appreciate how they work.

1.17 Use the `cal` command to display the calendar for the current year and current month. What commands did you use?

1.18 Run the `uptime` command on your system and write down the number of days it has been running for. Record the output of the command.

1.7 SHELL METACHARACTERS

Most of the characters other than letters and digits have special meaning to the shell. These characters are called shell metacharacters and cannot be used in shell commands as literal characters without specifying them in a particular way. Try not to use them in naming your files. Also, when these characters are used in commands, no space is required before or after them. However, you can use spaces before and after a shell metacharacter for clarity.

The shell metacharacters allow you to specify multiple files in multiple directories in one command line. We describe the use of these characters in subsequent chapters, but we give some simple examples here to explain the meanings of some commonly used metacharacters: *, ?, ~, and [ ]. The ? character is a wildcard character that matches any single character and * matches zero or more characters. The ?.txt string can be used for all the files that have a single character before .txt such as a.txt, G.txt, @.txt, and 7.txt. The [0-9].c string can be used for all the files in a directory that have a single digit before .c such as 3.c and 8.c. The lab1\/c string stands for lab1/c. Note the use of backslash (\) to quote (escape the special meaning of) the slash character (/). The following command prints the names of all the files in your current directory that have two-character file names and an .html extension, with the first character being a digit and the second being an uppercase or lowercase letter. The printer on which these files are printed is hp3right.

```
$ lpr -P hp3right [0-9][a-zA-Z].html
$
```

Note that [0-9] means any digit from 0 through 9 and [a-zA-Z] means any lowercase or uppercase letter.

The following command displays the names of all the files in your home directory that end with .c or .C, that is, the names of all your C and C++ source program files.

```
$ ls -C ~/*.[cC]
lab1.c   lab2.c   prog1.C
$
```

1.8 WEB RESOURCES

A huge number of Web repositories are available on the various topics of LINUX, from its history to the structure of an interactive map of its kernel structure. Table 1.4 lists some interesting Web sites that can provide further general and specific information on these topics.

1.9 SUMMARY

Although LINUX is about 12 years old, it is one of the most talked-about operating systems on the Internet. Tens of millions of users around the world use more than 250 varieties of LINUX today. It is used in a variety of devices ranging from powerful computer systems to wristwatches.

Table 1.4	Web Resources for LINUX	
Reference	**URL**	**Description**
1	www.linuxdoc.org	LINUX Documentation Project
2	www.kernel.org	LINUX Kernel Archives
3	www.memalpha.cx/Linux/Kernel	LINUX Kernel Version History
4	www.bitkeeper.com/history/history.gif	Graph of Kernel Releases
5	kernelmapper.osdn.com	An interactive map of the LINUX kernel structure
6	counter.li.org	Statistics and graphs on LINUX use growth rates worldwide
7	www.fokus.gmd.de/LINUX/LINUX-distrib.html	LINUX distributions
8	www.LINUXbase.org	LINUX standard base
9	www.linux.org	A resourceful Web site for LINUX
10	www.gnu.org	GNU/LINUX, an Open Software Project
11	www.opensource.org/history.html	History of the Open Source Initiative
12	www.mandrakelinux.com	Mandrake LINUX Web site
13	www.slackware.com	Slackware LINUX Web site
14	www.caldera.com	Caldera LINUX Web site
15	www.suse.com	SuSE LINUX Web site
16	www.redhat.com	Red Hat LINUX Web site
17	www.wired.com/wired/archives/5.08/linux.html	Article on Linus Torvalds and LINUX
18	www.linuxhq.com	LINUX Headquarters
19	www.linuxjournal.com	LINUX journal Web site
20	www.linuxmall.com	A Web site for various LINUX products
21	www. freahmeat.net	A resourceful Web site for LINUX
22	www. linuxsecurity.com	A resourceful Web site for LINUX Security

When you log on to a LINUX computer, the system runs a program called a shell that gives you a prompt and waits for you to type commands, one per line. When you type a command and hit <Enter>, the shell tries to execute the command, assuming that the first word in the command line is the name of the command. A shell program is therefore also called a command interpreter. A shell command can be built-in or external. The shell has the code for executing a built-in command, but the code for an external command is in a file. To execute an external command, the shell searches several directories, one by one, to locate the file that contains the code for the command. If the file is found, it is executed if it contains code (binary or shell script). The names of the directories that the shell searches to locate the file for an external command make up what is known as the search path. The search path is stored in a shell variable called *PATH* (for the Bourne Again shell) or *path* (for the TC shell). You can change the search path for your shell by adding new directory names in *PATH* or deleting some existing directory names from it.

Several shells are available for you to use. These shells differ in terms of convenience of use at the command line level and features available in their programming languages. The most commonly used shells in LINUX-based systems are the Bourne Again and TC. The Bourne Again shell is the superset of the Bourne shell and has an excellent programming language and rich command-level interface. The TC shell has several of the interactive features that Bash does but its programming features are less powerful.

For effective, efficient, easy, and secure use of the system, the system administrator sets up your work environment with various system setups. These setups are stored in environment variables such as *TERM* (for terminal type). You can change most of the setups per your taste.

There are several hundred commands, utilities, and tools in a typical LINUX system. Some of the most useful for a beginner are `mkdir` (make directory), `rmdir` (remove directory), `cd` (change directory), `ls` (list name of files in a directory), `pwd` (print name of the current/working directory), `lpr` (print files), `cat` (display files at one time), `more` (display files a screenful at a time), `less` (display files a screenful at a time), `cal` (display calendar), `date` (display today's date and current time), and `history` (display command history).

Certain characters, called shell metacharacters, have special meaning to the shell. Because the shell treats them in special ways, they should not be used in file names. If you must use them in commands, you need to quote them so that the shell will treat them literally.

1.10 QUESTIONS AND PROBLEMS

1. Go to the LINUX Documentation Project Web site, listed in Table 1.4, and read the "Manifesto." Describe the purpose of the project in your own words. Print out some of the FAQ and HOW TO documents for later reference.

2. Go to the LINUX Journal Web site (see Table 1.4), and click on the search button at the top of the page. You can enter any search criteria subject you want pertaining to LINUX, and you will get a listing of articles that are pertinent to this subject. Search for articles on Linus Torvalds. How many are there?

3. Browse the counter.li.org Web site and write down how many people are using LINUX in the country of your residence. Write down the names of the three countries that have the most number of LINUX users.

4. Describe the logon and logoff procedures on a LINUX/UNIX system. What are the three ways to log out?

5. What is a shell? What is its purpose? What is a login shell? How can you determine the name of your login shell? Give the command(s) that you can use for this purpose. Give names of three LINUX shells. Which are the most popular? Which shell do you normally use? Why?

6. What are the two types of shell commands? What are the differences between them?

7. Suppose that you want to change your login shell to Bash. What command will you use to do so? What command would you need to use on a networked system?

8. What is the name of the shell variable that holds the name of your login shell? How can you change your login shell under LINUX?

9. What is a login/home directory? How can you determine the name of your home directory? Give the command(s) that you can use for this purpose. Give the command for displaying the location of the home directory for the user david on your system.

10. What is the name of the shell variable that holds the name of your home directory? How can you change your home directory under a LINUX system?

11. What is your terminal type set to? What command did you use to get your answer?

12. What is the search path for a shell? What is the name of the shell variable that is used to maintain the search path for the Bourne Again and TC shells? Where (in which file) is this variable typically located? What is the search path set to in your environment? How did you find out? Set your search path so that your shell searches your current and your ~/bin directories while looking for a command that you type. In what order does your shell search the directories in your search path? Why?

13. Use the **man** command to display the online manual pages of the **grep** command. How many versions of grep does your system support? Write down the names of these versions. How would you display a brief description of the built-in command set?

14. What are hidden files? What are the names of the hidden files that are executed when you log on to a LINUX system?

15. What is a shell startup file? What is the name of this file for the TC shell? Where (in which directory) is this file stored?

16. Suppose that your login shell is a TC shell. You received a shell script that runs with the Bourne Again shell. How would you execute it? Clearly write down all the steps that you would use.

17. Create a directory called linux in your home directory. What command line did you use? What command would you use to create the directories called memos and personal in your home directory?

18. Give a command line for displaying the files lab1, lab2, lab3, and lab4. Can you give two more command lines that do the same thing? What is the command line for displaying the files lab1.c, lab2.c, lab3.c, and lab4.c? (Hint: Use shell metacharacters.)

19. Run the **man ls > ~/ls.man** command on your system. This command will put the man page for the **ls** command in the ls.man file in your home directory. Give the command for printing two copies of this file on a printer in your lab printer. What command line did you use?

20. Give a command line for printing all the files in your home directory that start with the string memo and end with .ps on a printer called tek2left. What command line did you use?

21. What history expansion expression (i.e., event designator) will you use to invoke the last command that you executed? What event designator will you use to invoke the last **make** command that you executed?

CHAPTER **2**

Files and File Processing

OBJECTIVES

- Discuss the LINUX and UNIX file concept and file types supported by LINUX/UNIX

- Describe the LINUX/UNIX file system structure

- Discuss the commonly used commands for creating, copying, moving, and removing directories

- Describe the commands for browsing the file system structure

- Describe the basic file processing operations and related commands

- Commands and primitives covered: `<`, `>`, `>>`, `|`, `cat`, `cp`, `cd`, `chmod`, `file`, `find`, `grep`, `gzexe`, `gunzip`, `gzip`, `ls`, `mkdir`, `more`, `mv`, `nl`, `pico`, `pr`, `rm`, `rmdir`, `vi`, `umask`, `wc`, `which`, `whereis`, `zcat`, `zmore`, `zcmp`, `zgrep`

2.1 INTRODUCTION

Computer system users typically work within a computer's file system structure. Hence, when using a computer system, a user is constantly performing file-related operations: creating, reading, writing/modifying, or executing files. Therefore the user needs to understand what a file is in LINUX and UNIX and how files can be organized and managed. In this chapter we describe the concept of a file in LINUX/UNIX, file types supported by LINUX/UNIX, and the LINUX/UNIX file system structure and how you can browse it. We also discuss the concept of relative and absolute pathnames, the search path for a shell, the creation of files and directories, some of the basic file operations, and the concept of file permission in LINUX/UNIX. The following file- and file system-related operations and aspects are discussed in this chapter.

- the concept of a file in LINUX/UNIX
- file types supported by LINUX/UNIX
- file system organization
- the File System Standard
- the concept of a directory
- creating, removing, moving, and listing directories
- browsing the file system structure
- creating text files
- displaying text files
- copying and moving files
- appending files
- removing /deleting files
- determining file size and other file attributes
- displaying the type of data in a file
- compressing and uncompressing files
- searching for files
- locating commands
- searching files

While discussing these operations, we also describe related commands and give examples to illustrate how these commands can be used to perform the needed operations.

2.2 FILES IN LINUX/UNIX

In LINUX and UNIX, a file is a sequence of bytes. This means that everything on your system, including I/O devices like keyboards, is a file. LINUX and UNIX do not support any file extensions, but you can use any extension for your files, as in memo.bak and prog.exe. Some LINUX/UNIX command do require extensions. For example the `gzip` and `gunzip` commands require the .gz extension. Similarly, all

C programming language compilers such as `gcc` (see Chapters 8–12) require the `.c` extension. LINUX and UNIX do support five file types: **ordinary file, directory, special/device file, named pipe (FIFO),** and **symbolic link.**

Ordinary files include text, graphic, executable, video, music, and postscript files. Directory files (commonly called directories) are containers that allow you to store any type of file, including subdirectories, under them. Special files represent devices such as keyboard, display screen, disks, and tapes. These devices are divided into two types: **character special files** and **block special** files. The character special files correspond to devices that perform character-oriented I/O, such as a keyboard. The block special files correspond to devices that perform I/O in terms of blocks or chunks of bytes, such as a disk drive. We discuss special files further in Section 2.3. A named pipe provides one of the several mechanisms on a LINUX system to allow processes on the same system to communicate with each other. A symbolic link file allows you to "point to" (i.e., reference) a file that may or may not reside under your home directory. It can be created by using the `ln -s` command and stores the pathname for the file it points to. The BSD-based UNIX systems also support a sixth file type, called socket. A socket is an endpoint for communication between processes; the processes may run on the same system or on different systems on a network.

2.3 FILE SYSTEM STRUCTURE

Three issues are related to the file system structure of an operating system. The first is how files in the system are organized from a user's point of view. The second is how files are stored on the secondary storage (usually a hard disk). The third is how files are created, removed, and manipulated. We discuss the first and third issue here; the discussion of the second issue is beyond the scope of this book but you can read any good book on operating system principles to learn about it.

2.3.1 FILE SYSTEM ORGANIZATION

The LINUX/UNIX file system is structured hierarchically (like an upside-down tree). Thus the file system structure starts with one main directory, called the **root directory,** and can have any number of files and subdirectories under it, organized in any way desired. This structure leads to a parent-child relationship between a directory and its subdirectories or files. A typical LINUX system contains hundreds of files and directories, organized as shown in Figure 2.1; the organization of UNIX files and directories is similar.

2.3.2 PATHNAMES: ABSOLUTE AND RELATIVE

A file or directory in a hierarchical file system is specified by a **pathname.** Pathnames can be specified in three ways: (1) starting with the root directory, (2) starting with the present working directory, and (3) starting with the user's home directory. When a pathname is specified starting with the root directory, it is called an **absolute pathname** because it can be used by any user from anywhere in the file system structure. For example, /home/faculty/sarwar/courses/ee446 is the absolute pathname for the ee446 directory under sarwar's home directory. The absolute pathname for the file called mid1 under sarwar's home directory is /home/faculty/sarwar/courses/ee446/exams/mid1.

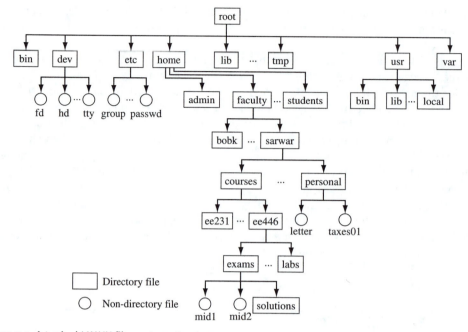

Figure 2.1 A typical LINUX file system structure

Pathnames starting with the present working directory or a user's home directory are called relative pathnames. When the user sarwar logs on, the system puts him into his home directory, /home/faculty/sarwar. The absolute pathname for a user's home directory is stored in a shell variable **HOME** (or home in TC shell). While in his home directory, sarwar can specify the file mid1 (see Figure 2.1) by using a relative pathname: ./courses/ee446/exams/mid1 or courses/ee446/exams/mid1. Sarwar (or anyone else) in the directory ee446 can specify the same file with the relative pathname exams/mid1. The owner (or anyone logged on as the owner) of the mid1 file can also specify it from anywhere in the file structure by using the pathname ~/courses/ee446/exams/mid1 or $HOME/courses/ee446/exams/mid1 (under the TC shell use $home in place of $HOME).

A typical LINUX/UNIX system has several disk drives that contain user and system files, but as a user, you don't have to worry about which disk drive contains the file that you need to access. In LINUX/UNIX, multiple disk drives and/or disk partitions can be **mounted** on the same file system structure, allowing their access as directories and not as named drives A:, B:, C:, and so on, as in MS-DOS and Microsoft Windows. Files and directories on these disks and/or partitions can be accessed by specifying their pathnames as if they were part of the file structure on one disk/partition. Doing so gives a unified view of all the files and directories in the system, and you don't have to worry about remembering the names of the drives and files (and directories) they contain.

2.3.3 HOME AND PRESENT WORKING DIRECTORIES

When you log on, the LINUX/UNIX system puts you in a specific directory, called your **home/login directory**. For example, the directory called sarwar in Figure 2.1 is the home directory for the user with login sarwar. While using the Bash or TC shell you can specify your home directory by using the tilde (~) character. The directory that you are in at any particular time is called your **present working directory** (also known as your **current directory**). The present working directory is also denoted **.** (pronounced dot). The parent of the present working directory is denoted **..** (pronounced dotdot).

You can use the **echo** and **pwd** commands to display the pathnames for your home or current working directory. In the following session, the first command is used to display the home directory and the second to display the current working directory. This example assumes that you are not in your home directory when these commands were executed. You can use the **pwd** command right after logging on to display the pathname of your home directory.

```
$ echo $HOME
/home/faculty/sarwar
$ pwd
/home/faculty/sarwar/courses
$
```

2.3.4 SEARCH PATH

The names of the directories that a shell searches to find the file corresponding to an external command comprise the **search path** for the shell. The search path for Bash is stored in the shell variable *PATH* and for TC shell in **path**. The directory names are separated by colons in Bash and by spaces in the TC shell. You can display your shell's search path by using the **echo $PATH** command in Bash and the **echo $path** command in the TC shell. The *PATH* (or *path*) variable is defined in a hidden file (also known as a dot file) called .profile or .login in your home directory. If you can't find the variable in one of those files, it is in the startup file (also a dot file) specific to the shell that you're using. You can change the search path for your shell by changing the value of this variable. To change the search path temporarily for your current session only, you can change the value of *PATH* at the command line and run the **export PATH** command to make the new value of the *PATH* variable available wherever it is accessed in future. For a permanent change, you need to change the value of this variable in the corresponding dot file. In the following example, the search path has been augmented by three directories, ~/bin, /sbin, and . (current directory). Moreover, the search path starts with ~/bin and ends with the current directory.

```
$ PATH=~/bin:/sbin:$PATH".
.
$ export PATH
$
```

2.4 SOME STANDARD DIRECTORIES AND FILES IN LINUX

Every LINUX system contains a set of standard files and directories organized according to the **File System Standard** (**FSSTND**) proposed in 1994. The standard directories contain some specific files. We describe briefly the purpose of each directory. The file system structure used by UNIX is similar.

Root directory (/)

The root directory is at the top of the file system hierarchy and is denoted as a slash (/). It contains some standard files and directories and, in a sense, it is the master cabinet that contains all drawers, folders, and files.

/BIN

Also know as the binary directory, the **/bin** directory contains binary (executable) images of most essential LINUX/UNIX commands for system administrators and users. Some of the general purpose commands in this directory are **bash, cat, chmod, cp, date, echo, kill, ln, ls, mail, mkdir, more, mv, ps, pwd, rm, rmdir, sh, stty, su, tcsh, uname,** and **vi.** Some of the commands for system restoration include **tar, gzip, gunzip,** and **zcat.** The /bin directory also contains some of the necessary networking commands, including **domainname** (or **nisdomainname**), **hostname, netstat,** and **ping.** The /usr/bin directory contains most of the user commands.

/BOOT

This directory contains all the files needed to boot the LINUX system, including the binary image of the LINUX kernel. (Some systems store the configuration files and kernel map in some other directories.) The kernel file name is vmlinux (or vmlinuz), followed by the version and release information. For example, on Red Hat LINUX 6.1, the kernel is in the /boot/vmlinux-2.2.5-15 file.

/DEV

The /dev directory, which is also known as the device directory, contains files corresponding to the devices (terminal, disk drive, CD-ROM drive, tape drive, modem, printer, etc.) connected to the computer. These files are also known as *special files,* and are divided into two groups: *character special files* and *block special files.* Some of the files in this directory are cdrom (for CD-ROM drive), console (for the console), fd (for floppy drive), hd (hard disk or a partition on a hard disk), isdn (for an ISDN connection), lp (for line printer), midi (for a midi interface), pty (pseudo terminal), ram (for a ram disk), and tty (for a terminal). A system may have several devices of each type. On a network-based system that the author uses, there are a total of 2,361 files in the /dev directory. The Red Hat 6.1 LINUX created 5,052 files in this directory, including 509 for hard disk drives/partitions and 20 for RAM disks.

/ETC

The /etc directory contains host specific files and directories. These files and directories contain system configuration files; they do not contain any binaries. The files in this directory are primarily for the use of the system administrator; however, an average user has read permission for most of these files. Some of the general files and directories in this directory are X11, bashrc, csh.login crontab, group, inittab, lilo.conf, linuxconf, localtime, motd, passwd, pine.conf, profile, securetty, shells, skel, syslog.conf, ttytype, and zshrc. The X11 directory contains the configuration files for the X Window System. Some of the networking-related files and directories in /etc are exports, ftpusers, gateways, host.conf, hosts, hosts.allow, hosts.deny, hosts.equiv, hosts.lpd, httpd, inetd.conf, inputrc, lynx.cfg, mail, mail.rc, networks, news, printcap, protocols, rc.d, resolv.conf, rpc, services, snmp, and uucp. Discussion of most of the files in this directory is beyond the scope of this textbook. We briefly discuss the /etc/passwd file toward the end of this section.

/HOME

The /home directory contains users' home directories. However, the setup for this file differs from host to host. On small systems, this directory contains the home directories for the users, such as /home/bobk. On large systems where home directories are shared by hosts by using the NFS protocol, the user home directories are usually subdivided into many groups of users such as /home/admin, /home/faculty, /home/staff, and /home/students. There are local variations to this scheme. In the system used by the authors, there are 43 subdirectories under /home that contain users' home directories, each containing home directories for administration, staff, students, and faculty belonging to various departments.

/LIB

The /lib directory contains a collection of related object image files for a given language in a single file called an **archive.** A typical LINUX/UNIX system contains libraries for C, C++, and FORTRAN. The archive files for one of these languages can be used by applications developed in that language. This allows software developers to use the prewritten and pretested functions in their software. The library images in the /lib directory are needed to boot the system and run some commands. In particular, it contains the standard C library /lib/libc.so.*, the math library libm.so.*, the shared dynamic linker /lib/ld/so, and some other shared libraries that are used by the commands in /bin and /sbin. The /lib/modules directory contains loadable kernel modules. Most of the remaining libraries are stored in the /usr/lib directory, but /lib contains all essential libraries.

/LOST+FOUND

The /lost+found directory contains all the files on the system not connected to any directory. A LINUX and UNIX tool, **fsck** (file system check), finds these files, which system administrators use to check a file system. System administrators decide the fate of the files in this directory.

/MNT

The /mnt directory is primarily used by system administrators to temporarily mount file systems by using the **mount** command. This directory on our system contains the cdrom, disk, and floppy mount points. Thus mounting of a device, such as a CD-ROM drive, allows you to access the files on a CD-ROM as files under the /mnt/cdrom directory.

/OPT

The /opt directory is used to install add-on software packages. The programs to be invoked by the users for a package should be located in the /opt/package_name/bin directory, where package_name is the name of the installed package. The manual pages for the package are located in the /opt/package_name/man directory.

/PROC

The /proc directory contains process and system information.

/ROOT

The `/root` directory is used on many LINUX systems as the home directory of the root account. This directory is completely protected from normal users.

/SBIN

The directories /sbin, /usr/sbin, and /usr/local/sbin contain system administration tools, utilities, and general root-only commands. Some of the general root-only commands in /sbin are `getty, init, update, mkswap, swapon,` and `swapoff.` The commands for halting the system are: `halt, re-boot,` and `shutdown.` The utilities for file system management are: `fdisk, fsck, fsck.ext2, fsck.minix, mkfs, mkfs.ext2, mkfs.minix, mkfs.msdos,` and `mkfs.vfat.` The minimum set of networking commands in `/sbin` are `ifconfig` and `route.`

/TMP

Used by several commands and applications, the /tmp directory contains temporary files. You can use this directory for your own temporary files as well. All the files in this directory are deleted periodically so that the disk (or a partition of disk) doesn't get filled with temporary files. The life of a file in the /tmp directory is set by the system administrator and varies from system to system, but is usually only a few minutes. On most systems the sticky bit is set for /tmp so that only the owner of a file can remove a file in it.

/USR

The /usr directory contains one of the largest sections of the LINUX/UNIX file system. It contains read-only data that can be shared between various hosts. On most LINUX systems, /usr contains at least the following subdirectories: X11R6, bin, doc, games, include, lib, local, man, sbin, share, src, and tmp. Table 2.1 gives a brief description of what these directories contain.

/VAR

The /var directory is used to contain the variable data (the data that keeps changing while the system is running). This data is maintained in several subdirectories but the discussion of most of the subdirectories is beyond the scope of this book. One of these directories is /var/spool/mail, which contains your incoming mail. When you read your new mail, it comes from a file in this directory set aside to contain your incoming mail. Once you have read the mail, it is put in a file in your home directory called mbox.

Table 2.1	Main Subdirectories in /usr
Subdirectory	**Contents**
X11R6	The X Window System, version 11 release 6, and files related to it
bin	Most of the user commands. It also contains interpreters such as perl, python, and tcl.
doc	Documentation for various tools, utilities, libraries, applications, and interpreters such as cc, gcc, Xfree86, GNOME, Mesa, and zsh.
games	Executables for games and educational software
include	C/C++ header files and directories that contain some specific header files, such as header files needed for writing network applications (/usr/include/netdb, /usr/include/netinet, etc.), GNU C++ header files (/usr/include/g++), and system specific header files (/usr/include/sys)
lib	Object files, libraries, and internal binaries (not to be executed directly by users or shell scripts). Some subdirectories contain libraries for specific tools or applications, such as gcc-lib, gnome-libs, netscape, perl5, tcl8.0, and xemacs.
local	Software (binaries and data) installed locally by the system administrator to be shared between hosts. Most systems contain the following directories under this directory: bin, doc, etc, games, lib, man, sbin, share, and src
man	The manual pages for the LINUX and UNIX commands, utilities, tools, and applications
sbin	Any non-essential commands and tools used by the system administrator and daemons
share	Read-only architecture independent data files, that is, data files that can be shared by various platforms (Pentium, Alpha, Sparc, etc.) for a given same OS
src	The source code for LINUX/UNIX and package management software (e.g., RPM: Red Hat Package Management)
tmp	A symbolic link to /tmp

/ETC/PASSWD

The /etc/passwd file contains one line for every user on the system and describes that user. Each line has seven fields, separated by colons. The following is the format of the line.

login_name:dummy_or_encrypted_password:user_ID:group_ID:user_info:home_directory:login_shell

The login_name is the login name by which the user is known to the system and is what the user types to login. The dummy_or_encrypted_password field contains the dummy password x (or *) or encrypted version of the password. If dummy passwords are stored in the /etc/passwd file, then the encrypted passwords are stored in /etc/shadow. The user_ID is an integer between 0 to 65535 assigned to the user; 0 is assigned to the superuser and 1–99 are reserved. The group_ID identifies the group that the user belongs to, and is also an integer between 0 and 65535 with 0–99 reserved. The user_info field contains information about the user, typically the user's full name. The home_directory field contains the absolute pathname for the user's home directory. The last field, login_shell, contains the absolute pathname for the user's login shell. The command corresponding to the pathname specified in this field is executed by the system when the user logs on. Back to back colons mean that the field value is missing, which is sometimes the case with the user_info field. The following line from the /etc/passwd file on our system is for the user davis.

davis:x:134:105:James A Davis:/home/student/davis:/bin/bash

In this line, the login name is davis, the password field contains x, the user ID is 134, the group ID is 105, the personal information is the user's full name James A Davis, the home directory is /home/student/davis, and the login shell is /bin/bash.

2.5 DIRECTORY OPERATIONS AND BROWSING THE FILE SYSTEM STRUCTURE

While using a LINUX or UNIX system, you normally create ordinary files by using tools such as editors and compilers. For example, you can use a text editor to create the source code file for your software in a particular programming language such as C, C++, and Java. Once you have created the source code, you can compile it to generate the executable (binary) code for it.

In order to organize your work systematically, you should create and maintain a hierarchical directory structure under your home directory. This requires operations of creating, copying, moving, and removing directories. So that you can move around your directory hierarchy, you need to be able to get into a directory and browse it. LINUX/UNIX provides commands for performing all of these tasks.

2.5.1 CREATING AND REMOVING DIRECTORIES

You can create a directory by using the `mkdir` command and remove an empty directory with the `rmdir` command. Both commands work with absolute or relative pathnames. Here are brief descriptions of these commands.

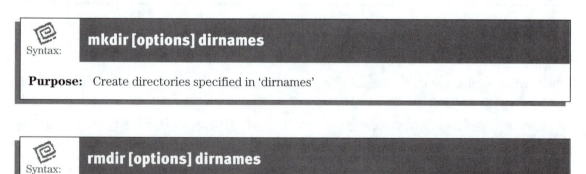

Syntax: **mkdir [options] dirnames**

Purpose: Create directories specified in 'dirnames'

Syntax: **rmdir [options] dirnames**

Purpose: Remove the empty directories specified in 'dirnames'

When executed with the **–p** option, these commands allow you to create and remove a sequence of directories with the parent-child relationship.

In the following session, the first command creates the courses directory in your current directory. The second command creates the cs475 directory under the newly created courses directory. The third command creates the personal directory under your current directory and the taxes directory under it. The fourth command removes the ~/temp directory. The last command removes all the directories in the pathname ~/personal/letters/travel, provided that they are empty. If any directory along the path is not empty, an error message is displayed.

```
$ mkdir courses
$ mkdir courses/cs475
$ mkdir -p personal/taxes
$ rmdir ~/temp
$ rmdir -p ~/personal/letters/travel
$
```

A nonempty directory (or directory hierarchy) can be removed with the **rm -r** command, as in **rm -r** courses. With the **rm -ir** command, you are prompted for permission to remove, and with **rm -rf**, the whole hierarchy is removed silently, without giving you any clues!

2.5.2 Moving and Copying Directories

You can move a directory to another location by using the **mv** command. If the destination is a directory, the source directory is moved under it. If the destination directory does not exist, it is created and contains the contents of the source directory. If the destination is a file, the source directory cannot be moved and an error message is displayed to inform you accordingly. Here is a brief description of the **mv** command.

Syntax:
mv [options] file1 file2
mv [options] file-list directory

Purpose: First Syntax: Move file1 to file2 or rename file1 as file2
          Second Syntax: Move all the files in 'file-list' to directory

Commonly used options/features:
    -f   Force the move regardless of the permissions of the destination file
    -i   Prompt the user before overwriting the destination down the search area

You can use the **cp -r** command to copy a directory hierarchy, along with its contents. Whether you use the **mv** or **cp -r** command, the timestamps for files change to current time. In the following session, we show the use of these commands. The first command moves the temp directory to the home directory. The second command generates an error message because destination (file1) is not a directory. The last command copies the complete directory hierarchy under (and including) the courses directory under your home directory as the courses.bak directory.

```
$ mv temp1 ~
$ mv dir1 file1
mv: cannot create directory `file1': File exists
$ cp -r courses ~/courses.bak
$
```

2.5.3 BROWSING THE FILE SYSTEM STRUCTURE AND LISTING DIRECTORIES

The **cd** command allows you to hop around in the directory structure. When executed without an argument, it puts you in your home directory. You can display the absolute pathname of your current directory by using the **pwd** command and the contents of a directory (the files and directories in it) with the **ls** command. The **ls** command is perhaps the most used LINUX and UNIX command and can be used with many options. Here is a brief description of this command.

Syntax: **ls [options] [pathname-list]**

Purpose: Display the names of the files in the directories and files in 'pathname-list'

Commonly used options/features:

−F	Display / after directories, * after binary executables, and @ after symbolic links
−a	Display names of all the files, including hidden files ., .., etc.
−i	Display long list that includes access permissions, hard link count, owner, group, file size (in bytes), and modification time

---

When used without an argument, this command displays the names of files and directories in your current directory. Some of the commonly used options of this command and their meaning are listed in Table 2.2. The **ls** command is mostly used with the **−l** option. We describe the output of the **ls −l** command in Section 2.6.2.

Table 2.2	Commonly Used Options of the `ls` Command with Their Meaning
Option	**Meaning**
-l	Display long listing of the files (of all types, except hidden files) in a directory
-a	Display all the files in a directory including the hidden files
-d	Display the long listing of a directory (and not its contents); usually used with the -l option as -ld
-t	Display files according to their timestamp (modification time) with the most recently modified file listed first; the -r option can be used to list files in the reverse order
-q	Display files according to their access time (and not modification time)
-s	Display files according to their size (as 1k blocks)

The -ltr options can be used to display the long listing of directories in the reverse order of their modify time. When used without a directory argument, the command lists the contents of the current working directory.

In the following session we show the use of these commands. The **cd** command without an argument places you in your home directory. The `ls -ld ~/temp` command displays the long listing of the ~/temp directory. The **cd courses/cs475** command puts you in the courses/cs475 directory under your home directory. The **pwd** command displays the absolute pathname of your current directory. The **cd** command following the **pwd** command places you in your home directory. The output of the **ls** command shows the names of the files in your current directory (which is also your home directory at this time). This listing does not include the hidden files (i.e., files whose names start with a dot) such as .bashrc. The `ls -a ~` command displays the names of all the files in your home directory, including the hidden files, the ones that start with a dot (.).

```
$ cd
$ ls -ld ~/temp
drwx------    2 sarwar    faculty    512 Oct  6 12:45
   /home/faculty/sarwar/temp
$ cd ~/courses/cs475
$ pwd
$ cd ..
$ pwd
/home/faculty/sarwar/courses
$ cd
$ ls
bin  books  courses  linuxtools  mail  personal  temp
```

```
$ ls -a ~
.                    .bash_profile    .emacs          .gtkrc          .nautilus
..                   .bashrc          .gconf          .ICEauthority   .pinerc
.addressbook         bin              .gconfd         input.c         .sawfish
.addressbook.lu      books            .gnome          .kde            .screenrc
.bash_history        cvsroot          .gnome-desktop  linuxtools      .Xauthority
.bash_logout         .ddd             .gnome_private  mail            .xsession-
   errors
$
```

In the following In-Chapter Exercises, you will browse the file system of your LINUX/UNIX machine, locate some information in it, and display and change your shell's search path.

IN-CHAPTER EXERCISES

2.1   Browse your LINUX/UNIX file system and find out the name of the file that contains the LINUX or UNIX kernel. What is the absolute pathname of this file?

2.2   Search the /etc/passwd file to locate the line for your user name. Write down this line. What are your user ID, group ID, home directory, and login shell?

2.3   Display your shell's search path with the **echo $PATH** (or **echo $path**) command. Then augment the search path so that it includes your home and current directories.

2.6 FILE PROCESSING

We now describe how text files can be created and manipulated in LINUX and UNIX, how you can obtain information about the attributes of a file (of any type), and how you can protect your files.

2.6.1 CREATING FILES

You can create text files in LINUX or UNIX by using a text editor. LINUX/UNIX has several native and non-native text editors such as **emacs, pico, vi, vim,** and **Xemacs.** A brief description of the vi and pico editors is given in Appendix A.

2.6.2 DISPLAYING FILE TYPE AND TYPE OF DATA IN A FILE

While browsing a file system structure, sometimes you need to display the type of a file. You can display a file's attributes, including its type, with the **ls -l** command. The output of this command contains one line per file with the first character specifying the type of the file. Without an argument, this command uses the current directory as its argument. Table 2.3 shows the type character and its meaning.

Table 2.3	File Type Character in the Output of `ls -l` Command and Its Meaning
Type Character	**Meaning**
–	ordinary file
b	block special file
c	character special file
d	directory
l	symbolic link
p	named pipe (FIFO)

In the following session, we use the `ls -l` command to display the types of the files in the ~/sample directory. The meaning of each field is described at the bottom of the session. The output of the command shows that books is a directory, input.c is an ordinary file, and dir1 is a symbolic link file.

```
$ ls -l ~/sample
lrwxrwxrwx   1   sarwar   faculty      4   Apr 28  13:12   bin -> /bin
drwxrwxr-x   2   sarwar   faculty   4096   Apr 28  10:10   books
-rw-rw-r--   1   sarwar   faculty    213   Apr  1  11:03   input.c
$
```

| File type and permissions | Hard link count | Owner | Group | Size (in bytes) | Timestamp | File name |

If you want to know the type of data stored in a file, you can use the `file` command.

In the following session, the file cat.man.gz command informs us that cat.man.gz contains data compressed with the `gzip` command and the file banner command displays that the banner file is an executable file on an Intel CPU-based machine. You can use the `file ~/*` command to display the types of data contained in all the files in your home directory.

```
$ file cat.man.gz
cat.man.gz: gzip compressed data, deflated, original filename, `cat.man',
last modified: Sun Apr 28 16:22:05 2002, os: Linux
$ file banner
banner: ELF 32-bit LSB executable, Intel 80386, version 1, dynamically
linked (uses shared libs), not stripped
$
```

In the following In-Chapter Exercises, you will use the `ls` and `file` commands to appreciate the type of output they generate.

2.6.3 VIEWING COMPLETE FILES

You can display the complete contents of one or more files on screen by using the **cat** command if you have the read permission for the file (see Chapter 5 for file access permissions). Here is a brief description of the command.

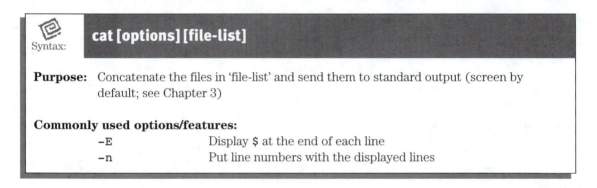

Syntax: **cat [options] [file-list]**

Purpose: Concatenate the files in 'file-list' and send them to standard output (screen by default; see Chapter 3)

Commonly used options/features:

`-E`	Display $ at the end of each line
`-n`	Put line numbers with the displayed lines

Because this command does not display file contents one screen or page at a time, you see only the last page of a file that is larger than one page in size. For example, the following command displays the contents of the student_records file in the present working directory. If the file is larger than one page, the file contents quickly scroll off the display screen.

```
$ cat student_records
John    Doe    ECE    3.54
Pam     Meyer  CS     3.61
Jim     Davis  CS     2.71
Jason   Kim    ECE    3.97
Amy     Nash   ECE    2.38
$
```

The `cat ~/courses/ee446/labs/lab1 ~/courses/ee446/labs/lab2` command displays the contents of files lab1 and lab2 in the directory ~/courses/ee446/labs. The command does not pause after displaying the contents of lab1.

You can use shell metacharacters to specify file names. The contents of all the files in the current directory can be displayed by using the `cat *` command. The `cat exam?` command displays all the files in the current directory starting with the string exam followed by one character. The contents of all the files in the current directory starting with the string lab can be displayed by using the `cat lab*` command. The `cat prog[1-3].C` command can be used to display files prog1.C, prog2.C, and prog3.C.

When the `cat` command is used without an argument, it takes input from standard input one line at a time and sends it to standard output. By default, standard input for a command is the keyboard and standard output is the display screen. Therefore, when the `cat` command is executed without an argument, it takes input from the keyboard and displays it on the screen one line at a time. The command terminates when the user presses `<Ctrl-D>`, the LINUX/UNIX end-of-file marker, on a new line.

At times you need to display the contents of a file with line numbers. You typically need to do so when, during the software development phase, a compilation of your source code results in compiler errors containing line numbers of the source program. You can use the `cat –n` or `nl` command to display lines in a file with line numbers, as in `cat –n lab1.C` or `nl lab1.C`. You can display files with a page header containing a time stamp, file name, and page number with the `pr` utility, as in `pr lab1.C`. We discuss the `pr` command further in Chapter 4.

You can use the `tac` (reverse of `cat`) command to display files in the reverse order.

2.6.4 VIEWING FILES ONE PAGE AT A TIME

If the file to be viewed is larger than one page, you can use the `more` or `less` command, also known as the LINUX/UNIX pagers, to display the file a screenful at a time. We discuss these commands one by one.

When run without a file argument, the more command, like the `cat` command, takes input from the keyboard one line at a time and sends it to the display screen. If file-list (a list of file names separated by spaces) is given as an argument, the command displays the contents of the files in file-list one screen at a time. To display the next screen, press the `<space bar>`. To display the next line in the file, press `<Enter>` (or `<Return>`). At the bottom left of a screen, the command displays the percentage of the file that has been displayed up to that point. To return to the shell, press the `<Q>` key. Here is a small description of the `more` command.

Syntax:

more [options] [file-list]

Purpose: Concatenate the files in file-list and send them to standard output (screen by default; see Chapter 3) a screenful at a time

Commonly used options/features:

`+/str`	Start two lines before the first line containing *str*
`-nN`	Display N lines per screen
`+N`	Start displaying the contents of the file at line number N

The **more sample letter memo** command displays contents of the files sample, letter, and memo in the present working directory a screenful at a time. The files are displayed in the order in which they are listed in the command.

The **more -n20 /usr/include/sys/param.h** command displays the contents of the /usr/include/sys/param.h file one page at a time with 20 lines per page.

The **less** command is similar to the **more** command but has more features. The **less** command can also be used to view a file page by page. It is similar to the **more** command but is more efficient and has many features that are not available in **more**. It has support for many of the **vi** command mode commands. For example, it allows forward and backward movement of file contents one or more lines at a time, redisplaying the screen, and forward and backward string search. It also starts displaying a file without reading the entire file, which makes it more efficient than the **more** command or the **vi** editor for large files. Here is a small description of the **less** command.

Syntax: **less [options] [file-list]**

Purpose: Display files in file-list one screenful at a time

Commonly used options/features:

-N	Display line numbers
-o file	When input is coming from a pipe, send output to 'file' as well as to screen; if 'file' exists, prompt for overwriting
-p pattern	Search for the first occurrence of 'pattern' in the file

---

While you are viewing a file with the **less** command, you can use a number of commands to browse through the file and perform other operations on it.

In the following session, we use the **less** command to display the bash.man file and use **!ps** to execute the shell command **ps** while the **less** command is still running. The **q** command is used to quit **less.** The **-N** option is used to display lines in the bash.man file with line numbers.

```
$ less -N bash.man
    1
    2
    3
    4    BASH2(1)                              BASH2(1)
    5
    6
    7    NAME
    8         bash2 - GNU Bourne-Again SHell
```

```
  9

 10   SYNOPSIS

 11        bash2 [options] [file]

 12

 13   COPYRIGHT

 14        Bash is Copyright (C) 1989-1999 by the Free

 15        Software Foundation, Inc.

 16

 17   DESCRIPTION

 18        -Bash is an sh-compatible command language
...
!ps
  PID TTY        TIME CMD
29181 pts/3 00:00:00 csh
29214 pts/3 00:00:00 bash
29894 pts/3 00:00:00 less
29916 pts/3 00:00:00 csh
29936 pts/3 00:00:00 ps
!done (press RETURN)
:q
$
```

2.6.5 Viewing the Head or Tail of a File

Having the ability to view the head (some lines from the beginning) or tail (some lines from the end) of a file is useful in identifying the type of data stored in the file. For example, the **head** operation can be used to identify a PostScript file or a uuencoded file, which have special headers. The LINUX and UNIX commands for displaying the head or tail of a file are **head** and **tail**. Without an argument, these commands take input from standard input. By default, both display 10 lines of a file.

The **head sample** command shows the first 10 lines of the file sample. The output of the **head sample memo1 phones** command is the first 10 lines of the files sample, memo1, and phones. The **head -5 sample** command displays the first 5 lines of sample.

The following command, which displays the first 10 lines of the file otto, shows that the file is a PostScript file. The output of the command gives additional information about the file, including the name of the software used to create it, the total number of pages in the file, and the page orientation. All of this information is important to know before the file is printed.

```
$ head otto
%!PS-Adobe-3.0
%%BoundingBox: 54 72 558 720
```

```
%%Creator: Mozilla (NetScape) HTML->PS
%%DocumentData: Clean7Bit
%%Orientation: Portrait
%%Pages: 4
%%PageOrder: Ascend
%%Title: Otto Doggie
%%EndComments
%%BeginProlog
$
```

The `tail` command is used to display the last portion (tail) of one or more files. It is useful to ascertain, for example, that a PostScript file has a proper end or that a uuencoded file has the required end on the last line. You can display any number of lines starting with a particular line, as well as display lines in the reverse order.

Like the `head` command, the `tail` command takes input from standard input if no file is given as argument. The `tail sample` command displays the last 10 lines of sample, and the `tail -5 sample` command displays the last 5 lines of sample. The tail +8 sample command displays all the lines in the sample file, starting with line 8. The `tail -5r sample` command displays the last 5 lines in reverse order (the last line of the file is the first displayed). The following `tail` commands show that files otto and data have proper postscript and uuencoded tails.

```
$ tail data
M;W4@:&%V90IN;W0@=')I960@;W5T(&9O<B!L;VYG('1I;64N("!(;;W=E=F5R
M+"!T;R!B92!S=6-C97-S9G5L+"!Y;W4@;75S=";!T<@I(96QL;RP@RP@&0A
"(0H`
`
end
$ tail -5 otto
8 f3
( ) show
pagelevel restore
showpage
%%EOF
$
```

The `-f` option of the `tail` command is very useful if you need to see the tail of a file that is growing. This situation occurs quite often when you are running a simulation program that takes a long time to finish (several minutes, hours, or days) and you want to see the data produced by the program as it is generated. It is convenient to use if your LINUX/UNIX system runs **X Window System**. In an X environment, you can run the `tail` command in an **xterm** (a console window) to monitor the data as it is generated and keep doing your other work concurrently. The following command displays the last 10 lines of the sim.data file and displays new lines as they are appended to the file. The command can be terminated by pressing <Ctrl-C>, as shown below.

```
$ tail -f sim.data
[ last 10 lines of sim.data ]
[ more data displayed as it is appended to sim.data ]
<Ctrl-C>
$
```

In the following In-Chapter Exercises, you will use the `more` (or `less`), `head`, and `tail` commands to appreciate their working.

IN-CHAPTER EXERCISES

2.6 Use the `more` (or `less`) command to view the /usr/include/stdio.h file. What is the value of the end-of-file constant?

2.7 Use the `head` and `tail` commands to view the beginning and end portions of a large text file.

2.6.6 DISPLAYING THE NIS DATABASE

You can use the `ypcat` command to display a map in the **NIS database,** a centralized repository of various pieces of systemwide information in a network environment. For example, you can use the `ypcat passwd` command to display password-related information about the login names on the screen. Similarly, you can display all systemwide aliases with the `ypcat aliases` command, the `ypcat hosts` command to display the hosts on your local area network, and the `ypcat services` command to display the Internet services supported by your networked system. You can use the `ypcat -x` command to display names of the NIS maps maintained on your system and their nicknames.

2.6.7 COPYING FILES

The LINUX and UNIX command for copying files is `cp`. You must have permission (see Chapter 5) to read the source file (the file to be copied) and permission to search the directories that contain the source and destination files. In addition, you must have write permission for the directory that contains the destination file if it does not exist already. Here is a brief description of this command.

If the destination file exists, you don't need write permission for the directory that contains it but you must have write permisson for the file. If the destination file exists, by default, it will be overwritten without informing you if you have permission to write to the file. To be prompted before an existing file is overwritten you need to use the `-i` option. If you don't have permission to write to the destination file, you'll be so informed. If you don't have permission to read the source file, an error message will appear on your screen.

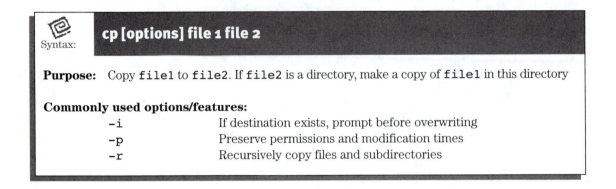

Syntax:

cp [options] file 1 file 2

Purpose: Copy `file1` to `file2`. If `file2` is a directory, make a copy of `file1` in this directory

Commonly used options/features:

`-i`	If destination exists, prompt before overwriting
`-p`	Preserve permissions and modification times
`-r`	Recursively copy files and subdirectories

In the following session, the `cp temp temp.bak` command makes a copy of temp in temp.bak. The first error message is reported because the letter file does not exist in the current directory. The second command reports an error message because temp.bak exists and the user does not have write permission for it. The last command fails because the user doesn't have permission to read the system file /etc/shadow.

```
$ cp temp temp.bak
$ cp letter letter.bak
cp: cannot access letter
$ cp memo temp.bak
cp: cannot create temp.bak: Permission denied
$ cp /etc/shadow ~/etc/shadow
cp: cannot open `/etc/shadow' for reading: Permission denied
$
```

The following command makes a copy of the .profile file in your home directory and puts it in the .profile.old file in the ~/sys.backups subdirectory. You should execute this command before changing your run-time environment (as specified in the ~/.profile file) so that you have a backup copy of the previous working environment in case something goes wrong when you set up the new environment.

```
$ cp ~/.profile ~/sys.backups/.profile.bak
$
```

The `cp -i lab* ~/courses/ee446/backups` command copies all the files in the current directory, starting with the string lab to the directory ~/courses/ee446/backups. With the `-i` option, this command prompts you for overwriting if any of the source files already exist in the backups directory.

If you want to copy a complete directory to another directory, you need to use the `cp` command with the `-r` option. This option recursively copies files and subdirectories from the source directory to the destination directory. It is a useful option that you can use to create backups of important directories periodically. Thus the following command recursively copies the ~/courses directory to the ~/backups directory.

```
$ cp -r ~/courses ~/backups
$
```

If you want to preserve permissions, use the **cp –a** or **cp –p** commands.

2.6.8 MOVING AND RENAMING FILES

Files can be moved from one directory in a file structure to another with the **mv** command. This operation in LINUX or UNIX may result in simply renaming a file if the source and destination files are on the same file system. A file system is a directory hierarchy with its own root stored on a disk or disk partition, mounted under (glued to) a directory. The files and directories in the file system are accessed through the directory under which they are mounted.

You must have write and execute access permissions to the directory that contains the existing file, but you do not need read, write, or execute permission to the file itself. Similarly, you must have write and execute access permissions to the directory that contains the target file, execute permission for every directory in the pathname of the target file, and write permission to the file if it already exists. If the destination file exists, by default it is overwritten without informing you. If you used the –i option, you are prompted before the destination file is overwritten.

The **mv temp temp.moved** command in the session that follows moves temp to temp.moved. In this case the temp file is renamed temp.moved. An error message is reported if temp does not exist, or if you do not have write or execute permission for the directory it is in. The command prompts you for moving the file if temp.bak already exists but you do not have write permission for it.

```
$ mv temp temp.moved
$
```

The **mv temp ~/backups/temp.old** command below moves temp to the ~/backups directory as the temp.old file.

```
$ mv temp ~/backups/temp.old
$
```

In the following session, the **mv –f temp temp.moved** command is a sure move; you can use it to force the move, regardless of the permissions for the target file-temp.moved in this case. The **mv dir1/* dir2** command moves all the files and directories (excluding hidden files) in dir1 to the dir2 directory. After the command is executed, dir1 contains hidden files only; the **ls –a** command can be used to confirm this status.

```
$ mv -f temp temp.moved
$ mv dir1/* dir2
$
```

2.6.9 REMOVING/DELETING FILES

When files are not needed anymore, they should be removed from a file structure to free up disk space to be reused for new files and directories. The LINUX and UNIX command for removing (deleting) files is **rm**. Here is a brief description of this command.

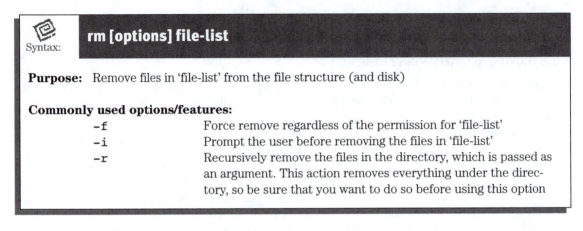

Syntax: **rm [options] file-list**

Purpose: Remove files in 'file-list' from the file structure (and disk)

Commonly used options/features:
-f	Force remove regardless of the permission for 'file-list'
-i	Prompt the user before removing the files in 'file-list'
-r	Recursively remove the files in the directory, which is passed as an argument. This action removes everything under the directory, so be sure that you want to do so before using this option

You need the search permissions for all the directory components in the pathnames and write and search permissions for the last directory (that contains the files to be deleted), but you do not need to have read or write permission to the files themselves. If you run the command and don't have the write permission for the file to be removed, the command displays your access permissions for the file and prompts you for an action.

The following command lines illustrate use of the **rm** command to remove one or more files from various directories.

```
$ rm temp
$ rm backups/temp.old
$ rm -f phones grades ~/letters/letter.john
$ rm ~/dir1/*
$ rm [kK]*.prn
$ rm [a-kA-Z]*.prn
$
```

The first command removes temp from the current directory. The second command removes the temp.old file from the backups directory. The third command removes the files phones, grades, and ~/letters/letter.john regardless of their access permissions. The fourth command removes all the files from ~/dir1 directory; the directories are not removed. The fifth command removes all the files in current directory that have the .prn extension and names starting with k or K. The sixth command removes all the files in the current directory that have the .prn extension and names starting with a lowercase letter from a through k or an uppercase letter.

The `rm` command with the `-r` option can be used to remove nonempty directories recursively. When used with the `-r` and `-f` options, the `rm` command removes the whole directory hierarchy regardless of the permissions for the files and directories in the hierarchy. Thus the following command recursively removes all the files and subdirectories in your ~/backups directory. This command is one of the commands that you must never execute unless you really know its consequences—the loss of all the files and directories in your ~/backups directory.

```
$ rm -rf ~/backups
$
```

You should generally combine the `-i` and `-r` options to remove a directory, recursively, as shown in the following command. The `-i` option is for interactive removal, and when you use this option, the `rm` command prompts you before removing a file.

```
$ rm -ir ~/personal
...
$
```

In the following In-Chapter Exercises, you will use the `mkdir`, `cp`, `mv`, and `rm` commands to appreciate how they work.

IN-CHAPTER EXERCISES

2.8 Create a directory called temp in your home directory. Copy the `ls`, `cat`, and `ftp` files from the /bin directory into this directory. Make duplicate copies of these files ls.bak, cat.bak, and ftp.bak, also in the same temp directory. Write down the commands that you used for performing these tasks.

2.9 Create a directory called backups in your home directory. Move the backup files from your ~/temp directory into the backups directory with a single command. What command did you use?

2.10 Remove the files in the ~/temp directory with a single command and then remove the ~/temp directory. What commands did you use? Remove the ~/backups directory with a single command. What command did you use?

2.6.10 DETERMINING FILE SIZE

You can determine the size of a file by using one of several LINUX/UNIX commands. The two commands commonly used for this purpose are `ls -l` and `wc`. As stated previously, the output of the `ls -l` command displays file size (in bytes) in the fifth field. In the following session, the size of the lab2 file is 163 bytes.

```
$ ls -l lab2
-r-xr--r--  1   sarwar    faculty    163   April 22 17:15   lab2
$
```

This command also displays the size of directory files when used with the **-ld** options. You can use it to get the sizes of multiple files by specifying the file names in the command line and separating them by spaces, as in **ls -l lab1 lab2**. You can use shell metacharacters with file names as in **ls -l ~/courses/ee446/***.

Whereas **ls -l** is a general-purpose command that can be used to determine most of the attributes of one or more files, including their sizes in bytes, **wc** is a special-purpose command that displays only file sizes. Here is a brief description of this command.

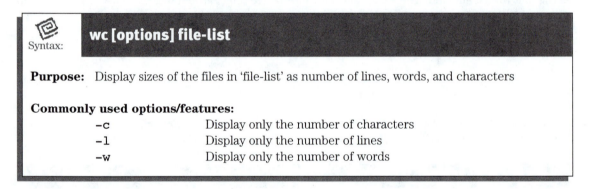

Syntax: **wc [options] file-list**

Purpose: Display sizes of the files in 'file-list' as number of lines, words, and characters

Commonly used options/features:
-c	Display only the number of characters
-l	Display only the number of lines
-w	Display only the number of words

The output of the **wc** command for every file is a line with four fields: line count, word count, character count, and file name. The command does not work with directories. You can use the **-c, -w,** or **-l** option to display the file size in bytes, words, or lines, respectively. The following session illustrates use of the **wc** command with and without options.

```
$ wc sample
       4        44       227 sample
$ wc letter sample test
      44       250      1687 letter
       4        44       227 sample
       2        12        90 test
      50       306      2004 total
$ wc -c letter sample test
    1687 letter
     227 sample
      90 test
    2004 total
```

```
$ wc -lw letter sample test
        44       250 letter
         4        44 sample
         2        12 test
        50       306 total
$
```

The first command displays that the sample file in the current directory has 4 lines, 44 words, and 227 bytes. The second command displays the line, word, and byte counts for the files letter, sample, and test in the present working directory. The last line in the output of this command also displays the total for all three files. The third command displays the number of characters in letter, sample, and test. The last command shows that multiple options can be used in a single command; in this case the output is the number of words and letters for the three files in the command line.

2.6.11 APPENDING TO FILES

Appending to a file places new data at the end of the named file. If the file does not exist, it is created to contain the new data. The append operation is useful when an application or a user needs to augment a file by adding data to it.

The **>>** operator is the append operator in LINUX and UNIX. You can use it according to the following syntax for appending files at the end of a file.

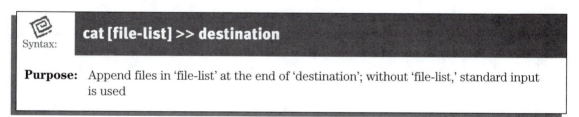

Syntax: **cat [file-list] >> destination**

Purpose: Append files in 'file-list' at the end of 'destination'; without 'file-list,' standard input is used

The **cat sample >> temp** command appends the contents of sample at the end of temp. You can append multiple files to a file, as in **cat memo1 memo2 memo3 >> memos.record**. This command appends the contents of the memo1, memo2, and memo3 files at the end of the memos.record file.

Without a file argument, the command can be used to append keyboard input at the end of a file. The following command takes input from the keyboard and appends it to a file called test.letter. The command terminates when you press **<Ctrl-D>** on a new line.

```
$ cat >> test.letter
November 14, 2000
Dear John:
This is to inform you ...

...
```

<Ctrl-D>

$

2.6.12 COMBINING FILES

You can use the following syntax to combine contents of multiple files and store them in a single file.

Syntax: **cat [file-list] >> destination**

Purpose: Concatenate data in files in 'file-list' and store the data in 'destination'

If file-list is not specified, keyboard input is saved in destination, allowing you to create text files with the **cat** command. When used in this manner, the command terminates when you press **<Ctrl-D>** on a new line. If the destination file does not exist, it is created.

The **cat data1 data2 data3 > data123** command saves the contents of files data1, data2, and data3 in the data123 file. The **cat memo* >** memos command saves all the memo files in the current directory in the memos file.

In the following In-Chapter Exercises, you will use the **wc** command and > and >> operators to appreciate the tasks that they perform.

IN-CHAPTER EXERCISES

2.11   What are the sizes of **ls**, **cat**, and **ftp** commands (i.e., the size of their executable code) in bytes? Use only one command to obtain the answer to the question. What command did you use?

2.12   Save the manual page for the **bash** command in the commands.man file. Then append the manual pages for the **tcsh** and **ping** commands at the end of this file. Write down the commands that you used for performing the above tasks.

2.13   Save the manual pages for the **traceroute**, **nslookup**, **ifconfig**, **netstat**, and **arp** commands in the NetCommands.man file. What command did you use for performing this task?

2.6.13 COMPARING FILES

If you need to compare two versions of a program code or other document, you can use the **diff** command. The command compares two files and displays differences between them in terms of commands that can be used to convert one file to the other. The following syntax is to be used for the **diff** command.

Syntax:

diff [options] [file1] [file2]

Purpose: Compare file1 with file2 line by line and display the differences between them as a series of commands that can be used to convert file1 to file2 or vice versa. Read from standard if – is used for file1 or file2

In the following example, we use the `diff` command to first compare file1 with itself and then compare file1 with file2. The first `diff` command does not produce any output because the files compared are the same. The second `diff` command compares file1 with file2 and produces an output that contains an instruction, `1c1`, followed by the first line in the first file and the first line in the second file. This instruction informs you to change the first line of file1 to the first line of file2 to make them the same files.

```
$ cat file1
Hello, World!
$ cat file2
Greetings!
$ diff file1 file1
$ diff file1 file2
1c1
< Hello, World!
--
> Greetings!
$
```

The file1 and file2 arguments can be directories. If file1 is a directory, `diff` searches it to locate a file named file2 and compares it with file2 (the second argument). If file2 is a directory, diff searches it to locate a file named file1 and compares it with file1 (the first argument). If both arguments are directories, the command compares all pairs of files in these directories that have the same names.

The `diff` command does not produce any output if the files being compared are the same. When used without any options, the `diff` command produces a series of instructions for you to convert file1 to file2 if the files are different. The instructions are **a** (add), **c** (change), and **d** (delete). The following session shows a sample use of the `diff` command.

```
$ diff Fall_OH Spring_OH
1c1
< Office Hours for Fall 2001
---
> Office Hours for Spring 2002
8a9
>        1:00 - 2:00 P.M.
12c13
<        3:00 - 4:00 P.M.
---
>
15,16d15
<        2:00 - 3:00 P.M.
<        4:00 - 4:30 P.M.
$
```

The instruction **1c1** asks you to change the first line in the Fall_OH file (Office Hours for Fall 2001) to the first line in the Spring_OH file (Office Hours for Spring 2002). Similarly, the instruction **12c13** asks you to change line 12 in Fall_OH (3:00–4:00 P.M.) to a blank line (note that nothing is given after the **>** symbol). The **8a9** instruction asks you to append line 9 in Spring_OH after line 8 in Fall_OH. The **15,16d15** instruction asks you to delete lines 15 and 16 from Fall_OH.

Most systems have a command called **diff3** that can be used to do a three-way comparison, that is, to compare three files. In the following example, we compare file1, file2, and file3. The output gives the descriptions of their differences, displaying the lines in which the three files differ.

```
$ diff3 file1 file2 file3
====
1:1c
2:1c
  Hello, World!
3:1c
  Greetings!
$
```

The **zdiff** and **zcmp** commands can be used to compare compressed files (see Section 2.6.14). The **zdiff** command uncompresses the files and passes them to the **diff** command, along with any options. The **zcmp** command uncompresses the files and passes them to the **cmp** command, along with any options. The **cmp** command stops at the first byte where the two files differ and reports the position on the screen. If one or both files are uncompressed, they are simply passed to the **diff** (or **cmp**) command. If only one file (file1, for example) is passed as an argument, then file1 and the uncompressed version of file1.gz are compared. For example, the zdiff bash.man.gz command is used to compare the uncompressed bash.man.gz and bash.man. The **zdiff.bash.man.gz tcsh.man.gz** command is used to compare the uncompressed versions of bash.man.gz and tcsh.man.gz files. The **zcmp** command can be used in a similar manner.

2.6.14 COMPRESSING FILES

Reduction in the size of a file, known as file compression, has both space and time advantages. A compressed file takes less disk space, less time to transmit from one computer to another in a network or Internet environment, and less time to copy. Compression takes time, but if a file is to be copied or transmitted several times, the time spent compressing the file could be just a fraction of the total time saved. In addition, if the compressed file is to be stored on a secondary storage device (e.g., a disk) for a long time, the savings in disk space is considerable. One consequence of compression is that the compressed file is not readable, but a compressed file can be converted back to its original form, making it readable. The compression process is fully reversible using the **uncompress** command.

The LINUX/UNIX operating system has several commands for compressing and decompressing files, and for performing various operations on compressed files. These commands include the traditional UNIX commands for compressing and decompressing files, **compress** and **uncompress**, and the GNU tools **gzexe**, **gzip**, **gunzip**, **zcat**, **zcmp**, **zforce**, **zmore**, and **zgrep**. We describe only the GNU tools here; the GNU commands (**gzip** and **gunzip**) are better than **compress** and **uncompress** because the compression algorithm used by **gzip** compresses better than the one used by the **compress** command. Also the **compress** command does not compress small files as well as the **gzip** command does.

THE GZIP COMMAND

The **gzip** command can be used to compress regular/ordinary files; it ignores symbolic links. The command reads the contents of files that are passed to it as parameters, analyzes their contents for repeated patterns, and then substitutes a smaller number of characters for these patterns by using **Lempel-Ziv** coding. A compressed file's contents are altogether different from the original file. The compressed file contains nonprintable control characters, so the screen display of a compressed file is simply a mass of control characters. See a brief description of this command on the next page.

The compressed files retain the access/modification times, ownership, and access privileges of the original files. The original file is removed from the file structure. With no file argument or with – as an argument, the **gzip** command takes input from standard input (keyboard by default), which allows you to use the command in a pipeline (see Chapter 3). We normally use the command with one or more files as its arguments.

THE GUNZIP COMMAND

The **gunzip** command can be used to perform the reverse operation and bring compressed files back to their original forms. The **gzip –d** command can also perform this task. With the **gunzip** command, the **–N**, **–c**, **–f**, **–l**, and **–r** options work just like they do with the **gzip** command.

Syntax: **gzip [options] [file-list]**

Purpose: Compress each file in 'file-list' and store it in filename.gz, where 'filename' is the name of the original file; if no file is specified in the command line or if – is used, gzip reads inputs from standard input

Commonly used options/features:

-N	Control compression speed (and compression ratio) according to the value of N, with 1 being fastest and 9 being slowest; slow compression compressing more
-c	Send output to standard output; input files remain unchanged
-d	Uncompress a compressed file
-f	Force compression of a file when its .gz version exists, it has multiple links, or the input file is standard input
-l	For compressed files given as arguments, display sizes of uncompressed and compressed versions, compression ratio, and uncompressed name
-r	Recursively compress files in the directory specified as argument

The following session shows the use of the two commands with and without arguments. We use the man **bash > bash.man** and **man tcsh > tcsh.man** commands to save the manual page for the Bourne Again and TC shells in the bash.man and **tcsh.man** files, respectively. The **gzip bash.man** command is used to compress the bash.man file and the **gzip –l bash.man.gz tcsh.man.gz** command is used to display some information about the compressed and uncompressed versions of the bash.man and tcsh.man files. The output of the command shows, among other things, the percentage compression achieved: 74.4% for bash.man and 71.7% for tcsh.man. The 74.4% compression means that the size of the compressed files is 25.6% of the original file. The **gzip bash.man.gz** command is used to show that **gzip** does not compress an already compressed file that has a .gz extension. If a compressed file does not have the .gz extension, **gzip** will try to compress it again. The **gunzip bash.man.gz** command is used to decompress the compressed file bash.man.gz. The **gzip –d bash.man.gz** command can be used to perform the same task. The **ls –l** commands have been used to show that the modification time, ownership, and access privileges of the original file are retained for the compressed file.

```
$ man bash > bash.man
$ ls -l bash.man
-rw------- 1 sarwar   faculty    284064 Nov 20 12:24 bash.man
$ gzip bash.man
```

```
$ ls -l bash.man.gz
-rw------- 1 sarwar faculty    72501 Nov 20 12:24 bash.man.gz
$ gzip bash.man tcsh.man
$ gzip -l bash.man.gz tcsh.man.gz
compressed uncompr. ratio uncompressed_name
   72501      284064 74.4% bash.man
   73790      261316 71.7% tcsh.man
  146291      545380 73.1% (totals)
$ gzip bash.man.gz
gzip: bash.man.gz already has .gz suffix - unchanged
$ gunzip bash.man.gz
$ ls -l bash.man
-rw------- 1 sarwar faculty 284064 Nov 20 12:24 bash.man
$
```

THE GZEXE COMMAND

The **gzexe** command can be used to compress executable files. Unlike with the **gzip** command, an executable file compressed with the **gzexe** command remains an executable file and can be executed by using the name of the executable file. Therefore an executable file is compressed with the gzexe command in order to save disk space and network bandwidth if the file is to be transmitted from one computer to another, for example, via e-mail over the Internet.

The following session illustrates the use of the **gzexe** command. Note that when the executable file banner is compressed with the **gzexe** command, a backup of the original file is created in **banner~**. After the **banner** file has been compressed, it can be executed as an ordinary executable file. The **gzexe -d banner** command is used to decompress the compressed file banner. The backup of the compressed version is saved in the **banner~** file.

```
$ file banner
banner: ELF 32-bit LSB executable, Intel 80386, version 1, dynamically
  linked (uses shared libs), not stripped
$ banner datafile 10
[ output of the banner command ]
$ gzexe banner
banner:                   58.0%
$ ls -l banner*
-rwx------ 1 sarwar faculty 5239  Nov 19 11:45 banner
-rwx------ 1 sarwar faculty 10881 Nov 19 11:44 banner~
$ banner datafile 10
```

```
[ output of the banner command ]
$ gzexe -d banner
$ ls -l banner*
-rwx------ 1 sarwar faculty 10881 Nov 19 11:48 banner
-rwx------ 1 sarwar faculty 5239  Nov 19 11:45 banner~
$
```

THE zcat COMMAND

Converting the compressed file back to the original and then displaying it is a time-consuming process because file creation requires disk I/O. If you want only to view the contents of the original file, you can use the LINUX/UNIX command **zcat** (the **cat** command for compressed files), which displays the contents of files compressed with **compress** or **gzip**. The command uncompresses a file before displaying it. The original file remains unchanged. The **zmore** command can be used to display the compressed files one screen at a time. When no file or – is given as a parameter, these commands read input from the keyboard. Both commands allow you to specify one or more files as parameters.

In the following session, the **gzip** command is used to compress the bash.man file and store it in the bash.man.gz file. The **zmore** command is used to display the contents of the original file. We did not use the **zcat** command because bash.man is a large, multipage file.

```
$ gzip bash.man
$ zmore bash.man.gz
--- > bash.man.gz < ---
BASH2(1)
NAME
      bash2 - GNU Bourne-Again SHell
SYNOPSIS
      bash2 [options] [file]
COPYRIGHT
      -Bash is Copyright (C) 1989—1999 by the Free Software Foundation,
  Inc.
DESCRIPTION
      -Bash is an sh-compatible command language interpreter that executes
  commands read from the standard input or from a file. Bash also
  incorporates useful features from the Korn and C shells (ksh and csh).
$
```

In the following In-Chapter Exercises, you will use the **gzip**, **gunzip**, and **zcat** commands to see how files can be compressed and uncompressed, and how compressed files can be displayed.

IN-CHAPTER EXERCISES

2.14 Save the manual page for the TC shell in the tcsh.man file into your home directory. Use the `ls -l` command to display the size of the manual page in bytes. Compress the tcsh.man file with the **gzip** command. How much disk space is saved if the compressed version of the file is saved instead of the uncompressed version? How did you obtain your answer? What file contains the compressed version of tcsh.man?

2.15 Display the compressed version with the **zcat** command.

2.16 Uncompress the compressed version of tcsh.man. What command did you use?

2.6.15 SEARCHING FOR FILES AND COMMANDS

At times you will need to find whether a particular file or command exists in your file system. Or, if you have multiple versions of a command, you might want to find out which one executes when you run the command. We discuss three commands that can be used for this purpose: `find`, `whereis`, and `which`.

THE FIND COMMAND

You can use the `find` command to search a list of directories that meet the criteria described by the expression (see command description) passed to it as an argument. The expression is used essentially to specify one or more of the file attributes being searched. The command searches the list of directories recursively; that is, all subdirectories at all levels under the list of directories are searched. The following is a brief description of the command.

Syntax:

Syntax: **find directory-list expression**

Purpose: Search the directories in 'directory-list' to locate files that meet the criteria described by the 'expression' (the second argument). The expression comprises one or more criteria (see the examples)

Output: None unless it is explicitly requested in 'expression'

Commonly used options/features:

`-exec CMD`	The file being searched meets the criteria if the command 'CMD' returns 0 as its exit status (true value for commands that execute successfully); 'CMD' must terminate with a quoted semicolon, that is, `\;`
`-inum N`	Search for files with inode number N
`-links N`	Search for files with N links

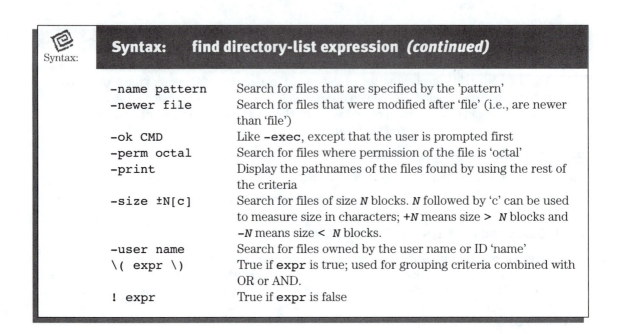

Syntax: find directory-list expression *(continued)*

-name pattern	Search for files that are specified by the 'pattern'
-newer file	Search for files that were modified after 'file' (i.e., are newer than 'file')
-ok CMD	Like **-exec**, except that the user is prompted first
-perm octal	Search for files where permission of the file is 'octal'
-print	Display the pathnames of the files found by using the rest of the criteria
-size ±N[c]	Search for files of size *N* blocks. *N* followed by 'c' can be used to measure size in characters; *+N* means size > *N* blocks and *−N* means size < *N* blocks.
-user name	Search for files owned by the user name or ID 'name'
\(expr **\)**	True if **expr** is true; used for grouping criteria combined with OR or AND.
! expr	True if **expr** is false

You can use [**-a**] or a space to logically AND, and **-o** to logically OR two criteria. Note that at least one space is needed before and after a bracket, [or], and before and after **-o**. A complex expression can be enclosed in parentheses, \(and \). The following are some illustrative examples.

The most common use of the **find** command is to search one or more directories for a file, as shown in the first example. Here, the command searches for the Pakistan.gif file in your home directory and displays the pathname of the directory that contains it. If the file being searched occurs in multiple directories, the pathnames of all the directories are displayed.

```
$ find ~ -name Pakistan.gif -print
/home/faculty/sarwar/myweb/Pakistan.html
$
```

The next command searches the /usr/include directory recursively for a file named socket.h and prints the absolute pathname of the file.

```
$ find /usr/include -name socket.h -print
/usr/include/sys/socket.h
$
```

You may want to know the pathnames for all the hard links (discussed in Chapter 11) to a file. The following command recursively searches the /usr and . (present working directory) directories for all the files that have an inode number 258072 and prints the absolute pathnames of all such files.

```
$ find /usr . -inum 258072 -print
/home/faculty/sarwar/myweb/LinuxTcpIP
$
```

The following command searches the present working directory for files that have the name **core** or have extensions .ps or .o, displays their absolute pathnames, and removes them from the file structure. Parentheses are used to enclose a complex criterion. Be sure that you use spaces before and after \(and **−o**. The command does not prompt you for permission to remove; in order to be prompted, replace **−exec** with **−ok**.

```
$ find . \( -name core -o -name '*.ps' -o -name '*.o' \) -print -exec rm
{} \;
[ output of the command ]
$
```

THE WHEREIS COMMAND

You can use the **whereis** command to find out whether your system has a particular command and, if it does, where it is in the file structure. You typically need to get such information when you are trying to execute a command that you know is valid but that your shell can't locate because the directory containing the executable for the command isn't in your search path. Under these circumstances, you can use the **whereis** command to find the location of the command and update your search path. The command not only gives you the absolute pathname of the command that you are searching for, but also the absolute pathname of its manual page if it is available on your system. The following is a brief description of the command.

Syntax: **whereis [options] [file-list]**

Purpose: Locate binaries (executables), source codes, and manual pages for the command in 'file-list'

Output: Absolute pathnames for the files containing binaries (executables), source codes, and manual pages for the command in 'file-list'

Commonly used options / features:

−b	Search for binaries (executables) only
−m	Search for manual pages only
−s	Search for source code only

The following examples illustrate use of the **whereis** command. The first command is used to locate the **ftp** command. The second command is used to locate the executable file for the **cat** command. The third command locates the information for the `find`, `gzip`, and `tar` commands. The last command locates the information about the `ifconfig` command.

```
$ whereis ftp
ftp:/usr/bin/ftp /usr/bin/ftp.expect /usr/share/man/man1/ftp.1.gz
$ whereis -b cat
cat: /bin/cat
$ whereis find gzip tar
find: /usr/bin/find /usr/share/man/man1/find.1.gz
gzip: /bin/gzip /usr/bin/gzip /usr/share/man/man1/gzip.1.gz
tar: /bin/tar /usr/include/tar.h /usr/share/man/man1/tar.1.gz
$ whereis ifconfig
ifconfig: /sbin/ifconfig /usr/share/man/man8/ifconfig.8.gz
$
```

In the outputs of these commands, the directories /bin, /sbin, and /usr/bin contain the executables for commands, the directory /usr/share/man contains several subdirectories that contain various sections of the LINUX/UNIX online manual, and the /usr/include directory contains header files.

THE WHICH COMMAND

In a system that has multiple versions of a command, the `which` utility can be used to determine the location (absolute pathname) of the version that is executed by the shell that you are using when you type the command. When a command doesn't work according to its specification, the `which` utility can be used to determine the absolute pathname of the command version that executes. A local version of the command may execute because of the way the search path is set up in the *PATH* variable (see Chapters 4 and 7). Or perhaps the local version has been broken due to a recent update in the code; it does not work properly with the new libraries that were installed on the system. The `which` command takes a command list (actually a file list for the commands) as argument and returns to standard output absolute pathnames for them.

In the following In-Chapter Exercises, you will use the `find` and `whereis` commands to practice locating files and commands.

IN-CHAPTER EXERCISES

2.17   Use the `find /usr/include -size -100c -print` command to display the names of all the header files that are smaller than 100 bytes. How many files on your system fall into this category?

2.18   Run the `ifconfig` command on your system. Chances are that you will not be able to run the command. Display the absolute pathname for the command with the `whereis` command. Rerun the `ifconfig` command using its full pathname. You will see two values for MTU. What are they?

2.6.17 SEARCHING FILES

LINUX and UNIX have powerful utilities for file searching that allow you to find lines in text files that contain a particular expression, string, or pattern. For example, if you have a large file that contains the records for a company's employees, one per line, you may want to search the file for lines containing information on John Johnsen. The utilities that allow file searching are `grep`, `egrep`, and `fgrep`. The following is a brief description of these utilities.

Syntax:	**grep [options] pattern [file-list]** **egrep [options] [string] [file-list]** **fgrep [options] [expression] [file-list]**

Purpose: Search the files in 'file-list' for given pattern, string, or expression; if no 'file-list', read input from standard input

Output: Lines containing the given pattern, string, or expression on standard output

Commonly used options/features:

-c	Print the number of matching lines only
-i	Ignore the case of letters during the matching process
-l	Print only the name of files with matching lines
-n	Print line numbers along with matched lines
-v	Print non-matching lines

Of the three, the `fgrep` command is the fastest but most limited; `egrep` is the slowest but most flexible, allowing full use of regular expressions; and `grep` has reasonable speed and is fairly flexible in terms of its support of regular expressions. In the following sessions, we illustrate the use of the middle-of-the-road `grep` command with some of the options shown in the description. We use the students file, displayed below with the `cat` command.

```
$ cat students
John Johnsen      john.johnsen@tp.com    503.555.1111
Hassaan Sarwar    hsarwar@k12.st.or      503.444.2132
David Kendall     d_kendall@msnbc.org    229.111.2013
John Johnsen      jjohnsen@psu.net       301.999.8888
Kelly Kimberly    kellyk@umich.gov       555.123.9999
Maham Sarwar      msarwar@k12.st.or      713.888.0000
Jamie Davidson    j.davidson@uet.edu     515.001.2932
Nabeel Sarwar     nsarwar@xyz.net        434.555.1212
$
```

The most common and simple use of the **grep** utility is to display the lines in a file containing a particular string, word, or pattern. In the following session, we display those lines in the students file that contain the string sarwar. The lines are displayed in the order they occur in the file.

```
$ grep sarwar students
Hassaan Sarwar      hsarwar@k12.st.or   503.444.2132
Maham Sarwar        msarwar@k12.st.or   713.888.0000
Nabeel Sarwar       nsarwar@xyz.net     434.555.1212
$
```

The **grep** command can be used with the **-n** option to display the output lines with line numbers. In the following session, the lines in the students file containing the string sarwar are displayed with line numbers.

```
$ grep -n sarwar students
2:Hassaan Sarwar      hsarwar@k12.st.or   503.444.2132
7:Maham Sarwar        msarwar@k12.st.or   713.888.0000
8:Nabeel Sarwar       nsarwar@xyz.net     434.555.1212
$
```

You can use the **grep** command to search a string in multiple files with **regular expressions** and **shell metacharacters.** In the following session, **grep** searches for the string include in all the files in the present working directory that end with .c (C source files). Note that the access permissions for server.c were set so that **grep** couldn't read it—the user running the command didn't have read permission for the server.c file.

```
$ grep -n include *.c
client.c: 21: #include    <stdio.h>
client.c: 22: #include    <ctype.h>
client.c: 23: #include    <string.h>
lab1.c: 13: #include      <stdio.h>
grep: can't open server.c
$
```

You can also use the **grep** command with the **-l** option to display the names of files in which the pattern occurs. However, the command does not display the lines that contain the pattern. In the following session, the ~/States directory is assumed to contain one file for every state in the United States and this file to contain the names of all the cities in the state (Portland, for example). The **grep** command therefore displays the names of files that contain the word Portland, that is, the names of states that have a city called Portland.

```
$ grep -l Portland ~/States
Maine
Oregon
$
```

The following command displays the lines in the students file that start with letters *A* through *H*. In the command, ^ specifies the beginning of a line.

```
$ grep '^[A-H]' students
Hassaan Sarwar   hsarwar@k12.st.or     503.444.2132
David Kendall    d_kendall@msnbc.org   229.111.2013
$
```

The `grep '\<Ke' students` command displays the lines that contain a word starting with the word (string) Ke. Note that \< is used to indicate start of a word. Single quotes are used in '\<Ke' to ensure that shell does not interpret any letter in the pattern as a shell metacharacter. The string \> is the end-of-word anchor. Thus the `grep 'net\>' students` command displays the lines that contain words that end with net. If we replace the string net with the string war, what would be the output of the command?

You can use the `-v` option to display the lines that do not contain the string specified in the command. Thus `grep -v "Kimberly|Nabeel" students` produces all the lines that do not contain the words Kimberly and Nabeel.

The `zgrep` command can be used to search compressed files. The command uncompresses compressed or `gzip`'ed files and passes them to the `grep` command along with any command line arguments. Multiple files can be passed as arguments to the command. The `zegrep` and `zfgrep` commands can be used to invoke the `egrep` and `fgrep` commands, respectively, instead of the `grep` command. The shell environment variable *GREP* can be set to any of the three `grep`-family commands (`grep`, `egrep`, and `fgrep`) to be invoked when `zgrep` is used. Thus, if *GREP* is set `egrep`, the execution of the `zgrep` command invokes the `egrep` command, and not the `grep` command.

In the following In-Chapter Exercises, you will use the `grep` command to understand its characteristics.

IN-CHAPTER EXERCISES

2.19 Use the `grep SOCK_STREAM /usr/include/bits/socket.h` command to determine the value of the symbolic constant SOCK_STREAM. What is the value of this variable?

2.20 Use the `grep PF_* /usr/include/bits/socket.h` command to display all the lines in the socket.h file that contain words starting with PF_. How many lines contain such words?

2.7 SUMMARY

In LINUX and UNIX, a file is a sequence of bytes. This simple, yet powerful, concept and its implementation lead to everything in the system being a file. LINUX/UNIX supports five types of files: ordinary file, directory, symbolic link, special file (device), and named pipe (also known as FIFO). The BSD-based systems support a sixth type, called socket. No file extensions are supported for files of any type, but applications running on a LINUX/UNIX system can require their own extensions. For example `.gz` extension is required by the `gzip` and `gunzip` commands. Similarly, the `.c` extension is required by all C programming language compilers such as `gcc` (see Chapters 8 through 12).

Every file in LINUX/UNIX has several attributes associated with it, including file name, owner's name, date last modified, link count, and the file's location on disk. You can display the attributes of a file with the `ls -l` command and display the size of a file in bytes, words, and characters with the `wc` command.

The LINUX/UNIX file structure is hierarchical, with a root directory and all the files and directories in the system being under it. Every user has a directory, called the user's home directory, which he or she gets into when logging on to the system. Multiple disk drives and/or disk partitions can be mounted on the same file system structure, allowing their access as directories and not as named drives A:, B:, C:, and so on, as in MS-DOS and Microsoft Windows. This approach gives a unified view of all the files and directories in the system, and users don't have to worry about remembering the names of drives and the files (and directories) that they contain.

Directories (primarily) can be created and removed under the user's home directory. The file structure can be navigated by using various commands (`mkdir`, `rmdir`, `cd`, `ls`, `dirs`, `pushd`, `popd`, etc.). The name of a file in the system can be specified by using its absolute or relative pathname. An absolute pathname starts with the root directory and a relative pathname starts with a user's home directory or present working directory. You can maintain a directory stack by using the `dirs`, `pushd`, and `popd` commands. This allows you to switch between various directories quickly.

The basic file operations involve creating text and executable files, displaying (all or part of) a file's contents, renaming a file, moving a file to another file, removing a file, determining a file's size, comparing files, combining files and storing them in another file, appending new contents (which may come from another disk file, keyboard, or output of a command) at the end of a file, and printing files. LINUX and UNIX provide several utilities that can be used to perform these operations.

The `vi` and `pico` editors can be used to create and edit text files. Binary/executable files can be created with a compiler such as `gcc`. The `cat` and `more` commands can be used to display all the contents of a file on the display screen. The > symbol can be used to send outputs of these commands to other files, and the >> operator can be used to append new contents at the end of a file. The `cat` command sends file contents as continuous text, whereas the `more` and `less` commands send them in the form of pages. Furthermore, the `more` and `less` commands have several useful features, such as displaying a page that contains a particular string. The `pg` command is similar to the `more` command. The `less` command is the most powerful of the three and has the most features.

The `head` and `tail` commands can be used to display the initial or end portions (head or tail) of a file. These helpful commands are usually used to find out the type of data contained in a file, without using the `file` command. In addition, the `file` command cannot decipher contents of all the files.

A copy of a file can be made in another file or directory by using the `cp` command. A file can be moved to another file by using the `mv` command. Depending on whether the source and destination files are on the same file system, using **mv** may or may not result in actual movement of file data from one location to another. If the source and destination files are on the same file system, the file data are not moved and the source file is simply linked to the new place (destination). If the two files are on different file systems, an actual copy of the source file is made at the new location and the source file is removed (unlinked) from the current directory. Files can be removed from a file structure by using the **rm** command. This command can also be used to remove directories recursively.

The size of a file can be determined by using the **ls -l** or **wc** command; both give file size in bytes. In addition, the wc command gives number of lines and words in the file. Both commands can be used to display the sizes of multiple files by using the shell metacharacters *, ?, [ ], and ^.

The **diff** command can be used to display differences between two files. The command, in addition to displaying the differences between the files, displays useful information in the form of a sequence of commands for the **ed** editor that can be used to make the two files the same. The **zdiff** and **zcmp** commands can be used to compare compressed files.

At times you will need to find whether a particular file or command exists in your file system. Or, if you have multiple versions of a command, you might want to find out which one executes when you run the command. Three commands can be used for this purpose: **find**, **whereis**, and **which**.

LINUX and UNIX have powerful utilities for file searching that allow you to find lines in text files that contain a particular expression, string, or pattern. These utilities are **grep**, **egrep**, and **fgrep**.

2.8 QUESTIONS AND PROBLEMS

1. What is a file in LINUX/UNIX?

2. Does LINUX/UNIX support any file types? If so, name them. Does LINUX/UNIX support file extensions?

3. What are special files in LINUX/UNIX? What are character special and block special files? Run the **ls /dev | wc -w** command to find the number of special files your system has.

4. Draw the hierarchical file structure, similar to the one shown in Figure 2.1, for your LINUX/UNIX machine. Show files and directories at the first two levels. Also show where your home directory is, along with files and directories under your home directory.

5. Give the command that you can use to list the absolute pathname of your home directory.

6. What shell are you using? What is the search path for your shell? How did you obtain your answer? What question(s) did you use?

7. Write down the line in the /etc/passwd file on your system that contains information about your login. What are your login shell, user ID, home directory, and group ID? Does your system contain the encrypted password in the /etc/passwd or /etc/shadow file?

8. Create a directory called memos in your home directory. Go into this directory and create a file memo.james by using one of the editors we discuss in Chapter 5. Give three pathnames for this file.

9. Give a command line for creating a subdirectory personal under the memos directory that you created in Problem 8.

10. Make a copy of the file memo.james and put it in your home directory. Name the copied file temp.memo. Give two commands for accomplishing this task.

11. Give the command for deleting the memos directory. How do you know that the directory has been deleted?

12. Why does a shell process terminate when you press `<Ctrl-D>` at the beginning of a new line?

13. Give a command line to display the types of all the files in your `~/linux` directory that start with the word chapter, are followed by digit 1, 2, 6, 8, or 9, and end with .eps or .prn.

14. Give a command line to display the types of all the files in the personal directory in your home directory whose filenames do not start with a, k, G, or Q and in which the third letter in the name is not a digit and not a letter (uppercase or lowercase).

15. Give a command line for viewing the sizes (in lines and bytes) of all the files in your present working directory

16. List 10 operations that you can perform on LINUX and UNIX files.

17. Give a command line for viewing the sizes (in lines and bytes) of all the files in your present working directory.

18. View the /usr/include/bits/socket.h file with the more (or less) command. What are the values of symbolic constants SOCK_STREAM and SOCK_DGRAM? What are the values of PF_INET and AF_INET?

19. What does the tail -10r ../letter.John command do?

20. Give a command for viewing the size of your home directory. Give a command for displaying the sizes of all the files in your home directory.

21. Give a command for displaying all the lines in the Students file, starting with line 25.

22. Give a command for copying all the files and directories under a directory courses in your home directory. Assume that you are in your home directory. Give another command to accomplish the same task, assuming that you are not in your home directory.

23. What do the following commands do?

    a. `rm -f ~/personal/memo*.doc`

    b. `rm -f ~/linuxbook/final/ch??.prn`

    c. `rm -f ~/linuxbook/final/*.o`

    d. `rm -f ~/courses/ece446/lab[1-6].[cC]`

24. Give a command line for moving files lab1, lab2, and lab3 from the ~/courses/ece345 directory to a newlabs.ece345 directory in your home directory. If a file already exists in the destination directory, the command should prompt the user for confirmation.

25. Give a command to display the lines in the ~/personal/Phones directory that are not repeated.

26. You have a file in your home directory called tryit&. Rename this file. What command did you use?

27. Give a command for displaying attributes of all the files starting with a string prog, followed by zero or more characters and ending with a string .c in the courses/ece345 directory in your home directory.

28. Refer to Problem 27. Give a command line if file names have two English letters between **prog** and .c. Can you give another command line to accomplish the same task?

29. Give a command line for displaying files gotlcha and M*A*S*H a screen at a time.

30. Give a command line for displaying the sizes of files that have the .jpg extension and names ending with a digit.

31. What is file compression? What do the terms compressed files and decompressed files mean? What commands are available for performing compression and decompression in LINUX and UNIX? Which are the preferred commands? Why?

32. Take three large files in your directory structure—a text file, a PostScript file, and a picture file—and compress them by using the compress command. Which file was compressed the most? What was the percentage reduction in file size? Compress the same file by using the gzip command. Which resulted in better compression, **compress** or **gzip**? Uncompress the files by using the **uncompress** and **gunzip** commands. Show your work.

33. Use the **find** command to display the names of all the header files in the /usr/include directory that are larger than 1000 bytes. Write down the command that you used to perform this task.

34. Use the **find** command to remove all the files in your home directory named core and those having the .bak extension. What command line did you use?

35. Use the **whereis** command to locate the manual pages for the **tar**, **strcmp**, and **socket** commands. What are the absolute pathnames for the files that contain these manual pages?

36. Use the **grep** command to search the /usr/include/bits/socket.h file and display the lines that contain the string SOCK_. What command line did you use?

## CHAPTER 3

Input/Output Redirection

OBJECTIVES

- To describe the notion of standard files—standard input, standard output, and standard error—and file descriptors

- To describe input and output redirection for standard files

- To discuss the concept of error redirection and appending to a file

- To explain the concept of pipes in LINUX/UNIX

- To discuss the `tee` utility

- To describe how powerful operations can be performed by combining pipes, file descriptors, redirection primitives, and the tee utility

- Commands and primitives covered: `&`, `|`, `<`, `>`, `>>`, `cat`, `grep`, `more`, `pr`, `sort`, `stderr`, `stdin`, `stdout`, `tee`, `tr`, `uniq`, `wc`

3.1 INTRODUCTION

All computer software commands perform one or more of three operations—input, processing, output; a typical command performs all three. The questions for the operating system are: Where does a shell command take its input from, where does it send its output, and where are error messages sent? If the input is not part of the command code (i.e., data within the code in the form of constants or variables), it must come from an outside source. This outside source is usually a file, although it could be an I/O device such as keyboard or a network interface card. Command output and error messages can go to a file as well. In order for a command to read from or write to a file, it must first open the file.

Every command in LINUX/UNIX has three files opened for it, called standard files. LINUX and UNIX have a set of powerful operators and commands that allow you to redirect a command's input, output, and errors by using the redirection operators and to connect output of a command to the input of another command by using the pipe operator. In this chapter, we discuss standard files, file descriptors, I/O and error redirection, connecting multiple commands together to perform complex operations on files, and the tee utility that allows you to save the output of a command to one or more files as well as send it to another command.

3.2 STANDARD FILES, FILE DESCRIPTORS, AND REDIRECTION OF STANDARD FILES

In LINUX/UNIX, three files are automatically opened by the kernel for each command for that command to read input from and send its output and error messages to. These files, known as **standard files**, are **standard input (stdin)**, **standard output (stdout)**, and **standard error (stderr)**. By default, these files are associated with the terminal on which the command executes. More specifically, the keyboard is standard input and the display screen (or the console at which you are logged in) is standard output and standard error. Therefore, every command, by default, takes its input from the keyboard, and sends its output and error messages to the display screen, as shown in Figure 3.1. In the remainder of this chapter, we use the terms monitor screen, display screen, console window, and display window interchangeably.

The LINUX/UNIX kernel associates a small integer number, called the file descriptor, with every open file. The upper limit on a descriptor value is system dependent but could be as large as 1023 or larger. You can use the `ulimit` command (see Chapter 6) to determine the limit on the number of files that a process can open simultaneously. On Mandrake 6.1 and RedHat 7.1, this value is 1024 by default and on SunOS the default value is 64. The file descriptors for stdin, stdout, and stderr are 0, 1, and 2, respectively.

Figure 3.1 Standard input, standard output, and standard error

You can use the LINUX/UNIX **redirection** features to detach the default files from stdin, stdout, and stderr and attach other files with them. We describe how these features work in this chapter. Our discussion is for Bash unless stated otherwise.

3.3 INPUT, OUTPUT, AND ERROR REDIRECTION

The default files (devices) attached to the standard files of a command can be changed to other files for a single execution of the command by using the LINUX/UNIX redirection features. The use of these features results in what is commonly known as input, output, and error redirection. We discuss these features one by one. Although the redirection features can be used across computers in a network environment, our discussion is limited to redirection on the same computer.

3.3.1 INPUT REDIRECTION

You can change the default device associated with stdin to a different file by using input redirection for one execution of a command. This allows the command to read input from the newly attached file instead of from the keyboard. The **<** (or **0<** — 0 is implicit default) operator can be used for input redirection according to the following syntax, where 0 is the file descriptor for stdin.

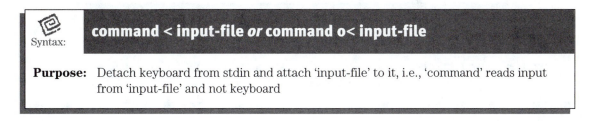

Syntax: **command < input-file** *or* **command o< input-file**

Purpose: Detach keyboard from stdin and attach 'input-file' to it, i.e., 'command' reads input from 'input-file' and not keyboard

The output of command and error messages still go to the display screen. In the following session, the `cat` and `grep` commands read input from the Phones file instead of from the keyboard. The outputs of the commands are still sent to the display screen.

```
$ cat < Phones
[ contents of Phones ]
$ grep "John" < Phones
[ output of the grep command ]
$
```

Although the end result is the same, the `cat < Phones` command is different from the `cat` Phones command, in which the Phones file is passed as a command line argument to the `cat` command; stdin of `cat` does not change.

The `cat` and `grep` commands read input from stdin if they are not passed file arguments in the command line. The `tr` command reads input from stdin only and sends its output to stdout. The `tr` command does not work with a file as a command line argument. Thus input redirection is often used with the `tr` command, as in the following session where it substitutes multiple consecutive spaces in the Phones file with a single space.

```
$ tr -s ' ' ' ' < Phones
[ contents of Phones with multiple consecutive spaces replaced with a
  single space ]

$
```

3.3.2 OUTPUT REDIRECTION

You can change the default device associated with stdout to a different file by using output redirection for one execution of a command. This allows the command to send its output to the newly attached file instead of to the display screen. The `>` (or `1>` — 1 is implicit default) operator can be used for output redirection according to the following syntax, where 1 is the file descriptor for stdout.

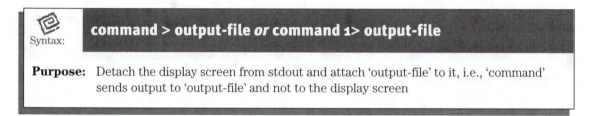

Syntax:	**command > output-file *or* command 1> output-file**

Purpose: Detach the display screen from stdout and attach 'output-file' to it, i.e., 'command' sends output to 'output-file' and not to the display screen

The input of command still comes from the keyboard and error messages still go to the display screen. In the following session, the `cat` command reads input from keyboard and saves it in the Phones file. If the Phones file already exists, it will be overwritten. The `grep` command reads its input from the Phones file (which is passed as a command line argument) and the command output goes to the Phones file. The output of the `find` command is redirected to the foo.paths file. The error messages of the commands are still sent to the display screen.

```
$ cat > Phones
[ your input ]
<Ctrl-D>
$ grep "John" Phones > Phones.bak
[ output of the grep command ]
$ find ~ -name foo -print > foo.paths
[ error messages ]

$
```

3.3.3 Error Redirection

You can change the default device associated with stderr to a different file by using error redirection for one execution of a command. This allows you to send error messages to the newly attached file instead of to the display screen. The **2>** operator can be used for error redirection according to the following syntax, where 2 is the file descriptor for stderr. You must specify 2 for stderr.

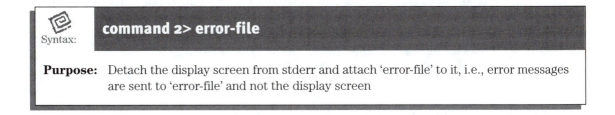

Syntax:

command 2> error-file

Purpose: Detach the display screen from stderr and attach 'error-file' to it, i.e., error messages are sent to 'error-file' and not the display screen

The input of command still comes from the keyboard and the command output still goes to the display screen. In the following session, the output of the find command goes to the display screen and error messages go to the find.errors file. The command reads its input from your home directory (~). The output of the `ls -l foo` command goes to the display screen and the error message goes to the error.log file. Thus, if foo does not exist, the error message `ls: foo: No such file or directory` goes into the error.log file, as shown below.

```
$ find ~ -name foo -print 2> find.errors
[ output of the find command ]
$ ls -l foo 2> error.log
[ output of the find command ]
$ cat error.log
ls: foo: No such file or directory
$
```

Keeping standard error attached to the display screen, and not redirected to a file, is useful in many situations. For example, when you execute the `cat lab1 lab2 lab3 > labs` command to concatenate files lab1, lab2, and lab3 into a file called labs, you would like to know whether any of the three input files is nonexistent or if you don't have the permission to read. In this case, redirecting error messages to a file does not make much sense, because you want to see the immediate results of the command execution.

Sometimes, in shell scripting in particular, you want to ignore the output of a command or error messages produced by a command (you don't want them to appear on screen or be saved in a file). You can do so by redirecting the output or error messages in a file called /dev/null. Anything that goes into this file never comes out; for this reason, we call it the LINUX/UNIX black hole. In the following command, we redirect the error messages of the `find` command to /dev/null.

```
$ find / -name ls -print 2> /dev/null
/bin/ls
$
```

You can use the following command to redirect both the output and error messages of the find command to /dev/null. Although, such a command does not make much sense when executed at the command line, it is sometimes used in shell scripts to check the execution status of a command (to determine whether the command executed successfully or not).

```
$ find / -name ls -print 1> /dev/null 2> /dev/null
$
```

3.3.4 REDIRECTING STDIN, STDOUT, AND STDERR IN ONE COMMAND

You can combine I/O and error redirection in a single command line. The position of error redirection in the command line is important because the command line content for file redirection is evaluated from left to right. In the following command, the **sort** command sorts lines in a file called students and stores the sorted data in the students.sorted file. Note again that 0, 1, and 2 are used to specify stdin, stdout, and stderr. If the **sort** command fails to start because the students file does not exist, the error message goes to the display screen and not to the file **sort.error**. This happens because at the time the shell determines that the students file does not exist, the standard error is still attached to the console.

```
$ sort 0< students 1> students.sorted 2> sort.error
$
```

For the following command, the error message goes to the sort.errors file if the sort command fails to start because the students file does not exist. This is because the shell processes the error redirection before it determines that the students file is nonexistent.

```
$ sort 2> sort.error 0< students 1> students.sorted
$
```

You don't have to redirect all the standard files. You can run a command with its stdin still attached to the keyboard but its stdout and stderr redirected. Similarly, you can run a command with its input coming from a file, its error messages going to another file, and its stdout still attached to the display screen. Thus the **sort 0< students 2> sort.error** command reads its input from the students file and sends an error message to the display screen if **sort** could not start because the students file did not exist; the output of the command still goes to the display screen. The **sort 2> sort.error 0< students** command reads its input from the students file and sends error messages

to the sort.error file; the output of the command still goes to the display screen. The **sort 1>**
students.sorted 2> sort.error command reads its input from the keyboard, sends its output
to the students.sorted file, and sends error messages to the sort.error file.

Standard output and standard error can be redirected to the same file. One way to do so is to
specify the same filename for output and error redirections, as in **cat lab1 lab2 lab3 1>**
cat.output 2> cat.errors. Another way to do this is to use the **2>&1** or **1>&2** operator. The
2>&1 operator informs the shell to attach the same file to stderr that is attached to stdout. It is used
in commands where you first specify output redirection and then use this operator to redirect stderr
to the same file. The **1>&2** operator informs the shell to attach the same file to stdout that is attached
to stderr. For the following command, the command output and error messages are saved in the
cat.output.errors file.

```
$ cat lab1 lab2 lab3 2> cat.output.errors 1>&2
$
```

You usually use the **1>&2** or **2>&1** operators to discard both the output of a command and its error message, as in the following command. Such commands are sometimes used in shell scripts to
check whether a command executes successfully.

```
$ find / -name foobar 2> cat.output.errors 1>&2
$
```

The redirections must be specified in the left to right order if one notation is dependent on another.
In the above command, first the standard error is changed to the cat.output.errors file and then standard output becomes a duplicate of standard error. Thus, the output and errors for the above command
both go to the same file, cat.output.errors. The **cat lab1 lab2 lab3 1> cat.output.errors 2>&1**
command performs that same task.

The following command, therefore, does *not* have the effect of the above two commands because
in this command standard error is made a duplicate of standard output *before* output redirection.
Therefore, stderr becomes a duplicate of stdout (the display screen at this time) first, and then standard output is changed to the cat.output.errors file. Thus, the output of the command goes to the file
cat.output.errors and errors go to the display screen.

```
$ cat lab1 lab2 lab3 2>&1 1> cat.output.errors
$
```

You can redirect stdout and stderr of a command to the same file in the TC shell with the **>&**
operator, as shown in the following command. The **%** sign is used as the prompt for the TC shell.

```
% cat lab1 lab2 lab3 >& cat.output.errors
%
```

The TC shell does not have an operator for redirecting stderr alone. You can attach stdout and stderr of a command to different files executing the command in a subshell (by enclosing the command in parentheses). In the following command, the output of the **find** command goes to the foo.paths file and error messages to the error.log file.

```
% (find ~ -name foo -print > foo.paths) >& error.log
%
```

By default, output and error redirections overwrite contents of the destination file. The Bash *noclobber* variable prevents you from overwriting files accidentally. You can set this variable by using the **set -C** command as shown below. If you want to set this variable permanently, place the **set -C** command in a startup file such as ~/.profile.

```
$ set -C
$
```

You can set and reset (unset) the *noclobber* variable in the TC shell with the **set** and **unset** commands as shown below.

```
% set noclobber
[ your interactive session ]
% unset noclobber
%
```

When the *noclobber* variable is set, you can force overwriting of a file by using the >| operator.

3.3.5 APPENDING DATA TO A FILE

You can append output or errors generated by a command at the end of a file by using the **>>** operator in place of the **>** operator. As with the **>** operator, **1>>** (append to stdout) and **2>>** (append to stderr) can be used for redirecting output and error, respectively, and appending them to a file. In the following command the output of the **cat** command is appended to the stuff file and the error messages are appended to the error.log file.

```
$ cat memo letter >> stuff 2>> error.log
$
```

In the following In-Chapter Exercises, you will practice the use of input, output, and error redirection features of LINUX/UNIX shells in a command line.

IN-CHAPTER EXERCISES

3.1   Write a shell command that displays the number of lines, words, and characters in a file called memo in your present working directory. Use input redirection.

3.2   Repeat Exercise 3.1, but redirect output to a file called counts.memo. Use I/O redirection.

3.3   Write a shell command that appends the files lab3, lab4, and lab5 at the end of the labs file. Any error messages are appended to the error.log file.

3.4   Write a TC shell command to locate the lab1 file in your home directory. Redirect the output and errors messages to the lab1.all file.

3.5   Repeat Exercise 3.4, but the output of the command should go to the find.lab1 file and any error messages to the error.log file.

3.6   Write a shell command to send the contents of the greetings file to doe1@domain.net by using the mail command. If the mail command fails, the error message should go to a file mail.error. Use input and error redirection.

3.7   Write a shell command that searches the root directory (/) for a file called **sort**. Ensure that error messages don't appear on the screen.

3.4 LINUX/UNIX FILTERS AND PIPES

The LINUX/UNIX operating system allows you to connect stdout of a command to stdin of another command. You can do so by using the **pipe** operator (|) according to the following syntax.

Syntax: **command1 | command2 | command3 | ... | commandN**

Purpose: Stdout of 'command1' is connected to stdin of 'command2', stdout of 'command2' is connected to stdin of 'command3', ..., stdout of 'commandN-1' is connected to 'commandN'

In general, any two commands can be connected via a pipe as long as one of them sends its output to stdout and the other reads its input from stdin. For example, in the following command, the **more** command takes output of the **ls –l** command as its input. The end result of this command is that the output of the **ls –l** command is displayed one screen at a time. It is important to mention here that no extra disk operation is performed for executing this command. The semantics of this command are shown in Figure 3.2.

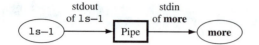

Figure 3.2 The semantics of the `ls -l | more` command

```
$ ls -l | more
[ output of the ls -l command displayed one screen at a time ]
$
```

Any task that can be performed with pipes can also be performed using only the redirection operator, but doing so requires many commands, temporary files, and expensive disk operations. For example, the task of the previous command can be performed by the following command sequence. First, a temp file is created that contains the output of the `ls -l` command. Then the contents of the temp file are displayed one page at a time. Finally, the temp file is removed.

```
$ ls -l > temp
$ more temp
[ output of the ls -l command displayed one screen at a time ]
$ rm temp
$
```

The LINUX and UNIX commands, called **filters,** read their input from stdin, process it in some fashion, and send it to stdout. Pipes and filters are frequently used in LINUX/UNIX to perform complicated tasks that cannot be performed with a single command. Some commonly used filters are `cat`, `grep`, `gunzip`, `lp`, `pr`, `sort`, `tr`, `uniq`, `wc`, and `zip.` The pipe and redirection operators can be used together in a command line.

The `sort` utility can be used to sort lines in a file. The `uniq` command allows you to remove consecutive repeated lines from a file. Suppose that you have a file called student_records that you want to sort and suppose that the file may have some repeated lines that you would like to see appear only once in the sorted file. An easy way to perform this task is to sort the file and send the output of the `sort` command to the `uniq` command via a pipe, as shown below.

```
$ sort student_records | uniq > sorted_students_records
$
```

There are times when you need to connect several commands together. The following command line demonstrates the use of multiple pipes, forming a **pipeline** of commands. In this command line, we have used the `sort`, `uniq`, and `grep` filters.

```
$ sort student_records | uniq | grep "John"
$
```

You can attach stdout and stderr of a command to stdin of another command in the TC shell by using the |& operator. Here is the syntax for doing so.

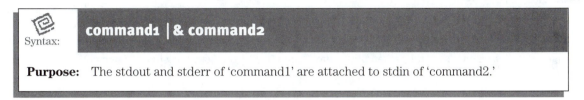

command1 |& command2

Purpose: The stdout and stderr of 'command1' are attached to stdin of 'command2.'

In the following command, stdout and stderr of the **cat** command are attached to the **grep** command, stdout of the **grep** command is attached to stdin of the **sort** command, and stdout of the sort command is attached to the JohnDoe file.

```
% cat file1 file2 |& grep "John Doe" | sort > JohnDoe
%
```

3.5 REDIRECTION AND PIPING COMBINED

The redirection operator and pipe alone cannot be used to redirect stdout of a command to a file as well as connect it to stdin of another command in a single command line. The **tee** utility can be used to accomplish this task. You can use the **tee** utility to tell the shell to send stdout of a command to one or more files as well as to the stdin of another command. Here is the syntax of the **tee** command.

tee [options] file-list

The **tee** utility is commonly used to read output of another command via a pipe, instead of reading keyboard input. Also, the command output is saved in the files in file-list and redirected to another command instead of being displayed on screen. The following is the commonly used syntax of this utility.

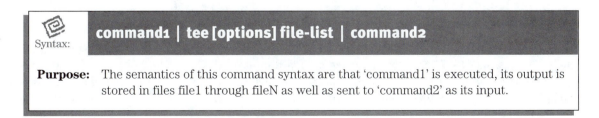

command1 | tee [options] file-list | command2

Purpose: The semantics of this command syntax are that 'command1' is executed, its output is stored in files file1 through fileN as well as sent to 'command2' as its input.

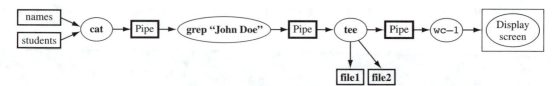

Figure 3.3 The semantics of the **cat tempfile | grep "John Doe" | tee file 1 file 2 | wc -l** command

An example use of the **tee** utility is given in the following command.

```
$ cat names students | grep "John Doe" | tee file1 file2 | wc -l
$
```

This command line extracts those lines from the names and students files that contain the string John Doe, pipes these lines to the **tee** utility which puts copies of these line in the two files file1 and file2 as well as sends them to **wc -l**, which sends its output to the display screen. Thus, those lines in the names and students files that contain the string John Doe are saved in file1 and file2 and the line count of such lines is displayed on the monitor screen. Figure 3.3 illustrates the semantics of this command line.

IN-CHAPTER EXERCISES

3.8 Write a shell command that sorts a file students.records and stores the lines containing Tom in a file called Tom.record. Use piping and I/O redirection.

3.9 Write a command to copy a file Scores to Scores.bak and send a sorted version of **Scores** to professor@college.edu via the **mail** command.

3.10 Write a TC shell command for copying a file Phones in your home directory to a file called Phones.bak (also in your home directory) by using the **cat** command and the **>&** operator.

Such commands are useful in a shell script where different operations have to be performed on file1 and file2 later in the script.

In the following In-Chapter Exercises, you will practice the use of input, output, and error redirection and piping features of LINUX/UNIX shells in a command line.

3.6 SUMMARY

For every command, LINUX/UNIX automatically opens three files to read input from and send output and error messages to. These files are called standard input (stdin), standard output (stdout), and standard error (stderr). By default, these files are attached to the terminal on which the command is executed. Thus, the command input is expected from the terminal keyboard and output and error messages go to the monitor screen. These default files can be changed to other files by using redirection operators: < for input redirection and > for output and error redirection.

In Bash, using integers 0, 1, and 2—known as file descriptors for the three standard files, respectively—can refer to stdin, stdout, and stderr. The > operator is used in conjunction with descriptor 2 to redirect error. The use of descriptors 0 and 1 with the operators < and >, respectively, is optional. The TC shell does not support redirection with file descriptors. Also, redirecting stdout and stderr of a command to different files is specified differently in the TC shell than it is in Bash.

The LINUX and UNIX commands that read input from stdin, process it in some fashion, and send it to stdout, are called filters. Examples of filters are **pr**, **sort**, **tr**, and **zip**. Stdout of a command can be connected to stdin of another command via a LINUX/UNIX pipe. Pipes are created in the main memory and are used to take output of a command and give it to another command without creating a disk file, effectively making two commands talk to each other. I/O and error redirection features and pipes can be used together to perform complicated operations with one command line. The **tee** utility can be used to save output of a command in one or more files as well as send it to stdin of another command.

3.7 QUESTIONS AND PROBLEMS

1. What are standard files? Name them and describe their purpose.

2. Sort a file data1 and put the sorted file in a file called data1.sorted. Give the Bash and TC shell commands for performing this task.

3. What is a LINUX/UNIX filter? Name five and give examples of their use.

4. Use the **tr** command to translate all uppercase letters in a file, called Grades, to lowercase and store the output in the grades file.

5. What is a LINUX/UNIX pipe? How is a pipe different from output redirection? Give an example to illustrate your answer.

6. What is the purpose of the **tee** command? Give an example of the use of this command.

7. Write LINUX/UNIX shell commands to carry out the following tasks.

   a. Count the number of characters, words, and lines in the a file called data1 and display the output on the screen.

   b. Count the number of characters, words, and lines in the output of the **ls –l** command and display the output on the screen.

   c. Perform the same task as in 7b, but redirect the output to a file called data1.stats.

8. Give the command line for searching a file datafile for the string Internet, sending the output of the command to a file called Internet.freq and sending any error message to a file error.log.

9. What do the following commands do? Specifically, where do the inputs of the commands come from, where do their outputs go, and where do the error messages go? Explain your answers.

   a. `cat 1> letter 2> save 0< memo`

   b. `cat 2> save 0< memo 1> letter`

c. `cat 1> letter 0< memo 2>&1`

d. `cat 0< memo | sort 1> letter 2> /dev/null`

e. `cat 2> save 0< memo | sort 1> letter 2> /dev/null`

10. Consider the following two commands.

    `cat memo letter 2> communication 1>&2`

    `cat memo letter 1>&2 2> communication`

    Where do output and error messages of the `cat` command go in each case if

    a. both files (memo and letter) exist in the present working directory

    b. one of the two files does not exist in the present working directory

11. What happens when the following commands are executed on your LINUX/UNIX system? Why do you think these commands produce the results that they do?

    `cat letter >> letter`

    `cat letter > letter`

12. Repeat Exercise 3.6, but append error messages at the end of mail.error.

13. Give a command line for displaying the number of users currently logged on the system. Give the command line that performs the above task by counting only once if a user is logged on multiple times.

14. What is the difference between the following commands?

    a. `grep "John Doe" Students > /dev/null 2>&1`

    b. `grep "John Doe" Students 2>&1 > dev/null`

15. Save the output of the **who** command in the who.log file and run the following command on your system. What does this command do? Explain your answer.

    `uptime | cat - who.log >> system.log`

16. Consider a file called employees that contains information about employees in a department, one line per employee. Give a command line for displaying the lines in the employees file that are not repeated.

17. Give a command line that displays a long listing for the most recently created directory.

18. Give a command line for displaying the number of users currently logged onto your system.

19. Give a command for displaying the login name of the user who was the first to log on to a system.

20. Give a command that reads its input from a file called Phones and removes unnecessary spaces from the file, sorts the file, and removes duplicate lines from that file.

Printer Control

OBJECTIVES

- To describe the LINUX/UNIX mechanism and command for printing files
- To describe commands for printer control
- Commands and primitives covered: `lpq, lpr, lprm,` lpstat

4.1 INTRODUCTION

In this chapter, we cover file printing fully, including commands related to printing and printer control. These commands include commands for printing files, checking the status of print requests/jobs on a printer, and canceling print jobs.

4.2 LINUX/UNIX MECHANISM FOR PRINTING FILES

The process of printing files is similar to the process of displaying files: in both cases the contents of one or more files are sent to an output device. In the case of displaying files the output device is a display screen, whereas in the case of printing files the output device is a printer. Another key difference results primarily from the fact that every user has an individual display screen but that many users share a single printer on a typical multiuser computer running LINUX/UNIX (or any **time-sharing**) operating system. Thus when you use the `cat` or `more` command to display a file, the contents of the file are sent immediately to the display screen by LINUX/UNIX. However, when you print a file, its contents are not sent immediately to the printer because the printer may be busy printing another file (yours or some other user's). To handle multiple requests, a **first-come first-serve** (**FCFS**) mechanism places a print request in a queue and processes the request in its turn when the printer is available.

LINUX/UNIX maintains a queue of print requests, called the **print queue,** associated with every printer in the system. Each print request, also called a **print job,** is assigned a number, called **job ID.** When you use a command to print a file, the system makes a temporary copy of your file, assigns a job ID to your request, and puts the job in the print queue associated with the printer specified in the command line. When the printer finishes its current job, it is given the next job from the front of the print queue. Thus your job is processed when the printer is available and your job is at the head of the print queue.

The work of maintaining the print queue and directing print jobs to the right printer is performed by a LINUX/UNIX process called the **printer spooler,** or **printer daemon.** The LINUX/UNIX printer daemon (**lpd**) starts execution in the background when the system boots up, and waits for your print requests. We discuss LINUX/UNIX daemons in Chapter 6. For now, think of a daemon as a process that runs while you are unaware of its presence because it does not interact with the terminal.

4.3 PRINTER CONTROL COMMANDS

LINUX and UNIX have many commands for printer control that allow you to print files, display the status of a print job, display the status of one or more printers on your local network, remove a print job from a print queue, test a printer, and control a printer, its print queue, and the printer daemon. Table 4.1 contains a list of the printing-related commands for LINUX/UNIX. The superuser—the system administrator—normally uses `lpc` and `lpstat`.

Table 4.1		List of Commands Related to Printing and Printer Control
Command		**Purpose**
System V UNIX	**LINUX and BSD UNIX**	
lp	lpr	Submit a file for printing
lpstat	lpq/lpstat	Display the status of print jobs for one or more printers
cancel	lprm	Remove or purge one or more jobs from the print queue
	lpc	Printer control command
	lptest	Generate a ripple pattern to test the printer

4.4 PRINTING FILES

As shown in Table 4.1, you can print files by using the `lpr` command. The following is a brief description of this command.

Syntax:

lpr [options] file-list

Purpose: Submit a print request to print the files in 'file-list'

Commonly used options / features:

-# N	Print N copies of the file(s) in 'file-list'; default is one copy
-P ptr	Submit the print request for the **ptr** printer
-T title	Print **title** on a banner page
-m	Send mail after printing is complete
-p	Format the output by using the **pr** command

The following session shows how to use the `lpr` command with and without options. The first `lpr` command sends the print request for printing the lab1.c file on the default printer. The second command sends the request for printing the prog1.java file on the hp2left printer. The third command prints three copies of the project.C file on the hp3right printer.

```
$ lpr lab1.c
$ lpr -P hp2left prog1.java
$ lpr -P hp3right -# 3 project.C
$
```

You can use the following command to print the lab1.c file with the header information on every page produced by the **pr** command. In this command, the output of the **pr** command that normally goes to stdout is sent to the **lpr** command via a pipe. The pipe operator (|) is discussed in Chapter 3.

```
$ pr lab1.c | lpr
$
```

You can also perform the above task with the **lpr -p lab1.c** command. You can print two copies of the lab1.c file on the hp5right printer with line numbers and a **pr** header on each page by using the following command. The **nl** command numbers the lines in the lab1.c file and sends them to the **pr** command via a pipe. The **pr** command inserts the header information on the page that it received from the **nl** command and sends it to the **lpr** command. The **lpr** command prints two copies of the final version on the hp5right printer. You can perform the same task with the **nl lab1.c | lpr –p – #2 –Php5right** command.

```
$ nl lab1.c | pr | lpr -#2 —Php5right
$
```

In the following In-Chapter Exercises, you will use the **lpr, nl**, and **pr** commands to appreciate the tasks they perform.

IN-CHAPTER EXERCISES

4.1   How would you print five copies of the file lab1.c on the printer cs_hp1? Write down the command.

4.2   Repeat the above task, incorporating commands to number all the lines and to print the **pr** header on the output.

It is important to note that you should NEVER try printing nontext files with the **lpr** command, especially files with control characters (e.g., executable files such as a.out). Doing so will not print what you want printed and will waste many printer pages. Don't even try testing it! If you do accidentally print a nontext file, turn off the printer immediately and run to your system administrator for help.

4.5 FINDING THE STATUS OF A PRINT REQUEST

You can use the **lpq** or **lpstat** command to display the status of print jobs on a printer. We discuss both of these commands here. The following is a brief description of the **lpq** command.

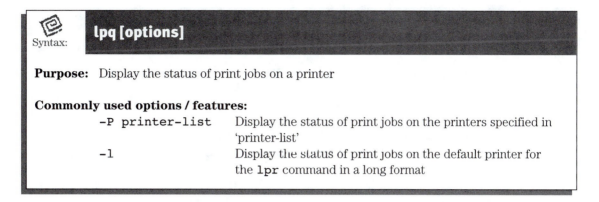

Syntax: **lpq [options]**

Purpose: Display the status of print jobs on a printer

Commonly used options / features:

-P printer-list   Display the status of print jobs on the printers specified in 'printer-list'

-l   Display the status of print jobs on the default printer for the `lpr` command in a long format

The most commonly used option of this command is **-P**. In the following session, the first command is used to display the status of print jobs on the hp5 printer. The output of the command shows that there are four jobs in the printer queue with job IDs 3991, 3992, 3993, and 3994. The active job (job ID 3991) is at the head of print queue and it is for printing the mail.bob file. When the printer is ready for printing, it will print the active job first. The second command shows that the hp3right printer has no job to print.

```
$ lpq -Php5
hp5 is ready and printing
Rank     Owner      Job           Files           Total Size
active   sarwar     3991          mail.bob        1056 bytes
1st      sarwar     3992          csh.man         93874 bytes
2nd      davis      3993          proposal1.nsa   2708921 bytes
3rd      tom        3994          memo            8920 bytes
$ lpq -Php3right
no entries
$
```

Here is a brief description of the `lpstat` command.

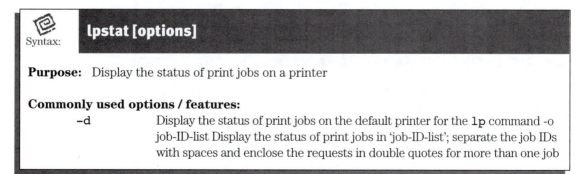

Syntax: **lpstat [options]**

Purpose: Display the status of print jobs on a printer

Commonly used options / features:

-d   Display the status of print jobs on the default printer for the `lp` command -o job-ID-list Display the status of print jobs in 'job-ID-list'; separate the job IDs with spaces and enclose the requests in double quotes for more than one job

Syntax: **lpstat [options]** *(continued)*

-o job-ID-list	Display the status of print jobs in 'job-ID-list'; separate the job
-p printer-list	Display the status of print jobs on the printers specified in 'printer-list'
-u user-list	Display the status of print jobs from the users in 'user-list'

Without any option, the `lpstat` command displays the status of all the print jobs that are printing or waiting in the print queue. We show some typical uses of the command.

The `lpstat -p` command shows the status of all printers on the network. You can specify the printer list to display the status of print jobs on them, as in `lpstat -p hp5` for displaying the status of print jobs on the hp5 printer.

In the following session, the `lpstat -u sarwar` displays all print jobs for the user sarwar. The output of the command shows that there are three print jobs submitted by sarwar—two to hp5 (job IDs 3998 and 3999) and one to hp4left (job ID 534).

```
$ lpstat -u sarwar
3991    sarwar  1056 Aug 17 17:48 on hp5
3992    sarwar 34726 Aug 17 17:48
534     sarwar 47268 Aug 17 17:49 on hp4left
$
```

In the following In-Chapter Exercises, you will use the `lpq` and `lpstat` commands to appreciate the tasks they perform.

IN-CHAPTER EXERCISES

4.3 Display the status of all your print jobs. What command did you use?

4.4 Display the status of all the printers on your system. What command did you use?

4.6 DISPLAYING THE NAMES OF PRINTERS ON YOUR SYSTEM

You can use the `lpstat -a` command to display all the printers that are up and accepting print jobs. The output of this command in the following session shows that your local network has 12 printers that are up and accepting print requests.

```
$ lpstat —a
ppr accepting requests since Wed Mar 12 13:33:11 PST 1997
tpr accepting requests since Wed Mar 12 13:33:13 PST 1997
jpr accepting requests since Wed Mar 12 13:33:10 PST 1997
cpr accepting requests since Wed Mar 12 13:33:09 PST 1997
wpr accepting requests since Wed Mar 12 13:33:13 PST 1997
spr accepting requests since Wed Mar 12 13:33:12 PST 1997
opr accepting requests since Wed Mar 12 13:33:11 PST 1997
mpr accepting requests since Wed Mar 12 13:33:10 PST 1997
qpr accepting requests since Wed Mar 12 13:33:12 PST 1997
apr accepting requests since Wed Mar 12 13:33:09 PST 1997
fpr accepting requests since Wed Mar 12 13:33:10 PST 1997
kpr accepting requests since Fri Apr 17 19:00:26 PDT 1998
$
```

For displaying the names of the printers only, you can use the `lpstat —a | cut —d' ' —f1` command. When this command line is executed, the output of the `lpstat —a` command is given as input to the `cut` command, which cuts the first word of each line of input and sends it to stdout (i.e., the display screen). To display the total number of printers on your system, you can use the `lpstat —a | cut —d' ' —f1 | wc —l` command, as shown below. The `wc —l` command displays the number of lines in its input. We discuss this command in detail in Chapter 13.

```
$ lpstat -a | cut -d' ' -f1 | wc -l
      13
$
```

In the following In-Chapter Exercises, you will use the `lpstat` and `cut` commands, along with the pipe operator, to display the printers on your system.

IN-CHAPTER EXERCISES

4.5 Run the `lpstat —a` and `lpstat —a | cut —d' ' —f1` commands on your system and show their outputs.

4.7 CANCELING PRINT JOBS

There may be times when you want to cancel your print request. You may suddenly realize that you have submitted the wrong file for printing, for example. You can use the `lprm` command to perform this task. The following is a brief description of the command.

Syntax: **lprm [options] [jobID-list] [user(s)]**

Purpose: Cancel print requests that were made with the `lpr` command, that is, remove these jobs from the print queue. The job IDs in 'jobID-list' are taken from the output of the `lpq` command

Commonly used options / features:

–	Remove all the jobs that you own
N	Remove the job with jobs ID 'N' from the print queue of the default printer
-P ptr	Specify the print queue for the 'ptr' printer
user	Attempt to remove any jobs queued belonging to the user 'user.' This option is useful only to the superuser, who is allowed to remove anyone's print jobs

---

The following `lprm` commands show how print jobs can be removed from a printer. The first command removes print job 3991 from the hp5 printer and the second removes all print jobs for the user john from the hp5 printer.

```
$ lprm -Php5 3991
3991 dequeued
$ lprm -Php5 john
3997 dequeued
3998 dequeued
$
```

When executed without an argument, the `lprm` command removes the job that is currently active, provided it is one of your jobs. You cannot remove others' print jobs from a printer. If `lprm` does not find a job in a print queue, it remains silent.

In the following In-Chapter Exercises, you will use the `lprm` command to appreciate the tasks that it performs.

IN-CHAPTER EXERCISES

4.6 Open the paper tray of your default printer. Send a print job to that printer. Then remove the job from the printer queue with the `lprm` command. Show your shell session for performing these steps.

4.8 CONTROLLING PRINTERS

The system administrator can use the `lpc` utility to perform various operations on printer daemons and queues, including disabling and enabling printers, terminating and restarting the print daemon, cleaning a print queue, turning a printer queue off, displaying the status of print daemons and queues, and manipulating print queues to print jobs in a particular order (to reorder print queues). Here is a brief description of this command.

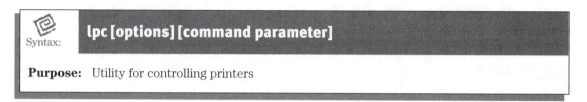

Syntax:

lpc [options] [command parameter]

Purpose: Utility for controlling printers

A common use of this utility by an average user is to display the status of printers. In the following session, we use the `lpc help` command to display the names of various commands that can be run under the `lpc` utility. The `lpc status hp5` command is used to display the status of the hp5 printer. The output of the command shows that the printer is up and running and has no print job in its queue.

```
$ lpc help

Commands may be abbreviated.   Commands are:

abort    enable   disable help    restart status   topq     ?
clean    exit     down    quit    start   stop     up
$ lpc status hp5
hp5:
        queuing is enabled
        printing is enabled
        no entries
        no daemon present
$
```

When used interactively, the `lpc` command displays the `lpc>` prompt and allows you to run any `lpc` command. In the following session we show the interactive use of the `lpc` utility. The `status` command is used to display the status of the hp3 and hp4 printers. The `quit` command is used to exit the lpc program. The `exit` command performs the same task.

```
$ lpc
lpc> status hp3 hp4
hp3:
        queuing is enabled
        printing is enabled
        no entries
        no daemon present
hp4:
        queuing is enabled
        printing is enabled
        no entries
        no daemon present
lpc> quit
$
```

You can use the `lpc status `ls /var/spool/lpd`` command to display the status of all the printers on your network. Note that the `ls` command is enclosed in back quotes (grave accents) and not forward quotes. If you don't have the permission to search and read any directory in the pathname /var/spool/lpd, an error message is reported.

The `lptest` command can be used to display the printer ripple pattern that displays the 96 printable ASCII characters in 96 lines with every character appearing in every position. By default 200 lines are displayed with a line length of 79 characters.

4.9 SUMMARY

LINUX and UNIX have a set of commands for printing and printer control. You can use the `lpr` command for printing files on a printer, the `lpq` command for checking the status of all print jobs on a printer (waiting, printing, etc.), the `lprm` command to remove a print job from a printer queue so that the requested file is not printed, the `lpstat` command for reporting the status of print jobs on printers, the `lpc` command for controlling printers and print daemons, and the `lptest` command to generate a ripple pattern for testing a printer.

4.10 QUESTIONS AND PROBLEMS

1. Describe the mechanism used by LINUX/UNIX for printing.
2. Clearly describe the terms print job, print queue, and print spooler (print daemon).
3. Name five commonly used printing-related tasks. Give LINUX/UNIX commands for performing these tasks.

4. What is a printer daemon? What is it called in LINUX/UNIX? How did you obtain your answer?

5. What is a print job? What is the job ID for a print request?

6. How would you print five copies of a file, called memo, on a printer called hp7? Give a command for performing this task.

7. Give a command line for producing 10 copies of the file report on the hp3 printer. Each page should contain a page header produced by the **pr** command.

8. Give a command line for checking the status of a print job with job ID 8971 on your default printer. How would you remove this print job from the print queue? What command would you use to check the status of a print job with job ID 9506 on the hp5 printer?

9. After submitting two print requests, you realize that you really wanted to print five copies of the file called letter. How would you remove the print jobs from the print queue?

10. Give the command for displaying the status of all the printers that your LINUX/UNIX computer has access to. What command did you use? Show the command and its output.

11. What command would you use to display the total number of printers on your system? Show the execution of the command and its output on your system.

12. Give a command for removing all your print jobs for the print queue.

13. Suppose that you are a system administrator of a LINUX/UNIX computer system. What command will you use to remove all print jobs for the user bill on the system?

## CHAPTER 5

File Security

OBJECTIVES

- To discuss briefly the basic mechanisms provided by LINUX and UNIX for file protection
- To describe in detail file protection based on access permission
- To discuss default permissions for files and directories
- To describe the mechanism used by LINUX and UNIX to set default permissions
- To discuss the commands for setting, displaying, and changing file permissions
- Commands and primitives covered: chmod, ls -l, ls -ld, touch, umask

---

5.1 INTRODUCTION

Although time-sharing systems such as LINUX and UNIX offer great benefits, protecting the hardware and software resources in them is a challenge. These resources include the I/O devices, CPU, main memory, and the secondary storage devices that store user files. We have limited the scope of this section to protecting a user's files from unauthorized access by other users. LINUX and UNIX provide three mechanisms for protecting your files.

The most fundamental scheme for protecting user files is to give every user a login name and a password, allowing a user to use a system (see Chapter 1). To prevent others from accessing your files, only you should know the password for your computer account. The second scheme protects individual files by converting them through encryption to a form that is completely different from the original version. You can use this technique to protect important files so that the contents of these files cannot be understood even if someone somehow gains access to them. The third file protection scheme protects your files by associating access privileges with them so that only a subset of users can access them for a subset of file operations. This technique is the primary focus of this chapter. We discuss how the basic file protection mechanism—using read, write, and execute access privileges—works in LINUX and UNIX and extend this discussion to describe advanced file protection with set UID, set GID, and sticky bits.

5.2 FILE PROTECTION BASED ON ACCESS PERMISSION

File protection based on access permission prevents users from accessing each others' files when they are not logged on as a file's owner. As file owner, you attach certain access rights to your files that dictate who can and cannot access them for various types of file operations. This scheme is based on the types of users, the types of access permissions, and the types of operations allowed on a file under LINUX/UNIX. Without such a protection scheme, users could access each others' files because the LINUX file system structure has a single root from which all the files in the system hang (see Figure 2.1).

5.2.1 TYPES OF USERS

Every user in a LINUX/UNIX system belongs to a group of users, as assigned by the system administrator when the user is allocated an account on the system. A user can belong to multiple groups, but a typical LINUX/UNIX user belongs to a single group. All the groups in the system and their memberships are listed in the file /etc/group (see Figure 2.1). This file contains one line per group, with the last field of the line containing the login names of the group members. The three types of users of a LINUX/UNIX file are: the owner of the file (known as the user); someone who belongs to the same group as the owner of the file; or an unconnected user (known as others—everyone else who has an account on the system). As the owner of a file you can specify who can access it.

Every LINUX/UNIX system has one special user who has access to all of the files on the system, regardless of the access privileges on the files. This user, commonly known as the superuser, is the administrator of the computer system. The login name for the superuser is root, and the user ID is 0.

5.2.2 TYPES OF FILE OPERATIONS/ACCESS PERMISSIONS

In LINUX and UNIX, three types of access permissions/privileges are associated with a file: read (r), write (w), and execute (x). The read permission allows you to read the file, the write permission allows you to write to or remove the file, and the execute permission allows you to execute (run) the file. The execute permission should be set for executable files only (files containing binary codes or shell scripts); setting it for any other type of file doesn't make sense.

Recall that a directory is a file, hence access rights pertain to them also. The read permission for a directory allows you to read the contents of the directory. Thus the `ls` command can be used to list the contents of a directory. The write permission for a directory allows you to create a new **directory entry** (file name and a pointer to a place that contains the file's attributes, including its location on disk) in it or to remove an existing entry from it. The execute permission for a directory allows you to search for a directory but not to read from or write to it. Thus, if you don't have execute permission for a directory, you can't use the `ls -l` command to list its contents or use the `cd` command to make it your current directory. The same is true if any component in a directory's pathname does not contain execute permission.

With three types of file users and three types of permissions, a LINUX/UNIX file has nine different types of permissions associated with it, three per user type, as shown in Table 5.1.

The value of X can be 1 (for permission allowed) or 0 (permission not allowed). Therefore 1 bit is needed to represent a permission type. So a total of three bits are needed to indicate file permissions for one type of user (user, group, or others). In other words, a user of a file can have one of the eight possible types of permissions for a file. These eight 3-bit values can be represented by octal numbers from 0 through 7, and in terms of r, w, and x as shown in Table 5.2, 0 means no permissions and 7 means all (read, write, and execute) permissions.

The total of nine bits needed to express permissions for all three types of file users results in possible access permission values of 000 through 777 (in octal) for file permissions. The first octal digit specifies permissions for the owner of the file, the second digit specifies permissions for the group that the owner of the file belongs to, and the third digit specifies permissions for everyone else. A bit value of 0 for a permission is also denoted dash (-), and a value of 1 is also denoted r, w, or x, depending on the position of the bit according to the table. Thus a permission value of 0 in octal (no permissions allowed) for a user of a file can be written as --- and a permission of 7 (all three permissions allowed) can be denoted rwx.

Table 5.1	Summary of File Permissions in LINUX/UNIX		
User Type	**Permission Type**		
	Read (r)	Write (w)	Execure (x)
User (u)	x	x	x
Group (g)	x	x	x
Others (o)	x	x	x

Table 5.2				Permission Values	
r	w	x	Ocatal Value	Permission Value in Terms of r, w, x, and -	Meaning
0	0	0	0	---	No permission
0	0	1	1	--x	Execute-only permission
0	1	0	2	-w-	Write-only permission
0	1	1	3	-wx	Write and execute permission
1	0	0	4	r--	Read-only permission
1	0	1	5	r-x	Read and execute permission
1	1	0	6	rw-	Read and write permission
1	1	1	7	rwx	Read, write, and execute permission

5.2.3 DEFAULT FILE ACCESS PRIVILEGES

When a new file or directory is created, LINUX sets its access privileges based on the argument of the
umask command. The following is a brief description of the command.

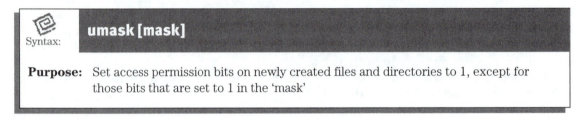

Syntax: **umask [mask]**

Purpose: Set access permission bits on newly created files and directories to 1, except for
those bits that are set to 1 in the 'mask'

The argument of the umask command is a **bit mask,** specified in octal, which identifies the protection bits that are to be turned off when a new file is created. The access permission value for a file
is computed by the expression

file access permission = default permissions - mask

where mask is the argument of the umask command and default permissions are 777 for an executable file or directory and 666 for a text file (i.e., no execute permission for text files). If a text file
contains a program script such as a Perl script or a shell script, you must explicitly add the execute
permission for the file so it can be executed. Symbolic links are always created with 777 access privileges, and device files are created with permissions specified in the mknod command. Therefore, if
the umask 013 command is executed, file access privileges for the newly created executable files and
directories are set to (777 - 013) = 764. Thus every new executable file or directory has its access privileges set to rwxrw-r--. The mask value of 777 disallows any access to newly created files and directories because all the bits in the mask (777) are set. In other words, the access privileges for the newly
created executable files and directories are set to (777 - 777) = 000.

A commonly used mask value is 022, which sets the default access privileges for newly created
executable files and directories to (777 - 022) = 755 and for text files to (666 - 022) = 644. The

authors of this textbook prefer a mask value of 077 so that their files are always created with full protection in place, that is, full access permissions for the owner and no permissions for anyone else. You can change access privileges for files on an as-needed basis by using the **chmod** command (see Section 5.2.5 below). In the following session, we use the **umask**, **touch**, and **ls -l** commands to show how the **umask** command affects the file permissions of the newly created files. The **touch** command without an argument can be used to create an empty file. The foo file created after the permissions mask has been set to 022 has its permissions set to 644, and the bar file and foobar directory created after the permissions mask has been set to 077 have their access privileges set to 600.

```
$ umask 022
$ touch foo
$ umask 077
$ touch bar
$ mkdir foobar
$ ls -l foo bar foobar
-rw-------  1  sarwar  faculty  0    Nov 5 16:16 bar
-rw-r--r--  1  sarwar  faculty  0    Nov 5 16:16 foo
drw-------  2  sarwar  faculty  512 Nov 5 16:16 foobar
$
```

The **umask** command is normally placed in a system startup file ~/.profile, ~/.login, or /etc/profile. It may also be placed in a shell startup file such as ~/.cshrc, /etc/zshrc, /etc/bashrc, /etc/csh.cshrc, /etc/skel/.bashrc, /etc/skel/.bash_profile, or /etc/skel/.zshrc.

When the command is executed without an argument, it displays the current value of the bit mask, as in

```
$ umask
777
$
```

IN-CHAPTER EXERCISES

5.1   Run the **umask** command without any argument to display the current value of the bit mask. What is it? With this mask, what will be the default permission on a text file and a directory? Why? Use the **mkdir** command to create a directory and a text file with the text editor of your choice and run the **ls -l** command to display their permissions. What are the permissions for the directory and the file?

5.2.4 Determining File Access Privileges

You can use the `ls` command with the `–1` or `–ld` option to display access permissions for a list of files and/or directories. Without a file argument, the command gives long lists for all the files (except hidden files) in the present working directory.

Consider the following session.

```
$ ls -1
total 20
drwxr-x---     2 sarwar   faculty      512 Mar   3 10:10 courses
-rwxrwxrwx     1 sarwar   faculty       12 Apr  14 11:03 labs
-rwxr--r--     1 sarwar   faculty      163 May   1 10:12 temp
$
```

As stated previously, the left-most character in the first field of the output indicates the file type (e.g., d for directory and - for ordinary file). The remaining nine characters in the first field show file access privileges for user, group, and others, respectively. The output shows that the owner has read, write, and execute access for the courses directory, users in the faculty group have read and execute permissions, and nobody else has any permissions. Every user has full permissions for the labs file. And, finally, the owner has full access and everyone else has read-only permission for the temp file.

If an argument of the `ls –1` command is a directory, the command displays the long lists of all the files and directories in it. You can use the `ls –ld` command to display long lists of directories only. When executed without an argument this command displays the long list for the current directory, as shown in the first command in the following session. The second and third commands show that when the `ls –ld` command is executed with a list of directories as its arguments, it displays the long lists for those directories only. If an argument to the `ls –ld` command is a file, the command displays the long list for the file. The fourth command, `ls –ld pvm/*`, displays the long lists for all the files and directories in the pvm directory.

```
$ ls -ld
drwx--x--x 2 sarwar faculty      11264 Jul  6 10:21 .
$ ls -ld ABET
drwx------ 2 sarwar faculty        512 Dec 18 1997 ABET
$ ls -ld ~/myweb/Images courses/ee446
drwx------ 3 sarwar faculty        512 Apr 30 09:52 courses/ee446
drwx--x--x 2 sarwar faculty       2048 Dec 18 1997
    /home/faculty/sarwar/myweb/Images
$ ls -ld pvm/*
drwx------ 3 sarwar faculty        512 Dec 18 1997 pvm/examples
drwx------ 2 sarwar faculty       1024 Oct 27 1998 pvm/qsort
```

```
-rw------- 1 sarwar faculty      1606 Jun 19 1995 pvm/Book_PVM
-rw------- 1 sarwar faculty      7639 Sep 11 1998 pvm/Jim_Davis
$
```

The following In-Chapter Exercises ask you to use the `ls -l` and `ls -ld` commands to see how they can be used to display access privileges for files and directories.

IN-CHAPTER EXERCISES

5.2 Use the `ls -l` and `ls -ld` commands to display the long list of the /etc/passwd file and your home directory. Write down the permissions on each. Do the permission values make sense? Why?

5.3 Display access privileges for all the files in your current directory. What command did you use?

5.2.5 CHANGING FILE ACCESS PRIVILEGES

You can use the **chmod** command to change access privileges for your files. Here is a brief description of the **chmod** command.

Syntax:

chmod [options] octal-mode file-list
chmod [options] symbolic-mode file-list

Purpose: Change or set permissions on files in 'file-list'

Commonly used options/features:

R	Recursively descend through directories changing/setting permissions for all of the files and subdirectories under the given directory
-f	Force specified access permissions

The **symbolic mode,** also known as **mode control word,** has the form <who><operator> <privilege>. The possible values for who are u, g, o, a, or a combination of u, g, and o. Remember that **u** is for user (owner), **g** for group, **o** for others, and **a** for all. The possible values for operator are + (add privilege), – (remove privilege), and = (set privilege). The possible values for privilege are r, w, x, u (user's current privileges), g (group's current privileges), and o (other's current privileges). We are not discussing the advanced privileges such as the sticky bit.

Note that u, g, or o can be used as a privilege with the = operator only. Multiple values can be used for who and privilege such as ug for the who field and **rx** for the privilege field. Some useful

Table 5.3	Examples of the chmod Command and Their Purposes
Command	**Purpose**
`chmod 700 *`	Set access privileges for all the files (including directories) in the current directory to read, write, and execute for the owner and no access privileges to anyone else
`chmod 700 ~`	Set access privileges for the home directory to read, write, and execute for the owner and no privileges for anyone else. (The authors use this command for their home directories; they do not trust anyone when it comes to security of their files, and they stop everyone at the main gate.)
`chmod 740 courses`	Set access privileges for courses to read, write, and execute for the owner and read-only for the group; noaccess for others
`chmod 751 ~/courses`	Set access privileges for ~/courses to read, write, and execute for the owner, read and search for the group, and search-only for others
`chmod 755 ~/labs`	Set access privileges for the ~/labs directory to read, write, and execute for the owner and read and execute for everyone else
`chmod u=rwx courses`	Set owner's access privileges to read, write, and execute for courses and keeps the group's and others' privileges at their present values
`chmod ugo-rw sample` or `chmod a-rw sample`	Don't let anyone read or write sample chmod a+x sample Let everyone execute sample
`chmod g=u sample`	Make sample's group privileges match its user's (owner's) privileges
`chmod a+x sample`	Let everyone execute sample
`chmod go= sample`	Remove all access privileges for the group and others for sample

examples of the chmod command and their purposes are listed in Table 5.3. Recall that the execute permission means search for directories.

The following session illustrates how access privileges for files can be determined and set. The **chmod** commands are used to change (or set) access privileges, and the **ls –l** (or **ls –ld**) commands are used to show the effect of the **chmod** commands. After the chmod 700 courses command has been executed, the owner of the courses file has all three access privileges for it, and nobody else has any privileges. The **chmod g+rx courses** command adds read and execute access privileges to the courses file for the group. The **chmod o+r courses** command adds the read access privilege to the courses file for others. The **chmod a–w *** command takes away the write access privilege from all users for all the files in the current directory. The chmod **700 [l–t]*** command sets access permissions 700 for all the files that start with letters *l* through *t*, as illustrated by the output of the last **ls –l** command, which shows access privileges for the files labs and temp changed to 700.

```
$ cd
$ ls -l
drwxr-x---    2   sarwar   faculty 512    Apr 23 09:37    courses
-rwxrwxrwx    1   sarwar   faculty 12     May 01 13:22    labs
```

```
-rwxr--r--  1  sarwar  faculty  163   May 05 23:13  temp
$ chmod 700 courses
$ ls -ld courses
drwx------  2  sarwar  faculty  512   Apr 23 09:37  courses
$ chmod g+rx courses
$ ls -ld courses
drwxr-x---  2  sarwar  faculty  512   Apr 23 09:37  courses
$ chmod o+r courses
$ ls -ld courses
drwxr-xr--  2  sarwar  faculty  512   Apr 23 09:37  courses
$ chmod a-w *
$ ls -l
dr-xr-x---  2  sarwar  faculty  512   Apr 23 09:37  courses
-r-xr-xr-x  1  sarwar  faculty  12    May 01 13:22  labs
-r-xr--r--  1  sarwar  faculty  163   May 05 23:13  temp
$ chmod 700 [l-t]*
$ ls -l
dr-xr-x---  2  sarwar  faculty  512   Apr 23 09:37  courses
-rwx------  1  sarwar  faculty  12    May 01 13:22  labs
-rwx------  1  sarwar  faculty  163   May 05 23:13  temp
$
```

The access permissions for all the files and directories under one or more directories can be set by using the **chmod** command with the **-R** option. The following command sets access permissions for all the files and directories under the directory called ~/MyWeb to 711 recursively. So that others could browse MyWeb the user would need to allow everyone read permission on all the files corresponding to the user's browsable Web pages, i.e., set 755 permissions on these files.

```
$ chmod -R 711 MyWeb
$
```

If you specify access privileges with a single octal digit in a **chmod** command, the command uses the single octal to set the access privileges for others; the access privileges for user and group are both set to 0 (no access privileges). If you specify two octal digits in a **chmod** command, the command uses them to set access privileges for group and others; the access privileges for user are set to 0 (no privileges). In the following session, the first **chmod** command sets others access privileges for the courses directory to 7 (rwx). The second **chmod** command sets group and others access privileges for the personal directory to 7 (rwx) and 0 (---), respectively. The **ls -l** command shows the results of these commands.

```
$ chmod 7 courses
$ chmod 70 personal
$ ls -l
d------rwx   2 sarwar   faculty   512 Nov 10 09:43 courses
d---rwx---   2 sarwar   faculty   512 Nov 10 09:43 personal
drw-------   2 sarwar   faculty   512 Nov 10 09:43 sample
$
```

Let's now look at what the read, write, and execute permissions mean for directories. As we stated before, the read permission on a directory allows you to read the directory's contents. Recall that the contents of a directory are the names of files and directories in it, that the write permission allows you to create a file in the directory or remove an existing file or directory from it, and that the execute permission for a directory is permission to search the directory. In the following session, write permission for the courses directory has been turned off. Thus you cannot create a subdirectory ee345 in this directory by using the `mkdir` command. Similarly, as you do not have search permission for the personal directory you cannot use the `cd` command to get into (change directory to) this directory. If the sample directory had a subdirectory for which the execute permission was turned on, you still could not change directory to it because search permission for sample is turned off. Finally, because read permission for the personal directory is turned off, you cannot display the names of files and directories in it by using the `ls` command.

```
$ chmod 600 sample
$ chmod 500 courses
$ chmod 300 personal
$ ls -ld
dr-x------   2 sarwar   faculty   512 Nov 10 09:43 courses
d-wx------   2 sarwar   faculty   512 Nov 10 09:43 personal
drw-------   2 sarwar   faculty   512 Nov 10 09:43 sample
$ mkdir courses/ee345
mkdir: cannot create directory "courses/ee345"; Permission denied
$ cd sample
bash: cd: sample: Permission denied
$ ls -l personal
ls: personal: Permission denied
$
```

The following session further elaborates the meaning of execute permission for directories, which allows you to search a directory but not read (list) its contents. The `mkdir -p test1/test2/test3` command creates a directory hierarchy in your current directory with test1 as the parent directory that has test2 as its child and test3 as its grandchild. The test1 directory has the execute permission but no read or write permission. This means that you cannot read/list its contents but you can search it. The test2 directory has read, write, and execute permission and therefore you can read its contents, create new files (or directories) in it, and search it. Thus the `ls test1` command produces an error message but the `ls test1/test2` command executes successfully.

```
$ mkdir —p test1/test2/test3
$ chmod 100 test1
$ chmod 700 test1/test2
$ ls test
ls: test1: Permission denied
$ ls test1/test2
test2
$
```

The following In-Chapter Exercises ask you to use the **chmod** and `ls —ld` commands to see how they work, and to enhance your understanding of LINUX and UNIX file access privileges.

IN-CHAPTER EXERCISES

5.4 Create three directories called courses, sample, and personal by using the **mkdir** command. Set access permissions for the sample directory so that you have all three privileges, users in your group have read access only, and other users of your system have no access privileges. What command did you use?

5.5 Use the `chmod o+r sample` command to allow others read access to the sample directory. Use the `ls —ld` sample command to confirm that others have read permission for the directory.

5.6 Use the session preceding these exercises to understand fully how the read, write, and execute permissions work for directories.

5.3 SPECIAL ACCESS BITS

In addition to the nine commonly used access permissions bits described in this chapter (read, write, and execute for user, group, and others), three additional bits are of special significance. These bits are known as the **set-user-ID (SUID) bit, set-group-ID (SGID) bit,** and **sticky bit.**

5.3.1 THE SET-USER-ID (SUID) BIT

We've previously shown that the external shell commands have corresponding files that contain binary executable codes or shell scripts. The programs contained in these files are not special in any way in terms of their ability to perform their tasks. Normally, when a command executes, it does so under the access privileges of the user who issues the command, which is how the access privileges system described in this chapter works. However, a number of LINUX and UNIX commands need to write to files that are otherwise protected from users who normally run these commands. An example of such a file is /etc/passwd, the file that contains a user's login information (see Chapter 2). Only the superuser is allowed to write to this file to perform tasks such as adding a new login and changing a user's group ID. However, LINUX/UNIX users normally are allowed to execute the **passwd** command to change their passwords. Thus, when a user executes the **passwd** command, the command changes the user password in the /etc/passwd file on behalf of the user who runs this command. The problem is that we want users to be able to change their passwords, but at the same time they must not have arbitrary write access to the /etc/passwd file so that information about other users in this file cannot be compromised.

As we stated before, when a command is executed, it runs with the privileges of the user running the command. Another way of stating the same thing is that, when a command runs, it executes with the "effective user ID" of the user running the command. LINUX/UNIX has an elegant mechanism that solves the problem stated in the preceding paragraph—and many other similar security problems—by allowing commands to change their effective user ID and become privileged in some way. This mechanism allows commands such as **passwd** to perform their work without compromising the integrity of the system. Every LINUX/UNIX file has an additional protection bit, called the SUID bit, associated with it. If this bit is set for a file containing an executable program for a command, the command takes on the privileges of the owner of the file when it executes. Thus, if a file is owned by root and has its SUID bit set, it runs with superuser privileges and this bit is set for the **passwd command**. Thus, when you run the **passwd** command, it can write to the /etc/passwd file (replacing your existing password with the new password), even though you do not have access privileges to write to the file.

Several other LINUX and UNIX commands require root ownership and SUID bit set because they access and update operating system resources (files, data structures, etc.) that an average user must not have permissions for. Some of these commands are **lp**, **mail**, **mkdir**, **mv**, and **ps**. Another use of the SUID bit can be made by the authors of a game software that maintains a scores file. When the SUID bit is set for such software, it can update the scores file when a user plays the game, although the same user cannot update the scores file by explicitly writing to it.

The SUID bit can be set by the **chmod** command by using octal or symbolic mode, according to the following syntaxes.

Syntax:

```
chmod 4xxx file-list
chmod u+s file-list
```

Here, **xxx** is the octal number that specifies the read, write, and execute permissions, and the octal digit 4 (binary 100) is used to set the SUID bit. When the SUID bit is set, the execute bit for the user is set to **s** if the execute permission is already set for the user; otherwise it is set to **S**. The following session illustrates use of these command syntaxes. The first **ls –l cp.new** command is used to show that the execute permission for the cp.new file is set. The **chmod 4710 cp.new** command is used to set the SUID bit. The second `ls -l cp.new` command shows that the x bit value has changed to **s** (lowercase). The following two `chmod` commands are used to set the SUID and execute bits to 0. The `ls -l cp.new` command is used to show that execute permission has been taken away from the owner. The `chmod u+s cp.new` command is used to set the SUID bit again, and the last `ls -l cp.new` command shows that the bit value is **S** (uppercase) because the execute bit was not set before the SUID bit is set.

```
$ ls -l cp.new
-rwx---x---  1  sarwar      faculty  12  May 08 20:00   cp.new
$ chmod 4710 cp.new
$ ls -l cp.new
-rws--x---  1  sarwar      faculty  12  May 08 20:00   cp.new
$ chmod u-s cp.new
$ chmod u-x cp.new
$ ls -l cp.new
-rw---x---  1  sarwar      faculty  12  May 08 20:00   cp.new
$ chmod u+s cp.new
$ ls -l cp.new
-rwS--x---  1  sarwar      faculty  12  May 08 20:00   cp.new
$
```

Although the idea of the SUID bit is sound, a SUID bit can compromise the security of the system if it is not implemented correctly. For example, if the permissions of any SUID program file are set to allow write privileges to others, others can change the program in this file or overwrite the existing program with another program. Doing so would allow others to execute your new program with superuser privileges.

5.3.2 THE SET-GROUP-ID (SGID) BIT

The SGID bit works in the same manner the SUID bit does, but it causes the access permissions of the process to take on the group identity of the group to which the owner of the file belongs. This feature is not as dangerous as the SUID feature because most privileged operations require superuser identity regardless of the current group ID. The SGID bit can be set by using either of the following two command syntaxes.

Syntax:

chmod 2xxx file-list
chmod g+s file-list

Here, **xxx** is the octal number specifying the read, write, and execute permissions, and the octal digit 2 (binary 010) specifies that the SGID bit is to be set. When the SGID bit is set, the execute bit for the group is set to **s** if the group already has the execute permission; otherwise it is set to **S**. The following session illustrates the use of these command syntaxes. The command **chmod 2751 cp.new** sets the SGID bit for the cp.new file and sets its access privileges to **751** (**rwxr-x--x**). The rest of the commands are similar to those in Section 5.3.1.

```
$ ls -l cp.new
-rwxr-x--x  1   sarwar   faculty   12   May 08 20:00   cp.new
$ chmod 2751 cp.new
$ ls -l cp.new
-rwxr-s--x  1   sarwar   faculty   12   May 08 20:00   cp.new
$ chmod g-s cp.new
$ chmod g-x cp.new
$ ls -l cp.new
-rwxr----x  1   sarwar   faculty   12   May 08 20:00   cp.new
$ chmod g+s cp.new
$ ls -l cp.new
-rwxr-S--x  1   sarwar   faculty   12   May 08 20:00   cp.new
$
```

You can set or reset the SUID and SGID bits by using a single **chmod** command. Thus the command **chmod ug+s cp.new** can be used to perform this task on the cp.new file. You can also set the SUID and SGID bits along with the access permissions bits (read, write, and execute) by preceding the octal number for access privileges by 6, because the left-most octal digit 6 (binary 110) specifies that both the SUID and SGID bits be set. Thus the command **chmod 6754 cp.new** sets the SUID and SGID bits for the cp.new file and its access privileges to 750.

5.3.3 THE STICKY BIT

The last of the 12 access bits, the sticky bit, can be set to ensure that an unprivileged user may not remove or rename files of other users in a directory. You must be the owner of a directory or have appropriate permissions to set the sticky bit for it. The sticky bit is commonly set for shared directories that contain files owned by several users.

Originally, this bit was designed for the UNIX system to inform the kernel that the code segment of a program is to be shared or kept in the main memory or the swap space owing to frequent use of the program. Thus, when this bit is set for a program, the system tries to keep the executable code for the program (process) in memory after it finishes execution—the processes "sticks around in the memory." If for some reason, memory space occupied by this program is needed by the system for loading another program, the program with the sticky bit set is saved in the **swap space** (a special area on the disk used to save processes temporarily). That is, if the sticky bit is set for a program, the program is kept either in memory or on the swap space after it finishes its execution. When this program is executed again, with the program code in memory, program execution starts right away. If the program code is on the swap space, the time needed for loading it is much shorter than if it were stored on disk as a LINUX/UNIX file. The advantage of this scheme, therefore, is that if a program with the sticky bit on is executed frequently, it is executed much faster.

This facility is useful for programs such as compilers, assemblers, and editors, and commands such as `ls` and `cat`, which are used frequently in a typical computer system environment. Care must be taken that not too many programs have sticky bit set, or system performance will suffer because of lack of free space, with more and more space being used by the programs whose sticky bit is set. This historical use of the sticky bit is not needed in newer UNIX systems and LINUX systems, because they use virtual memory systems that do not remove the most recently used pages or segments of recently executed processes. The sticky bit is now used to ensure that someone other than the owner of a directory cannot remove a file under the directory even if he or she has write permission for the directory. The person with write permission for the directory can still create files and/or directories under this directory. This allows you to put an extra security wall around your shared directories.

The sticky bit can be set by using either of the following command syntaxes.

Syntax:
chmod 1xxx file-list
chmod +t file-list

Here, xxx is the octal number specifying the read, write, and execute permissions, and the octal digit 1 (binary 001) specifies that the sticky bit is to be set. When the sticky bit is set, the execute bit for others is set to **t** if others already has execute permission; otherwise it is set to **T**. The following session illustrates the use of these syntaxes. The `chmod 1775 testSticky` command sets the sticky bit for the testSticky directory and sets its access privileges to 775. The rest of the command lines are similar to those explained in Sections 5.3.1 and 5.3.2 and need not be explained further.

```
$ chmod 1775 testSticky
$ ls -l
total 1
drwxrw-r-t 2 sarwar faculty 512 Oct 28 12:24 testSticky
$ chmod 760 testSticky
$ chmod +t testSticky
$ ls -l
total 1
drwxrw---T 2 sarwar faculty 512 Oct 28 12:24 testSticky
$
```

The following In-Chapter Exercise asks you to use the **chmod** and **ls −l** commands to see how they can be used to set the SUID, SGID, and sticky bits and display their values.

IN-CHAPTER EXERCISES

5.7   Run the above sessions on your system to enhance your understanding of the SUID, SGID, and sticky bits facilities.

5.4 FILE PERMISSIONS AND TYPES

The file permissions and types are stored together in a 16-bit location: the lower 9 bits for file access privileges, the next 3 bits for special permission bits (SUID, SGID, and sticky bits), and the uppermost 4 bits for file type. Further discussion of the bits used to specify file type is beyond the scope of this textbook. You can find values of all access and file types bits in the /usr/include/sys/stat.h file and a detailed discussion on this topic in a more advanced book on LINUX/UNIX programming.

5.5 SUMMARY

A time-sharing system has to ensure protection of one user's files from unauthorized (accidental or malicious) access by other users of the system. LINUX/UNIX provides several mechanisms for this purpose, including one based on access permissions. Files can be protected by informing the system what type of operations (read, write, and execute) are permitted on the file by the owner, group (the users who are in the same group as the owner), and others (everyone else on the system). These nine commonly used access permissions are represented by bits. In addition, there are three special permission bits that allow us to implement advanced protection. These bits are: set-user-ID (SUID) bit, set-group-ID (SGID) bit, and the sticky bit. When a user tries to access a file, the system allows or disallows access based on the file's access privileges.

Access permissions for files can be viewed by using the **ls −l** command. When used with directories, this command displays attributes for all the files in the directories. The **ls −ld** command can be used to view access permissions for directories. The owner of a file can change access privileges on it by using the **chmod** command. The **umask** command allows the user to specify a bit mask that informs the system of access permissions that are disabled for the user, group, and others. When a file is created by a LINUX/UNIX system, it sets access permissions for the file according to the mask given in the **umask** command (i.e., the parameter for the **umask** command). In a typical system, the access permissions are set to (777 - mask) for a new executable file or directory and to (666 - mask) for a text file.

The SUID and SGID bits allow the user to execute commands such as **passwd**, **ls**, **mkdir**, and **ps** that access important system resources to which access is not allowed otherwise. The sticky bit can be set for a directory to ensure that an unprivileged user may not remove or rename files of other users in that directory. Only the owner of a directory, or someone else having appropriate permissions, can set the sticky bit for the directory. It is commonly set for shared directories that contain files owned by several users. Historically, the sticky bit has served another purpose. It can be set for frequently used utilities so that LINUX/UNIX keeps them in the main memory or on a fixed area on the disk, called the swap space, after their use. This feature makes subsequent access to these files much faster than if they were to be loaded from the disk as normal files.

5.6 QUESTIONS AND PROBLEMS

1. What are the three basic file protection schemes available in LINUX/UNIX?

2. How does file protection based on access permissions work? Base your answer on various types of users of a file and the types of operations they can perform. How many permission bits are needed to implement this scheme? Why?

3. How do the read, write, and execute permissions work in LINUX/UNIX? Illustrate your answer with some examples.

4. Create a file test1 in your present working directory and set its access privileges to read and write for yourself, read for the users in your group, and none to everyone else. What command did you use to set privileges? Give another command that would accomplish the same thing.

5. The user sarwar sets access permissions to his home directory by using the command **chmod 700 $HOME**. If the file cp.new in his home directory has read permissions set to 777, can anyone read this file? Why or why not? Explain your answer.

6. What is the effect of each command? Explain your answers.

   ```
   chmod 776 ~/lab5
   chmod 751 ~/lab?
   chmod 555 *.c[
   chmod 711 ~/*
   chmod u+rx ~/bin

   umask 0077

   ls -l

   ls -ld

   ls -l ~/personal

   ls -ld ~/personal
   ```

7. What does the execute permission mean for a directory, a file type for which the execute operation makes no sense?

8. What **umask** command should be executed to set the permissions bit mask to 037? With this mask, what default access privileges are associated with any new file that you create on the system? Why? Where would you put this command so that every time you log onto the system this mask is effective?

9. Give a command line for setting the default access mode so that you have read, write, and execute privileges, your group has read and execute permissions, and all others have no permission for a newly created executable file or directory. How would you test it to be sure that it works correctly?

10. Give **chmod** command lines that perform the same tasks that the **mesg n** and **mesg y** commands do. (*Hint:* Every hardware device, including your terminal, has an associated file in the /dev directory.)

11. Some LINUX/UNIX systems do not allow users to change their passwords with the **passwd** command. How is this restriction enforced? Is it a good or bad practice? Why?

## CHAPTER 6

LINUX/UNIX Processes

OBJECTIVES

- To discuss the process concept
- To describe the concept of foreground and background processes and daemons in LINUX/UNIX
- To discuss various commands in LINUX and UNIX for process and job control
- To describe the process hierarchy in LINUX and UNIX
- To discuss the process and file attributes in LINUX and UNIX
- Commands and primitives covered: `<Ctrl-C>`, `<Ctrl-Z>`, `bg`, `fg`, `jobs`, `kill`, `limit`, `ps`, `pstree`, `top`, `ulimit`

6.1 INTRODUCTION

A process is a program in execution. The LINUX system creates a process every time you run an external command. The process is removed from the system when the command finishes its execution. Process creation and termination is the only mechanism used by the LINUX/UNIX system to execute external commands. In a typical time-sharing system such as LINUX/UNIX, which allows multiple users to use a computer system and run multiple processes, hundreds of thousands of processes are created and terminated every day. The system runs several of these processes simultaneously. In LINUX and UNIX, processes can run in the background or foreground. A background process runs at lower priority and allows you to use shell while the process runs. Because a background process runs at a lower priority, a command that takes a long time to finish is a good candidate for background execution.

The shell executes commands by creating child processes using the **fork** and **exec** system calls. When a process uses the **fork** system call, the LINUX/UNIX kernel creates an exact main memory image of the process. An internal command is executed by the shell itself. An external binary command is executed by the child shell overwriting itself by the code of the command via an **exec** call. For an external command comprising a shell script, the child shell executes the commands in the script file one by one.

We discuss the following process-related topics and operations and their associated commands in this chapter.

- the concept of processes, jobs, and daemons in LINUX/UNIX
- displaying process attributes
- foreground, background, and suspended processes
- displaying jobs
- switching processes between foreground and background
- suspending processes
- suspending and resuming a shell process
- terminating processes
- running processes sequentially and simultaneously
- LINUX/UNIX process hierarchy

6.2 PROCESSES, JOBS, AND DAEMONS

When you type a command and hit `<Enter>`, the shell executes the command. When the command is fully processed (i.e., done), the shell returns by displaying the shell prompt. While your command executes, you don't have access to your shell and therefore cannot execute any other commands until the current command finishes and the shell returns. When commands execute in this manner, we say that they execute in the **foreground.** When a command executes in the foreground, it keeps control of the keyboard. You can have only one process in a console window (on a window-based system) or terminal (on a non-window–based system).

You can suspend a foreground process by pressing `<Ctrl-Z>`. This returns control to your shell process. You can run a command in the **background** by ending the command with an ampersand (`&`).

The background execution of a command allows you to use the shell while the command executes. A suspended or background process is also known as a **job.**

In the following session, the first `find` command executes in foreground. Until the command finishes, you don't get the shell prompt and cannot use the shell for work. The second `find` command runs in the background and allows you to use the shell as it runs. The value in brackets returned by the shell is the **job number** (or job ID) for the process and the other number is its **process identifier (PID)**. So, the job number for the `find` command in the session below is 1 and its PID is 23467.

```
$ find / -name foo -print > foo.paths 2> /dev/null
[ wait until the command finishes execution ]
$ find / -name foo -print > foo.paths 2> /dev/null &
[1] 23467
$
```

Although any background process can be called a daemon, in LINUX and UNIX jargon a **daemon** is a system process running in the background. Daemons are frequently used in LINUX/UNIX to offer various types of services to users and to handle system administration tasks. For example, the print, e-mail, telnet, Web browsing, and finger services are provided via daemons. The printing services are provided by the printer daemon, `lpd`. The finger service is handled by the finger daemon, `fingerd`. The e-mail service is provided by the `smtpd` daemon. The Web-browsing service is handled by the `httpd` daemon and the telnet service is provided by the `telnetd` daemon. The `inetd`, commonly known as the LINUX/UNIX superserver, handles various Internet services by spawning various daemons at system boot time. Access the /etc/inetd.conf file to view the services that are offered by this daemon on your system. This file has one line for every service that `inetd` offers.

Multiple processes are executed on a system with a single CPU (or with more processes than the number of CPUs) running a time-sharing system such as LINUX or UNIX by multiplexing the CPU time (i.e., allowing a process to use the CPU briefly and switching it to another process). The LINUX/UNIX kernel code that performs this task is known as the CPU scheduler.

6.3 PROCESS AND JOB CONTROL

The LINUX/UNIX kernel is responsible for several activities related to process and job management, including process creation, process termination, running processes in the foreground and background, suspending processes, maintaining process status, and switching processes from foreground to background and vice versa. As a LINUX/UNIX user you can request these process and job control tasks by using the shell commands discussed in this section.

6.3.1 DISPLAYING PROCESS ATTRIBUTES

Every LINUX/UNIX process has several attributes, including process ID (PID), process ID of the parent (PPID), process name, process state (running, suspended, swapped, zombie, etc.), the terminal the process was executed on, the length of time the process has run, and process priority. The `ps` command can be used to display these attributes.

The **ps** command accepts options for the System V, BSD, and GNU versions of the **ps** command. The System V options may be grouped and must be preceded by a dash, the BSD options may also be grouped and must not be preceded by a dash, and the GNU options are preceded by two dashes. The options of different types may be mixed. The following is a brief description of the **ps** command. We don't discuss the GNU options here; you can use the **man ps** command to see the GNU options.

Syntax: **ps [options]**

Purpose: Report process status

Output: Attributes of process running on the system

Commonly used options / features:
System V Options

-a	Display information about all the processes executing on your terminal, including those of other users
-e/-A	Display information about all the processes running on the system
-l	Display long list (14 columns) of the status report
-u [ulist]	Display information about processes belonging to the users with the UIDs or user names in 'ulist' (UIDs or user names separated by commas); the default user is the one running the command

BSD Options

U [ulist]	Display information about processes belonging to the users with the UIDs or user names in 'ulist' (UIDs or user names separated by commas); the default user is the one running the command
a	Display information about all the processes executing on your terminal, including those of other users
e	Display information about all the processes running on the system
l	Display long list (14 columns) of the status report
x	Select processes without controlling ttys

You can use the **ps al** command to know the user IDs (UIDs) of the users whose processes are currently running on the system.

The output of the **ps** command shows four fields when executed without options. The output of the **ps** command below shows that five processes are attached to the terminal pts/2: tcsh (a TC shell), **bash** (a Bourne Again shell), **pine** (e-mail software), **banner**, and **ps**, belonging to the user who ran the command. The PIDs of tcsh, bash, pine, banner, and ps are 7628, 7666, 7828, 7829, and 7830, respectively. The **tcsh** process, the first one in the list and the one with the smallest PID, is called the **session leader** process (i.e., your login shell process); all other processes created in this session are its children or grandchildren. Under LINUX and UNIX, the execution of a shell process starts a **session** and the processes that execute under it are the components of this session. Each session is assigned a session identifier (SID) and the processes in a session have the same SID.

```
$ ps
  PID TTY              TIME CMD
 7628 pts/2        00:00:00 bash
 7666 pts/2        00:00:00 bash
 7828 pts/2        00:00:00 pine
 7829 pts/2        00:00:03 banner
 7830 pts/2        00:00:00 ps
$
```

You can use the **a** (or **−a**) option to display all the processes associated with your terminal, including the ones that you ran in the background in a previous session. The output of the **ps a** command below shows an additional process, the login process, which is executed whenever you logon; your login shell (**bash**) is a child of this process. The session leader process is tagged with a dash (**−**) in front of it (**−bash** in the following example). Furthermore, the output of the command shows an additional column that shows the execution status of each process. The possible status values and there meaning are shown in Table 6.1. In the following session, we have the first three processes sleeping, the **pine** process stopped, and **banner** and **ps a** processes runnable (on a computer with a single CPU, one of them is actually running and the other is waiting for the CPU to be assigned to it).

```
$ ps a
  PID TTY       STAT    TIME COMMAND
 7627 pts/2     S       0:00 login − sarwar
 7628 pts/2     S       0:00 -bash
 7666 pts/2     S       0:00 bash
 7828 pts/2     T       0:00 pine
 7829 pts/2     R       0:31 banner
 7831 pts/2     R       0:00 ps a
$
```

Table 6.1	Some Process States and Their Meaning
Process State	**Meaning**
D	Uninterruptible sleep (usually doing I/O or waiting for it)
N	Low-priority process (a process that has been niced)
R	Runnable process: waiting to be scheduled to use CPU
S	Sleeping
T	Traced or stopped
Z	A zombie (defunct) process
W	A process that is completely swapped on the disk (no resident pages)

You can use the –e, -A, or e option to select all the processes on the system. A frequently used group of options is aux, which displays detailed information about all processes with usernames. The following is a sample run of the **ps aux** command. The state value SW for some of the processes means that these processes are sleeping and they have been swapped out on the disk completely and have no page in the main memory (this is done for processes that do not awake often). The percentage CPU use is computed by the expression cputime/realtime. For the following example, CPU use percentage is highest for the banner process. The pine process for the user murty is using the most amount of space of all the processes that are currently running. Read the man page for the **ps** command to get information about other fields.

```
$ ps aux | more
USER       PID   %CPU   %MEM    VSZ    RSS    TTY     STAT   START   TIME    COMMAND
root         1   0.0    0.1    1140    384    ?       S      Dec18   0:03    init [3]
root         2   0.0    0.0       0      0    ?       SW     Dec18   0:00    [kflushd]
root         3   0.0    0.0       0      0    ?       SW     Dec18   0:00    [kupdate]
root         4   0.0    0.0       0      0    ?       SW     Dec18   0:00    [kpiod]
root         5   0.0    0.0       0      0    ?       SW     Dec18   0:00    [kswapd]
bin        250   0.0    0.2    1144     60    ?       S      Dec18   0:00    portmap
root       266   0.0    0.2    1296    524    ?       S      Dec18   0:00    ypbind (master)
root       271   0.0    0.2    1324    584    ?       S      Dec18   0:00    ypbind (slave)
...
root      7503   0.0    0.3    1716    876    ?       S      09:44   0:00    telnetd: lhotse.u up.edu [ansi]
root      7504   0.0    0.6    2240   1360    pts/0   S      09:44   0:00    login -- murty
murty     7505   0.0    0.5    2148   1240    pts/0   S      09:44   0:00    -csh
murty     7539   0.0    1.0    4540   2292    pts/0   S      09:44   0:01    pine
root      7544   0.0    0.3    1716    880    ?       S      09:54   0:00    telnetd: upsun26. egr.up.edu [xterm]
root      7545   0.0    0.6    2240   1360    pts/1   S      09:54   0:00    login -- vegdahl
vegdahl   7546   0.0    0.5    2216   1312    pts/1   S      09:54   0:00    -csh
root      7626   0.0    0.3    1716    880    ?       S      10:01   0:00    telnetd: upppp18. egr.up.edu [ansi]
root      7627   0.0    0.6    2240   1360    pts/2   S      10:01   0:00    login -- sarwar
sarwar    7628   0.0    0.5    2136   1228    pts/2   S      10:01   0:00    -tcsh
sarwar    7666   0.0    0.5    2056   1208    pts/2   S      10:13   0:00    bash
sarwar    7828   0.0    0.5    4044   1192    pts/2   T      11:04   0:00    pine
sarwar    7829   99.7   0.1    1104    292    pts/2   R      11:04   22:12   banner
sarwar    7857   0.0    0.4    2744   1036    pts/2   R      11:27   0:00    ps aux
sarwar    7858   0.0    0.1    1164    440    pts/2   S      11:27   0:00    more
$
```

The **ps axf | more** command can be used to display all process hierarchies on the system. You can display a tree of processes, showing the parent-child and sibling relationships between processes, by using the **f** option.

The **ps l** command shows the long listing of processes on the system. Table 6.2 briefly describes the meanings of various fields in the output of the command.

```
$ ps l
   F  UID   PID   PPID  PRI  NI  VSZ   RSS   WCHAN   STAT  TTY    TIME   COMMAND
 100  121  7628   7627    0   0  2136  1228  rt_sig  S     pts/2  0:00   -tcsh
 000  121  7666   7628   10   0  2060  1244  wait4   S     pts/2  0:00   bash
 000  121  7828   7666    0   0  4044  1192  do_sig  T     pts/2  0:00   pine
 000  121  7829   7666   18   0  1104  292   -       R     pts/2  49:22  banner
 000  121  8007   7666   17   0  2740  1012  -       R     pts/2  0:00   ps l
$
```

In the following In-Chapter Exercises, you will use the **ps** command with and without optional argument to appreciate the type of output it generates.

IN-CHAPTER EXERCISES

6.1   Run the shell commands used in this section on your system. How do the outputs on your system compare with the ones given here? What processes are running in your current session? Can you identify your login shell? What is it?

6.2   In the output of the **ps l** command, identify the runnable, stopped, and sleeping processes. Write down your user ID, process ID of your session leader (shell) process, and the priorities of all the processes.

Table 6.2	Brief Description of Various Fields of the Output of the ps l Command
Field	**Meaning**
F	Flags: Flags associated with the process. Indicates things like whether the process is a user or kernel process, and why the process stopped or went to sleep.
UID	User ID: Process owner's user ID
PID	Process ID: Process ID of the process
PPID	Parent PID: PID of the parent process

Table 6.2	Brief Description of Various Fields of the Output of the ps 1 Command *(continued)*
Field	**Meaning**
PRI	Priority: Priority number of a process that dictates when the process is scheduled. The smaller the priority number of a process, higher its priority
NI	Nice Value: The nice value of a process; another parameter used in the computation of a process's priority number
VSZ	Virtual Size: The number in this field is the size of the memory image of a process (code+data+stack) in blocks
RSS	Resident Set Size: The amount of physical memory in kilobytes; it does not include space taken by the page table and kernel task structure for the process
WCHAN	Wait Channel: Null for running processes, or processes that are ready to run and are waiting for the CPU to be given to them. For a waiting or sleeping process, this field lists the event the process is waiting for—the kernel function where the process resides
STAT	Process State
TTY	Terminal: This field shows the terminal name a process is attached to
TIME	Time: The time (in minutes and seconds) a process has been running for, or ran for before sleeping or stopping
COMMAD	Command: This field lists the command line that was used to start this process. The **-f** option is needed to see the full command line, otherwise only the last component of the pathname is displayed

6.3.2 FOREGROUND, BACKGROUND, AND SUSPENDED PROCESSES

In LINUX and UNIX, processes can run in the background or foreground. A foreground process is created when you type an external command (the name of a file containing binary code or a shell script) and hit **<Enter>**. A background process runs at a lower priority and allows the user to use shell while the process runs. Because a background process runs at a lower priority, a command that takes a long time is a good candidate for background execution. You can use the **fg** command to bring a background process to foreground and the **bg** command move a foreground process into the background. Here is the syntax of the **fg** command.

Syntax: **fg [%jobid]**

When the **fg** command is executed without a job number (jobid), it brings the **current job** into foreground. The job that is presently using the CPU is called the current job.

In the following session, three `find` commands are executed in the background. When the `fg` command is executed it brings the `find / -inum 23456 -print &` command into the foreground. The `fg %3` command brings job number 3 into the foreground. A string that uniquely identifies a job can also be used in place of a job number. Enclose the string in double quotes if it has spaces in it. The third `fg` command in the following session illustrates this use of a string. Using `find` alone will not work because more than one command starts with this string.

```
$ find / -inum 23456 -print > pathnames 2> /dev/null &
[1] 13590
$ find / -name foo -print > foo.paths 2> /dev/null &
[2] 13591
$ find / -name foobar -print > foobar.paths 2> /dev/null &
[3] 13596
$ fg
find / -inum 23456 -print > pathnames 2> /dev/null
<Ctrl-C>
$ fg %3
find / -name foobar -print > foobar.paths 2> /dev/null
<Ctrl-Z>
$ fg %"find / -name foob"
find / -name foobar -print > foobar.paths 2> /dev/null
$
```

While running a command in the foreground, you may have to suspend the command in order to go back to shell to do something under the shell and then return back to the suspended process. A foreground process can be suspended by pressing `<Ctrl-Z>`. A suspended process can be put in the foreground by using the `fg` command and in the background by using the `bg` command (described later in this section). The foreground and suspended processes can be moved to the background by using the `bg` command. The syntax of this command is exactly like the syntax of the `fg` command. Here is the syntax of the `bg` command.

Syntax: **bg [%jobid-list]**

If there are multiple suspended processes, the `fg` command without an argument brings the current process into the foreground, and the `bg` command without argument resumes execution of the current process in the background. In the following example, we use the bg command to move the current job into the background and the **bg %4** command to move job number 4 in the background. Both jobs were previously suspended with <Ctrl-Z>.

```
$ bg
[1]      find / -inum 23456 -print&
$ bg %4
[4]      vi chapter13&
$
```

As indicated in the command syntax, you can use the **bg** command with a list of job numbers for moving multiple suspended jobs into the background. Thus the **bg %1 %3** command can be used to move jobs 1 and 3 into the background.

6.3.3 DISPLAYING JOBS

You can use the **jobs** command to determine the job numbers of all suspended (stopped) and background processes and to determine the current process. Here is the syntax of the **jobs** command.

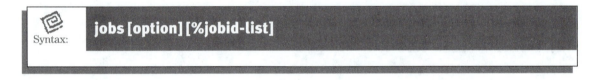

Syntax: **jobs [option] [%jobid-list]**

The optional argument 'jobid-list' can be a list of job numbers starting with **%** and separated by spaces. The **jobs** command can be used with the only option, **-l**, to display PIDs of the processes as well. In the following session the **jobs -l** command displays the job and process IDs of the jobs, status of each job, and the command line used to run a job. The current job is marked with the **+** sign and the previous job is marked with the **-** sign.

```
$ jobs -l
[1]  + 13583 Stopped      find / -inum 23456 -print 2> /dev/null 1&>2
[2]  - 13586 Running      find / -name foo > foo.paths 2> /dev/null&
[3]    13587 Running      find / -name foobar > foobar.paths 2> /dev/null&
[4]    13589 Stopped      vi chapter13
$
```

In the following In-Chapter Exercise, you will use the **fg**, **bg**, and <Ctrl-Z> commands with and without optional argument to appreciate how they work.

IN-CHAPTER EXERCISES

6.3 Run the shell commands used in this and the previous sections on your system. What are the job and process IDs of the three **find** commands? What are the job and process IDs of the current job?

6.3.4 SUSPENDING AND RESUMING A SHELL PROCESS

The **suspend** command can be used to suspend the current shell process. The **fg** command can be used to return to the last suspended shell. The following session shows the use of **suspend** under the Bourne Again and TC shells. The first suspend command is used to suspend (stop) the **tcsh** process and takes you to its parent process, a bash process. This is confirmed by using the **jobs** command. The **ps a** command also shows the **tcsh** process to be stopped (in **T** state). The **fg** command is used to bring back the **tcsh** process. Then a **bash** process is started under the current **tcsh** process and the second **suspend** command is used to suspend the **bash** process. The last **fg** command is used to bring back the suspended **bash** process. Note that on some systems, the messages displayed by the **suspend** command in TC and Bash shells are different.

```
% suspend

[1]+  Stopped                 tcsh
$ jobs
[1]+  Stopped                 tash
$ ps a
  PID TTY        STAT    TIME COMMAND
20932 pts/0      S       0:00 login — sarwar
20967 pts/0      S       0:00 bash
21071 pts/0      T       0:00 -tcsh
21101 pts/0      R       0:00 ps a
$ fg
tcsh
% bash

$ suspend

[2]+  Stopped                 bash
% fg
bash

$
```

In the following In-Chapter Exercise, you will use the **suspend**, **jobs**, **ps a**, **fg**, and **bash** (or **tcsh**) commands to appreciate how a shell process can be suspended and brought back.

IN-CHAPTER EXERCISES

6.4   Run the shell commands used in this section on your system and appreciate how your current shell process can be suspended. If your current shell is Bash, use the **tcsh** command to run a TC shell.

6.3.5 RUNNING COMMANDS SEQUENTIALLY AND SIMULTANEOUSLY

A set of commands can be run in a group as separate processes or as one process. Multiple commands can be run from one command line as separate processes by using a semicolon (;) as the command separator; enclosed in parentheses these commands can be executed as one process. Commands can be executed concurrently by using an ampersand (&) as the command separator. You can use all of these features in a single command line.

The following session shows some examples illustrating the above features. The first command line executes the **date**, **echo**, and **pwd** commands sequentially. The second command line executes the **date**, **echo**, and **who** commands simultaneously. The lines starting with integers in brackets such as [1] inform you of the job ID and PID of the processes that run in parallel. The third command line executes the **date** and **who** commands sequentially as one process and runs this process in parallel with the **find** command.

```
$ date; echo "Go Kings! "; pwd
Wed Apr 17 12:15:26 GMT+5 2002
Go Kings!
/home/faculty/msarwar
$ who & echo "Go Kings! " & date
[1] 28987
04020045 pts/0    Apr 16 21:44 (mba1pc34.lums.edu.pk)
[2] 28988
msarwar   pts/1    Apr 17 09:24 (sheranwala.lums.edu.pk)
04020031 pts/2    Apr 17 01:20 (bscpc28.lums.edu.pk)
04020031 pts/3    Apr 17 01:22 (bscpc28.lums.edu.pk)
root      pts/4    Apr 15 16:20
root      pts/6    Apr 15 16:51
Go Kings!
Wed Apr 17 12:17:42 GMT+5 2002
```

```
[1]-   Done                      who
[2]+   Done                      echo "Go Kings! "
$ find / -name passwd -print 2> /dev/null & (who; date)
[ Output of commands ]
$
```

In the following In-Chapter Exercise, you will appreciate how you can run multiple commands sequentially and simultaneously by specifying them in one command line by using the ; and & operators.

IN-CHAPTER EXERCISES

6.5 Run the shell commands used in this section on your system and appreciate how you can use the ; and & operators to specify multiple commands to be run sequentially and simultaneously in one command line.

6.3.6 ABNORMAL TERMINATION OF COMMANDS AND PROCESSES

When you run a command it normally terminates after successfully completing its task. A command can terminate prematurely, however, because of a bad argument that you passed to it, such as a directory argument to the **cp** command, or because your executing program contains an infinite loop. At times you may also need to terminate a process abnormally. The need for abnormal termination occurs when you run a process with a wrong argument (e.g., a wrong file name to a **find** command) or when a command is taking too long to finish. We address abnormal termination in relation to both foreground and background processes.

TERMINATING A FOREGROUND PROCESS

You can terminate a foreground process by pressing **<Ctrl-C>**. In the following session, we run the **find** command but soon realize that we gave the wrong file name. We press **<Ctrl-C>** to terminate the command.

```
$ find / -name foo -print > foo.paths 2> /dev/null
[ command output ]
<Ctrl-C>
$
```

TERMINATING A BACKGROUND PROCESS

You can terminate a background process in one of two ways: (1) by using the **kill** command or (2) by bringing the process into the foreground using the **fg** command and then pressing **<Ctrl-C>**. The primary purpose of the **kill** command is to send a **signal** (also known as a **software interrupt**) to a process. The LINUX/UNIX operating system uses a signal to get the attention of a process. Any one of more than 60 signal types (in Red Hat 7.2; 30 in Mandrake 6.1) can be sent to a LINUX/UNIX process. A process can take one of three actions upon receiving a signal:

1. Accept the default action as determined by the LINUX/UNIX kernel
2. Ignore the signal
3. Intercept the signal and take a programmer-defined action

For most signals the default action, in addition to some other events such as generating a "core" file, always results in termination of the process. Ignoring a signal doesn't have any impact on the process. A programmer-defined action is specified in the process as a program statement, and it can take control of the process at a specific piece of code in the process.

The `kill` command can be used to send any type of signal to a process. The following is a brief description of the `kill` command.

Syntax:
kill [-signal_number] -proc list
kill -l

Purpose: Send the signal for 'signal_number' to processes whose PIDs or jobIDs are specified in 'proc-list'; jobIDs must start with `%`. The command `kill -l` returns a list of all signal numbers and their names

Commonly used signal numbers:

1	Hang up (log out or hang up the phone line while using a system via a modem)
2	Interrupt (`<Ctrl-C>`)
9	Sure kill
15	Software signal (default signal number)

Without a signal number, the command sends signal number 15 to the process whose PIDs are specified as arguments. The default action for this signal is termination of the process that receives it. This signal can be intercepted and ignored by a process, as can most of the other signals. In order to terminate a process that ignores signal 15 or other signals, signal number 9, known as **sure kill,** must be sent. The following session presents some instances of how the `kill` command can be used.

```
$ kill 1845 1850
$ kill -2 1851
[1] Terminated        find / -inum 23456 -print >inumpaths 2>/dev/null
$ kill -9 1837
[3]+ Killed           a.out
$
```

In the first case, signal number 15 is sent to processes with PIDs 1845 and 1850. In the second case, signal number 2 (`<Ctrl-C>`) is sent to a process with PID 1851. In both cases, if the specified signal numbers are not intercepted, the processes are terminated. In the third case, the `a.out` process (process ID 1837) ignores signal numbers 2 (`<Ctrl-C>`) and 15 (software signal) and we use the `kill -9 1837` command to terminate it. After executing the `kill` command, you can use the `ps` command to ensure that the desired process has terminated.

Process ID 0 can be used to refer to all the processes created during the current login. Thus the `kill -9 0` command terminates all processes resulting from the current login (i.e., all the processes in your current session) and logs you out. The `kill` command also works with job numbers; job numbers are peceded by the `%` character.

Most modern shells, including Bash and Tesh, preserve the background processes when you log out. This means that when a shell terminates, all its children processes keep running.

When the parent of a process terminates, its children become **zombie** processes when they exit. The zombie processes are finished for all practical purposes and don't reside in the main memory, but they still have some kernel resources allocated to them and can't be taken out of the system. Zombie processes are, therefore, unwanted. All zombies (and their children) are eventually adopted by the "granddaddy," the init process, which removes them from the system. In general, any dying process is said to be in the zombie state.

IN-CHAPTER EXERCISES

6.6   Practice the termination of foreground and background processes by using some of the `find` commands used in this chapter.

6.4 PROCESS HIERARCHY IN LINUX/UNIX

When you turn on your LINUX system, LILO (LInux LOader) locates the LINUX kernel and loads it into memory. It initializes various hardware components such as the disk controller. The LILO process then switches to protected mode, loads the operating system, and executes the code that initializes the various kernel data structures such as the inode and file tables. This process has PID 0. It now starts the init process (PID 1) that carries out the rest of the bootup process. The init process starts the daemons `kflushd`, `kupdate`, `kpiod`, and `kswapd`, with PIDs 2, 3, 4, and 5, respectively. The init process then initializes the file systems and mounts the root file system. It then attempts to execute the `/sbin/init` program, which runs the mingetty process (usually called the getty process) on every active terminal line. The getty process sets the terminal attributes, such as baud rate, as specified in the /etc/termcap file. It then displays the `login:` prompt, inviting you to log onto the system.

At the `login:` prompt, when you type your login name and press `<Enter>`, the getty process forks a child. The child uses the **exec** call to become a login process with your login name as its parameter. The login process prompts you for your password and checks the validity of your login name and password. If it finds that both are correct, the login process forks a child that executes to become your login shell. If the login process doesn't find your login name in the /etc/passwd file or finds that the password you entered doesn't match the one in the /etc/passwd (or /etc/shadow) file, it displays an error message and terminates. Control goes back to the getty process, which redisplays the `login:` prompt.

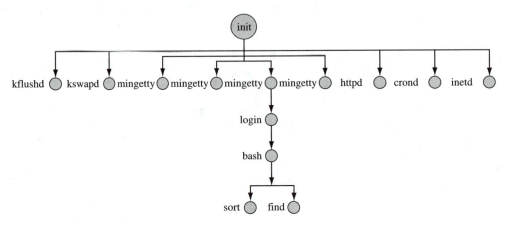

Figure 6.1 LINUX process heirarchy

Once in your login shell, you can do your work and terminate the shell by pressing **<Ctrl-D>**. When you do so, the shell process terminates and control goes back to the getty process, which displays the **login:** prompt, and life goes on.

Figure 6.1 shows the process hierarchy of a LINUX system schematically; the UNIX process hierarchy is very similar. This process diagram shows a system with one user running two processes, **sort** and **find**, with the Bash shell as the user's login shell.

Thus, when you log on to a LINUX/UNIX system, the system creates the first process for you, called the login process, which then creates your login shell. In Chapter 1 (Section 1.3), we explained how you determine the type of your login shell (Bash, TC, Z, etc.). The login shell interprets and executes your commands by creating processes for all the commands that you execute.

Two LINUX/UNIX processes exist throughout the lifetime of a system: the swapper and init processes. The getty process, which monitors a terminal line, lives for as long as the terminal is attached to the system. Your login and login shell processes live for as long as you are logged on. All other processes are usually short-lived and stay for as long as a command or utility executes.

The **ps -e f** (Section 6.3.1) or **pstree** command can be used to display the process tree of currently running processes on the system in a graphical form, showing the parent-child relationship. The **pstree** command displays a more compact diagram than the **ps -e f** command.

6.5 DISPLAYING PROCESS ATTRIBUTES IN LINUX/UNIX

The **ulimit** command can be used under Bash to display many process and file attributes, including the maximum number of processes a user can run simultaneously. The same task can be performed under Tesh by using the **limit** command. Both commands can be used to display limits on a number of hardware and operating system resources. You can use the **help ulimit** command under Bash to find out more details about the command. The following session shows the use of these commands to determine the process limit under Mandrake 6.1, which is 256. The process limit on Red Hat 7.2 is 2048 (on some systems it is 2047).

```
$ ulimit -u
256
$ tcsh
% limit maxproc
maxproc          256
%
```

You can use the `ulimit –a` command to display all of the process and file attributes on your system. The output of this command on Red Hat 7.2 shows that there is virtually no limit on the size of a process and that a process can open a maximum of 1024 files.

In the following In-Chapter Exercise, you will use the `limit` and `ulimit` commands to appreciate the type of output they generate.

IN-CHAPTER EXERCISES

6.7 Run the shell commands used in this section on your system. How do the outputs on your system compare with the ones given here?

6.6 SUMMARY

A process is a program in execution. Because LINUX/UNIX is a time-sharing system, it allows execution of multiple processes simultaneously. On a computer system with one CPU, processes are executed concurrently by scheduling the CPU time and giving it to each process for a short time, called a quantum (or a time slice). Each process is assigned a priority by the LINUX/UNIX system, and when the CPU is available, it is given to the process with the highest priority.

Every LINUX/UNIX process has several attributes, including process ID (PID), process ID of the parent (PPID), process name, process state (running, suspended, swapped, zombie, etc.), the terminal the process was executed on, the length of time the process has run, and process priority. The **ps** command can be used to display these attributes. The **pstree** command can be used to display process hierarchies.

LINUX/UNIX processes can be run in the background or the foreground. A foreground process controls the terminal until it finishes, so the shell can't be used for anything else for as long as a foreground process runs. When a process runs in the background, it returns the shell prompt so that the user can do other work as the process executes. Because a background process runs at a lower priority, a command that takes a long time is a good candidate for background execution.

A set of commands can be run in a group as separate processes or as one process. Multiple commands can be run from one command line as separate processes by using a semicolon (`;`) as the command separator; enclosed in parentheses these commands can be executed as one process. Commands can be executed concurrently by using ampersand (`&`) as the command separator. Background processes are created by terminating command lines with **&**. System processes (which are executed to provide a service such as printing) executed in the background are called daemons.

Actions such as suspending processes, moving them from the foreground to the background and vice versa, displaying their status, interrupting them via signals, and terminating them are known as job control, and LINUX/UNIX has a set of commands that allow these actions. Foreground processes can be moved to the background by suspending them by pressing `<Ctrl-Z>`, followed by executing the `bg` command. Background processes can be moved to the foreground by using the `fg` command. Commands that are suspended or run in the background are also known as jobs. The `jobs` command can be used to view the status of all your jobs. A foreground process can be terminated by pressing `<Ctrl-C>`. The suspend command can be used to suspend the current shell process.

The `kill` command can terminate a process using its PID or job ID. The command can be used to send various types of signals, or software interrupts, to processes. Upon receipt of any signal except one, a process can take the default (kernel-defined) action, take a user-defined action, or ignore the signal. No process can ignore the sure kill, which has been put in place by the LINUX designers to make sure that every process running on a system could be terminated. Bash and TC shells preserve the background processes when you log out.

The `ulimit` command can be used to display many process and file attributes, including the number of processes a user can run simultaneously.

6.7 QUESTIONS AND PROBLEMS

1. What is a process? How is it known inside the LINUX/UNIX system?

2. What is CPU scheduling? How does a time-sharing system run multiple processes on a computer system with a single CPU? Be brief but precise.

3. What are the main states that a process can be in? What does each state indicate about the status of the process?

4. Name three process attributes.

5. What are foreground and background processes in LINUX/UNIX? How do you run shell commands as foreground and background processes? Give an example for each.

6. In LINUX/UNIX jargon, what is a daemon? Give five examples of five daemons.

7. Give the command that displays the status of all running processes on your system.

8. Give the command that returns the total number of processes running on your system.

9. Give the sequence of steps (with commands) for terminating a background process.

10. Create a zombie process on your LINUX/UNIX system. Use the `ps` command to show the process and its state.

11. Give two commands to run the `date` command after 10 seconds. Make use of the `sleep` command; read the manual page for this command to find out how to use it.

12. Run a command that would reminds you to leave for lunch one hour into a session after one hour by displaying the message "Time for Lunch!"

13. Give a command line for running the `find` and `sort` commands in parallel.

14. What does the following command do?

    ```
    (who; date) & (cat temp; uname & whoami)
    ```

15. Give an example of a LINUX/UNIX process that does not terminate with `<Ctrl-C>`.

16. Run the following commands on one command line so that they do not terminate when you log out. What command line did you use?

```
find / -inum 23476 -print > all.links.hard 2> /dev/null

find / -name foo -print > foo.paths 2> /dev/null
```

17. Run the following sequence of commands under your shell. What are the outputs of the three **pwd** commands? Why are the outputs of the last two **pwd** commands different?

```
$ pwd
$ bash
$ cd /usr
$ pwd
...
$ <Ctrl-D>
$ pwd
...
```

18. Use the **pstree** and **ps** commands to find out how many mingetty processes are running on your system. Show your command runs with outputs.

19. Do you know of a foreground process that cannot be terminated with `<Ctrl-C>`? How do you terminate this process?

20. What are signals in LINUX/UNIX? Give three examples of signals. What are the possible actions that a process can take upon receiving a signal? Write commands for sending these signals to a process with PID 10289.

21. Run the `kill -l` command on your system to display all the ~~singals~~ signals that your system supports along with their numbers. What are the numbers for the following signals: SIGCHLD and SIGSEGV? When are these signals generated?

22. Assume that you run a program containing an infinite loop in the foreground. How would you terminate the execution of this program?

File System Backup and Restoration

OBJECTIVES

- To describe how files and directories can be archived and restored in LINUX/UNIX

- To explain restoration of a subset of archived files

- Commands and primitives covered: `;`, `|`, `( )`, `cd`, `cp`, `file`, `grep`, `ls`, `tar`, `uncompress`

7.1 INTRODUCTION

The LINUX/UNIX operating system has several utilities that allow you to archive (pack) your files and directories on a tape or in a single file. The system administrators normally use a tape as the storage media for archiving complete file system structures as backups, so that when a system crashes for some reason, files can be recovered. In a typical installation, the backup is done every day during off hours (late night or early morning) when the system is not normally used.

As a normal LINUX/UNIX user, you can also archive your work if you like. You normally need to do this to archive files related to a project so you could transfer them to someone via e-mail or ftp, or store them on a secondary storage media (tape, floppy, CD-ROM, etc.). The primary reason for making an archive is the convenience of dealing with (sending, receiving) a single file instead of a complete directory hierarchy. Without an archive, the sender may have to send several files and directories (a file structure) that the receiver would have to restore in the correct order. Without an archiving facility, depending on the size of the file structure, the task of sending, receiving, and reconstructing the file structure can be very time-consuming.

LINUX and UNIX have several utilities that can be used for archiving files. These utilities, also known as the low-level backup programs, include **tar**, **cpio**, **afio** (an enhanced version of **cpio**), and **dump**. There are **shell scripts** that allow you to carry out complete and **incremental backups** (backup of new files and files that were changed since the last backup) on different types of storage media; these are known as high-level backup programs. Some of these programs are **amanda**, **backup**, **KBackup**, **tbackup**, **lbu** (LINUX Backup Utility), and **tob**. We discuss the **tar** utility here because it is one of the easiest to use and it is widely used. Also, many software packages are distributed in the **tar** format. In this chapter we discuss the GNU version of the tar utility. Discussion of most of the other utilities can be found in a good book on LINUX/UNIX system administration.

7.2 ARCHIVING AND RESTORING FILES USING tar

The **tar** (**t**ape **ar**chive) utility was originally designed to save file systems on tapes as a backup, so that files could be recovered in case of a system crash. The **tar** utility is still used for that purpose, but it is also commonly used these days to pack a directory hierarchy as a disk file. This saves disk space as well as transmission time while electronically transmitting a directory hierarchy. In this section, we describe how you can use the **tar** utility to archive and retrieve files. A brief description of the utility is given below.

Syntax:	**tar [options] [files]** **The use of - in front of an option is not mandatory**

Purpose: Archive (copy in a particular format) files to or restore files from tape (which can be an ordinary file); directories are archived and restored recursively

Commonly Used Options / Features:

Option Format:	Function_letter [Modifier]
Function_letter:	
c	Create a new tape and record archive **files** on it.

Syntax:	tar [options] [files] The use of - in front of an option is not mandatory *(continued)*

Commonly Used Options / Features:

r	Record files at the end of tape (append operation)
t	List tape's contents (names of files archived on it) in a format like `ls -l`
u	Update tape by adding files on it if not on or if modified since last written to tape.
x	Extract (restore) files from tape; entire tape if none specified.

Modifier:	
f Arch	Use 'Arch' as the archive for archiving or restoring files. Default is /dev/rmt0. If Arch is –, standard input is read (for extracting files) or standard output is written (for creating an archive)—a feature used when `tar` is used in a pipeline.
h	Follow symbolic links.
l	Display error messages if links are not found.
v	Use verbose mode: display the pathnames of the files and directories being archived or extracted.

7.2.1 Archiving Files

You can use the `tar` command with the `c` or `r` options for archiving a list of files and/or directories. The `c` option creates a brand new archive, whereas the `r` option appends files at the end of the current archive. The most common use of the `tar` command is with the `c` option.

In the examples discussed in this chapter, we will use the directory structure given in Figure 7.1. In this diagram, rectangles represent directories and circles represent files.

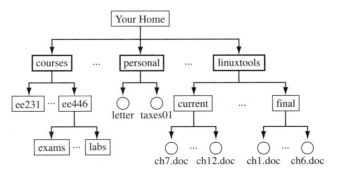

Figure 7.1 A sample file structure

If you want to create an archive of the linuxtools directory on a tape drive /dev/rmt0 (the name may be different on your system), you can use the following command after changing directory to linuxtools. Unless you are the system administrator (or own the LINUX/UNIX machine you are using), in all like-lihood you don't have the access permissions to use (read from or write to) the tape drive. Thus, the shell will give you an error message as shown below. However, if you do have proper access permissions for the given file (i.e., the tape drive), an archive of the linuxtools directory is created on the tape in the given tape drive. Not only do you need access privileges to /dev/rmt0, you also need to **mount** it first.

```
$ tar cf /dev/rmt0 .
tar: Cannot open /dev/rmt0: Permission denied
tar: Error is not recoverable: exiting now
$
```

You can create an archive of your files and directories on a disk file, in a directory that you have the write permission to, by using the command shown in the following session. In this example, we make ~/linuxtools our current directory and create a tar archive of this directory in a file called linuxtools.tar. Note that .tar is not an extension required by the **tar** utility. You should use it to be able to identify a **tar** archive by looking at its name. With no such extension, you have to use the **file** command to identify your tar archive files, as shown in the last command line in the following session (in case that you have forgotten what the **file** command does!). You can use the **v** (verbose) option to display the names of files and directories as they are archived.

```
$ cd ~/linuxtools
$ tar cf linuxtools.tar .
tar: linuxtools.tar is the archive; not dumped
$ ls -l
drwx------   2 sarwar        512 Jul 22 13:21 current
drwx------   2 sarwar        512 Jul 22 13:21 final
-rw-------   1 sarwar    2064896 Jul 22 13:47 linuxtools.tar
$ file linuxtools.tar
linuxtools.tar: GNU tar archive
$
```

You can also create the **tar** archive of your current directory by using the command shown in the following session. The – argument can be used to inform tar that the archive is to be sent to standard output, which is redirected to the linuxtools.tar file. Note that the **find** command is enclosed in grave accents (back quotes) and not forward quotes. The output of the **find . -print** command is the names of all the files and directories in your current directory, which are passed to the **tar** command as its parameters. These file and directory names are taken as the list of files to be archived by the **tar** command. The archive of the current directory is created in the linuxbook.tar file.

```
$ tar cf - `find . -print` > linuxtools.tar
tar: ./linuxtools.tar is the archive; not dumped
tar: ./linuxtools.tar is the archive; not dumped
$
```

The **-z** option of the GNU version of the **tar** utility can be used to generate the compressed version of the **tar** archive. This option can also be used to restore the compressed version of a **tar** archive. The use of **-z** eliminates use of the **gzip** utility to compress an archive, or the use of **gunzip** utility to uncompress a compressed file and then untar (resotre/unpack) it with the **tar** command; the two-step process can be performed by the **tar** command alone. In the following session, we use the first **tar** command to create a compressed archive of the current directory in the ~/backup.tar.gz file and use the second **tar** command to uncompress and untar it in the ~/backups directory.

```
$ tar -zcf ~/backup.tar.gz .
$ tar -zxf ~/backup.tar.gz ~/backups
$
```

IN-CHAPTER EXERCISES

7.1   Create a tape archive of the labs directory hierarchy (or whatever directory contains your labwork and /programs) in your home directory. What command line(s) did you use? What is the name of your archive file?

7.2.2 RESTORING ARCHIVED FILES

You can restore an archive by using the function option **x** of the **tar** command. The restoration can be complete or partial, that is, you can restore everything in an archive or a subset of the files in it.

7.2.2.1 COMPLETE RESTORATION

You can run the following command sequence to restore the linuxtools.tar archive and place it in the ~/backups directory. The **cp** command copies the archive file to the directory (~/backups) where the archived files are to be restored. The **cd** command is used to make the destination directory the current directory. Finally, the **tar** command is used to do the restoration of the archived files in your current directory. After the files and directories in linuxtools.tar have been restored, the ~/backups directory contains the current and final directories and all the files (and directories) under them.

```
$ cp linuxtools.tar ~/backups
$ cd ~/backups
$ tar xf linuxtools.tar
$ ls -l
```

```
drwx------    2 sarwar        512 Jul 22 13:21 current
drwx------    2 sarwar        512 Jul 22 13:21 final
-rw-------    1 sarwar    2064896 Jul 22 13:47 linuxtools.tar
$
```

Note that the linuxtools.tar file remains intact after the restoration is complete. This makes sense considering that the primary purpose of the **tar** archive is to back up files; the archive should remain intact after restoration in case the system crashes after restoration but before it is archived again.

IN-CHAPTER EXERCISES

7.2 Copy the archive file that you created in Exercise 7.1 to a file called labs.tar. Unarchive labs.tar in a directory called labs.backup in your home directory. Show the commands that you used for this task.

7.2.2.2   PARTIAL RESTORATION

Sometimes you may have to restore a subset of files in a **tar** archive. Selective restoration is possible with the function option **x** as long as you know the pathnames of the files to be restored. If you don't remember the pathnames of the files to be restored, you can use the function option **t** to display the pathnames of files and directories in the archive file. You can use the **v** option to display a long list of file attributes. The output of the **tar tv** command is in a format similar to the output of the **ls -l** command, as shown in the following sample. As marked in the sample output, the first field specifies file type and access permissions, the second field specifies login name and group name of the owner of the file, the third field shows the file size in bytes, next two fields show the date and time the file was last modified, and the last field shows the pathname of the file as stored in the archive.

```
-rw------- sarwar/faculty 121344 2001-10-06 16:10 ./current/ch10.doc
```
| File type and permissions | login_name group_name | File size | Modification date and time | File name |

If an archive contains a large number of files, you can pipe the output of the **tar t** command to the **more** command for page-by-page view. If you know the name of the file but not its pathname, you can pipe output of the **tar t** command to the **grep** command. Files can be restored or their pathnames viewed selectively as well. The following session shows some examples.

```
$ tar tvf linuxtools.tar
drwx------ sarwar/faculty        0 2001-10-06 00:14:56 ./
-rw------- sarwar/faculty        0 2001-08-23 19:42:22 ./.lastlogin
drwx------ sarwar/faculty        0 2001-10-06 00:02:12 ./current/
```

```
-rwxrw---- sarwar/faculty 204288 2001-08-23 19:11:22 ./current/ch7.doc
...
-rwxrw---- sarwar/faculty 334848 2001-08-23 09:24:15 ./final/ch6.doc
$ tar tvf linuxtools.tar | grep ch10.doc
-rw------- sarwar/faculty 121344 2001-08-23 19:11:22 ./current/ch10.doc
$
```

If you want to restore the file ch10.doc in the ~/linuxtools/current directory, you can use the following command sequence. Be sure that you give the pathname of the file to be restored, and not just its file name.

```
$ cd ~/linuxtools
$ tar -xvf ~/backups/linuxtools.tar ./current/ch10.doc
./current/ch10.doc
$
```

The output of the **tar** command shows that the file ch10.doc has been restored in the ~/backups/current directory. You can confirm this result by using the `ls -l ~/backups/current` command. The restored file remains archived in the ~/backups/linuxtools.tar file.

IN-CHAPTER EXERCISES

7.3 List the attributes of the files in the archive that you created in Exercise 7.1 and identify the sizes of all the files in it. What command did you use?

7.4 Restore the file called lab1.c from the archive created in Exercise 7.1. What command did you use to perform the task?

7.2.3 COPYING DIRECTORY HIERARCHIES

You can use the **tar** command to copy one directory to another directory. You can also use the **cp -r** command to do so, but the disadvantage of using **cp -r** is that the file access permissions and file modification times aren't preserved: The access permissions of the copied files and directories are determined by the value of umask, and the modification time is set to current time. Also, the **-r** option is not available on all LINUX/UNIX systems.

More commonly, the **tar** command is used to archive the source directory, create the destination directory, and unpack (untar) the archived directory in the latter directory. The entire task can be performed with one command by using command grouping and piping. You can use the following command to copy the whole directory hierarchy in your current directory to the ~/linuxbook/backups directory. The **tar** command to the left of the pipe creates the archive of the current directory and passes it as input to the **tar** command on the right side of the pipe. Recall that the commands in parentheses (on the right) are executed under a subshell.

```
$ tar -cf - . | ( cd ~/linuxbook/backups; tar -xvf - )
./
./ch1.doc
./ch2.doc
...
./ch21.doc
$
```

In the following session the ~/linuxbook/examples directory is copied to the ~/linuxbook/examples.bak directory. The `tar` command to the left of the pipe sends the archive to stdout, and the `tar` command to the right of the pipe unpacks the archive that it receives at its stdin. (Note: Don't hit `<Enter>` after `cd`; the line wraps around due to line length and the length of the pathname for the examples.bak file. Alternatively, you can type \ after `cd`, hit `<Enter>` on the first line, and continue typing on the second line.)

```
$ ( cd ~/linuxbook/examples; tar -cvf - . ) | ( cd
  ~/linuxbook/examples.bak; tar -xvf - )
./
./.lastlogin
./Tcsh/
./Tcsh/if_demo1
...
./Bash/timeit
$
```

The advantages of using this command line are that both the `cd` and `tar` commands are available on all LINUX/UNIX systems and that the copied files retain the access permissions and file modification times of the source files.

IN-CHAPTER EXERCISES

7.5 Use the command formats discussed in this section to practice copying directory hierarchies with the `tar` command.

7.3 SOFTWARE DISTRIBUTIONS IN THE tar FORMAT

Companies often use the tar command when distributing their software because it results in a single file for the customer to copy and a savings in disk space compared to the unarchived directory hierarchies that may contain the software to be distributed. Also, most companies keep their distribution packs (in the `tar` format) on their Internet sites, which their customers can download via the `ftp` command. Thus the **tar** format also results in less copying time and reduced work by the customer, who uses only one get (or **mget**) command (an **ftp** command) versus several sequences of commands if directory hierarchies have to be downloaded.

Because the sizes of software packages are increasing, owing to their graphical interfaces and multimedia formats, archives are compressed before they are put on ftp sites. The users of the software need to uncompress the downloaded files before restoring them.

Let's consider a file, tcsh-6.06.tar.Z, that we downloaded from an ftp site. In order to restore this file, we have to uncompress and untar it, as shown in the following command sequence.

```
$ uncompress tcsh-6.06.tar.Z
$ tar xvf tcsh-6.06.tar
[command output]
$
```

If the compressed archive has the **.gz** extension, we will use the **gunzip** command to uncompress the archive instead of using the **uncompress** command. Alternatively, we could use the **–zxf** option of the **tar** command (as discussed in Section 7.2.1) to uncompress and **untar** with a single command.

If a software pack is distributed on a secondary storage media (floppy, tape, or CD-ROM), you need to copy appropriate files to the appropriate directory and repeat these commands.

If you want to distribute some software that is stored in a directory hierarchy, you first need to make an archive for it by using the **tar** command and then compress it by using the **gzip** command (or some other similar utility). These steps create a **tar** archive in a compressed file that can be placed in an **ftp** repository or on a Web page or sent as an e-mail attachment.

Disk file backups are also commonly used to pack large, inactive or infrequently used files to save disk space.

7.4 SUMMARY

LINUX and UNIX have several utilities for creating archive (backup) copies of your files and directories. These utilities include **afio**, **cpio**, **dump**, and **tar**. The **tar** command is the most commonly used. The backups can be in the form of tape or disk files. For tape backups, not only do you not only need access privileges to the tape device file but you also need to mount it first. The disk file backups are commonly used for software distributions, but can also be used to pack large inactive files to save disk space as well. You can unpack a **tar** archive completely or partially (i.e., unpack a subset of files and directories in the archive). You can also use the **tar** command to copy directory hierarchies from one place on your file system structure to another.

7.5 QUESTIONS AND PROBLEMS

1. What is the meaning of the term **archive**?
2. What is the **tar** command used for? Give all possible uses of this command.

3. What are the names of the device files for the tape drives on your system? What are the access permissions on these files? Give the command line that you used to obtain your answer, along with the command output.

4. Give a command line for creating a **tar** archive of your current directory in the ~/home.tar file.

5. Give commands for restoring the above backup in the ~/backup directory.

6. Give a command line for copying your home directory in the ~/home.back directory such that the access privileges and file modify times are preserved.

7. Why is the **tar** command preferred over the **cp -r** command for creating backup copies of directory hierarchies?

8. Suppose that you download a file, linuxtools.tar.gz, from an ftp site. As the file name indicates, it is a tar archive file in compressed form. Give the sequence of commands for restoring this archive and installing it in your ~/linuxtools directory.

9. Give the command for displaying the long listing of all the files and directories in the linuxtools.tar.gz file.

10. What command will you use to restore only the ch10.doc file from this archive in the ~/linuxtools directory?

CHAPTER **8**

Program Development Process

OBJECTIVES

- To give an overview of programming at various levels

- To describe briefly the interpreted and compiled languages

- To explain briefly the classes of programming languages and some important programming paradigms

- To discuss the compilation and interpretation processes

- To describe how C, C++, and Java programs are compiled and executed

- To discuss briefly the software engineering life cycle

- To list some important Web resources

- Commands and primitives covered: None

8.1 INTRODUCTION

A typical LINUX/UNIX system has support for several high-level programming languages, both inter-preted and compiled. These languages include C, C++, Java, Perl, LISP, and FORTRAN. Most of the application software for the LINUX/UNIX platforms is written in the C language, the language in which the LINUX/UNIX operating system is written. Thus a range of software development tools are avail-able on the LINUX/UNIX platform for developing software in the C language. Many of these tools can also be used for developing software in other programming languages such as C++ and Java.

The LINUX/UNIX operating system has a wealth of software development tools for program gener-ation and static and dynamic analysis of programs. They include tools for editing source code, indent-ing source code, compiling and linking, handling module-based software, creating libraries, profiling, verifying source code for portability, source code management, debugging, tracing, and performance monitoring. In the remaining chapters, we describe some of the commonly used tools in the develop-ment of software in the C and, to some extent, C++ and Java languages. The depth of coverage of these tools varies from brief to detailed, depending on their usefulness and how often they are used in prac-tice. In this chapter, we describe briefly various types of programming languages that can be used to write computer software. In doing so, we also discuss different categories of programming languages, programming language paradigms, interpretation and compilation processes, and the software engi-neering lifecycles. We list some useful Web resources at the end of the chapter.

8.2 AN OVERVIEW OF COMPUTER PROGRAMMING LANGUAGES

Computer programs can be written in a wide variety of programming languages. The native language of a computer is known as its **machine language,** the language comprising the instruction set of the CPU inside the computer. Recall that the instruction set of a CPU consists of instructions that the CPU understands. These instructions enable the performance of various types of operations on data, such as arithmetic, logic, shift, and I/O operations. Today's CPUs are made of **bi-state devices** (devices that operate in on or off states), so the CPU instructions are in the form of 0s and 1s (0 for the off state and 1 for the on state). The total number of instructions for a CPU and the maximum length (in bytes) of an instruction are CPU-dependent. The CPUs based on complex instruction set computers (CISC) have several hundreds of complex instructions, while CPUs based on reduced instruction set comput-ers (RISC) have far fewer simple instructions. Programs written in a CPU's machine language are known as **machine programs,** commonly known as **machine codes.** The machine language programs are the most efficient because they are written in a CPU's native language. However, they are the most difficult to write because the machine language is very different from any spoken language; the pro-grammer has to write these programs in 1s and 0s, and a change in one bit can cause major problems. Debugging machine language programs is a very challenging and time-consuming task as well. For these reasons, programs are rarely written in machine language today.

In assembly language programming, machine instructions are written in English-like words, called mnemonics. Because programs written in assembly language are closer to the English language, they are relatively easier to write and debug. However, these programs must be translated into the machine language of the CPU used in your computer before you can execute them. This process of translation is carried out by a program called an **assembler.** You have to execute a command to run an assembler, with the file containing an assembly language program as its argument. Although assembly languages are becoming less popular, they are still used to write time-critical programs for controlling real-time systems (e.g., controllers in drilling machines for oil wells) that have limited amounts of main storage.

In an effort to bring programming languages closer to the English language—and to make programming and debugging tasks easier—high-level languages (HLLs) were developed. Commonly used high-level languages are Ada, C, C++, Java, Javascript, BASIC, FORTRAN, LISP, Pascal, Perl, and Prolog. Some of these languages are interpreted (e.g., Javascript, Perl, BASIC, and LISP), whereas others are compiled (e.g., C, C++, and Java). Programs written in an **interpreted language** are executed one instruction at a time by a program called an **interpreter,** without translating them into the machine code for the CPU used in the computer. Programs written in **compiled languages** must be translated into the machine code for the underlying CPU before they are executed. This translation is carried out by a program called a **compiler,** which generates the assembly version of the high-level language program. The assembly version has to go through further translation before the executable code is generated. This translation is carried out by a program, called an **assembler.** The compiled languages run many times faster than the interpreted languages because compiled languages are executed directly by the CPU, whereas interpreted languages are executed by a piece of software (an interpreter).

However, the Java language is not compiled in the traditional sense. Java programs are translated into a form known as the **Java Bytecode,** which is then interpreted by an interpreter, called the **Java Virtual Machine (JVM)**. You can also compile Java programs with a just-in-time (JIT) compiler to run directly on a native processor.

To simplify further the task of writing computer programs, languages at a higher level even than the HLLs were developed. They include scripting and visual languages such as LINUX/UNIX shell programming in Bash (or another shell), Perl, and visual BASIC. Some of these languages are interpreted; others are compiled. Figure 8.1 shows the proximity of various types of programming languages to the hardware, ease of their use, and relative speed at which programs are executed. Although fourth generation languages were supposed to be even more English-like, they aren't, so some would argue against languages like Perl and Visual Basic being classified as fourth-generation laguages and categorize them instead as different types of HHLs.

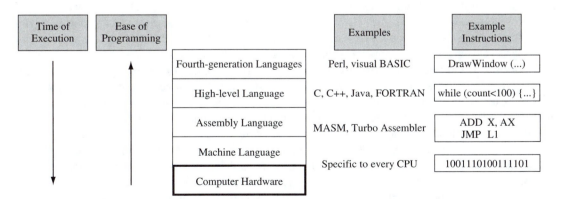

Figure 8.1 Levels of programming languages, with examples, ease of their programming, and speed of execution

As the level of programming languages goes high, the task of writing programs becomes easier and programs become more readable. The trade-off is that programs written in HLLs, if not properly optimized as they are compiled, may take longer to run. For interpreted programs, the increase in program running time is due to the fact that another program (the interpreter) runs the program. For compiled languages, the compilation process takes time and the resulting machine code is usually bigger than it would be if written in an assembly language by hand. However, time saved because of ease of programming in HLLs far outweighs the increase in code size. Furthermore, today's compiler technology allows excellent optimization of a program to reduce its size and execution time. Figure 8.1 also shows some language statement examples to demonstrate the increased readability of programs as the level of programming languages increases.

8.3 PROGRAMMING LANGUAGES AND PROGRAMMING PARADIGMS

There are many classes of programming languages and every such class forces you to write programs by using a particular programming model or paradigm. For example, the programming style that uses object-oriented (OO) features of a language is known as the object-oriented programming paradigm. We briefly describe the various categories of programming languages, and the procedural and object-oriented programming paradigms.

8.3.1 PROGRAMMING LANGUAGES

Programming languages are often classified as imperative, functional/applicative, logic, and object-oriented. In this section, we describe briefly these language classes.

In an **imperative programming language,** programs are written by using variables to store data, using assignment statements to change data, and iterative repetition (although most imperative laguages do allow recursive repetition). Most of the popular languages, including C, C++, Java, BASIC, COBOL, and FORTRAN, fall in the bin of imperative languages. Imperative languages are usually compiled but they can be interpreted too. The majority of scientific, business, Web, and system softwares are written in imperative languages. Most of the contemporary operating systems are written in C or C++. For example, UNIX and LINUX are written in C and Windows operating systems are written in C++. The bulk of scientific applications are written in FORTRAN, C, and C++. Most business software is written in COBOL and most new Web applications are written in Java.

In a **functional programming language,** computations are done by passing parameters to functions. In these languages, there are no concepts of variables, assignment statement, and iteration; repetitions are carried out by making recursive calls to functions. Some of the well-known functional languages are LISP, Scheme, ML, and Haskell. LISP and its variants are a popular choice for writing artificial intelligence (AI) applications. Outside the domain of AI, one of the most popular text editors for UNIX-like systems, called Emacs, is written in LISP, as is the popular computer-aided design software, AutoCAD.

In **logic programming languages** (also known as **rule-based programming languages**), computations are performed by specifying rules and letting the language implementation execute these rules in an order to perform the desired computation. One of the most popular logic programming languages is Prolog. Like functional languages, the logic programming languages are also used for solving problems related to AI, such as writing expert systems.

Object-oriented programming languages provide support for **abstract data types,** known as **classes.** A class consists of a data portion and operations on data specified as functions, called **methods.** An instance of a class (which is like a variable in a language like C) is called an **object.** Computations in object-oriented programming languages are carried out via **instantiation** of objects and communication between them that result in **method invocations.** Some of the well-known languages that are designed for object-oriented programming are Smalltalk 80, Eiffel, and Java. Languages such as C++ and Ada 95 provide features to support object-oriented programming. Although most of the object-oriented languages are imperative, CLOS is an object-oriented version of the functional language LISP. The bulk of the new application software is written in object-oriented programming languages Because Java was designed for the Web, it is the language of choice for writing Web applications.

Scripting languages allow you to place a list of commands, known as a **script**, in a file. The commands in the script are executed, one by one, by the language interpreter. These languages were pioneered by **sh**, the scripting language for the Bourne shell on UNIX. Most of the scripting languages were written for UNIX platforms. Some of the popular scripting languages are awk, tcl, tk, bash, Perl, BASIC, and Javascript.

Marking languages such as **Hypertext Markup Language (HTML),** although called languages, are not really programming languages. Such languages are used to specify the general appearance of a document, usually to be displayed as a Web page.

We encourage you to browse the Web sites listed in Table 8.1 in the last section of this chapter to get more information on the languages that interest you more.

8.3.2 PROGRAMMING PARADIGMS

Although every programming language category results in a programming paradigm, two of the most commonly used programming paradigms are procedural and object-oriented. We describe them here briefly.

In the **procedural programming paradigm,** data are passed to subprograms (functions or procedures) that process data to produce the desired results. For example, if the median of the integers in an array is to be found, the array is passed as a parameter to a function that processes the array to perform the desired task. Most of the imperative languages such as C, FORTRAN, BASIC, and Perl are designed for the procedural style of programming. Although it contains object-oriented programming features, C++ also allows you to write programs in the procedural style of programming.

In the **object-oriented programming paradigm,** also known as the **data-oriented programming paradigm,** the focus is on objects that contain data and operations (i.e., methods) associated with the data. Considering the above example of finding the median of numbers in an array in an object-oriented paradigm, we would have an array object that contains the integer array as its data and a method for finding the median of integers in the array. The median operation on the array object is performed by invoking its median finding method. The upside of using the OO programming paradigm is that the resultant software is highly modular, which makes it easy to maintain. The downside is that the software is much larger than the corresponding procedure-oriented software. It is not uncommon for even a medium-size object-oriented software to spread over many files; becoming well-versed in file management is a much more important issue for OO software developers than it is for procedure-oriented software developers.

8.4 THE COMPILATION PROCESS

Since many of the programming languages used on a LINUX/UNIX system are compiled, we need to describe briefly the compilation process before moving on. As we stated in Section 8.2, computer programs written in compiled languages must be translated to the machine code of the CPU used in the computer system on which they are to execute. This translation is usually a three-step process consisting of compilation, assembly, and linking. The compilation process translates the source code (e.g., a C++ program) to the corresponding assembly code for the CPU used in the computer system. The assembly code is then translated to the corresponding machine code, known as object code. Finally, the object code is translated to the executable code. The linking phase is required regardless of whether you have other object modules, or whether your program uses any library call. Figure 8.2 outlines the translation process.

The object code consists of machine instructions, but isn't executable because the source program may have used some library functions that the assembler can't resolve references to because the library functions' code isn't in the source file(s). The **linker** performs the task of linking (connecting) the object code for a program (which may be in multiple files or modules) to the object code in one or more libraries. The output of the linker is the executable code for the computer on which the program was compiled, assembled, and linked.

8.5 THE INTERPRETATION PROCESS

Many of the programming languages available on LINUX/UNIX are interpreted, such as Perl, awk, LISP, Javascript, and shell scripting language (e.g., Bash and Tesh). It is therefore important to understand how programs written in such languages are executed.

Programs written in an interpreted language are executed by another program, called the **language interpreter,** one statement or command at a time. Unlike programs written in a compiled language, programs written in an interpreted language don't need any translation before they can be executed. The interpreter reads the program one statement at a time and tries to execute it, as shown in Figure 8.3.

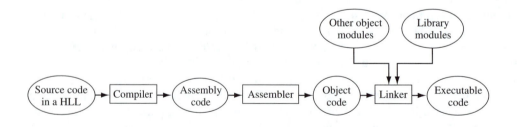

Figure 8.2 The process of translating a high-level language program into executable code

Figure 8.3 Execution of a program written in an interpreted language

8.6 COMPILING C, C++, AND JAVA PROGRAMS

The translation of C and C++ programs goes through a preprocessing stage before it is compiled. The **preprocessor** performs several operations on the source program before the modified source program is given to the compiler. Some of the main tasks performed by the preprocessor are

■ Inserting the files specified with the #include directive

■ Expanding macros (specified with the #define directive)

■ Processing conditional compilation specified with the #if directive

■ Handling continuation line concatenation (for C only).

The continuation line feature allows you to break a statement into multiple lines by terminating partial statements with the backslash and new line characters. When the preprocessor encounters a backslash at the end of a line, it removes the backslash and new line characters and concatenates the line with the next line. This feature is used in multiline preprocessor directives in C because they terminate with a new line character.

Figure 8.4 outlines the compilation process for C and C++ programs. The entire translation process is carried out by a single compiler command. After the executable code has been generated and stored in a file by the compiler, it can be executed by typing the file name (and any program arguments) in a command line (or clicking the icon for the executable in a GUI system). We discuss various LINUX and UNIX compilers in Chapter 9. The compilers and interpreters for various languages are located in the /usr/bin directory.

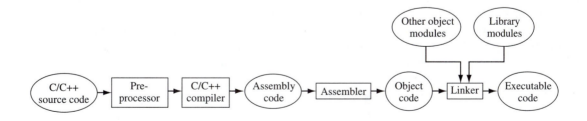

Figure 8.4 The process of translating C and C++ programs into executable code

A Java program can also be compiled with a just-in-time (JIT) compiler to produce the executable code for the underlying machine. Or, you can translate a Java program into Java Bytecode to be interpreted (executed) by the Java Virtual Machine.

In the following In-Chapter Exercises, you will use the LINUX/UNIX `ls`, `cd`, `more`, `whereis`, and `grep` commands, along with the LINUX/UNIX piping feature to identify the locations for the various compilers and interpreters and read about them by using the man command.

IN-CHAPTER EXERCISES

8.1 Browse the /bin directory on your system to determine which of the following compilers exist on your LINUX/UNIX system: `cc`, `gcc`, `CC`, `g++`, `java`, and `f77`. What commands did you use to accomplish this task?

8.2 Read the manual pages for `gcc`, `g++`, and `java` compilers to learn more about them.

8.7 THE SOFTWARE ENGINEERING LIFE CYCLE

A software product is developed in a sequence of phases, collectively known as the **software life cycle.** Several life-cycle models are available in the literature and used in practice. The life cycle used for a specific product depends on its size, the nature of the software to be developed (scientific, business, etc.), and the design methodology used (object-oriented or classical). Some of the commonly used life-cycle models are **build-and-fix, water-fall,** and **spiral.** The common phases in most life-cycle models are requirement analysis, specifications, planning, design, coding (i.e., program development), testing, installation, and maintenance. A full discussion of life-cycle models and their phases is outside the scope of this textbook, but we discuss the coding phase in detail in the remaining chapters of this book—in particular, the LINUX/UNIX program development tools that can be used in this phase.

The program development process consists of three steps: program generation, static analysis of the source code, and dynamic analysis of the executable code. The purpose of the **program generation phase** is to create source code and generate the executable code for the source code. Hence it involves tools for editing text files, indenting the source code properly, compiling the source code, handling module-based software, creating libraries, managing the source code, and controlling revisions. The **static analysis phase** consists of verifying the source code for portability and measuring metrics related to the source code (e.g., the number of calls to a function and the time taken by each function). The **dynamic analysis phase** consists of debugging, tracing, and monitoring the performance of the software, including testing it against product requirements. In the remaining chapters of this book we describe LINUX/UNIX tools for all three steps. The depth of discussion on each tool depends on its usefulness, the frequency of its use, and how widely it is available on various LINUX/UNIX platforms.

8.8 WEB RESOURCES

Table 8.1 lists useful Web sites for some of the famous programming languages.

Table 8.1	Web Resources for LINUX Well-Known Programming Languages	
Reference	**URL**	**Description**
1	www.perl.com	The Perl Language Homepage
2	cm.bell-labs.com/cm/cs/who/dmr/chist.html	History of the C Language by Dennis Ritchie
3	www.research.att.com/~bs/C++.html	C++ Language Page Maintained by Bjarne Stroustrup the Designer of the Language
4	java.sun.com	The Source of Java Technology
5	developer.java.sun.com/developer/online Training/Programming/BasicJava1/	Essentials of the Java Programmming Language
6	www.gnu.org/software/java/java.html	GNU and the Java Language
7	www.haskell.org	The Haskell Home Page
8	home.planet.nl/~revorvo/cobol.htm	Links to Most Interesting COBOL Sites
9	www.sics.se/SICS-reports/SICS-T—93-01—SE/report_10.html	A Nice Web Page on the Prolog Language
10	www.eiffel.com	The Eiffel Language Homepage
11	www.smalltalk.org	The Smalltalk Language Homepage
12	www.visualbasic.org	Association of Visual Basic Professionals
13	gcc.gnu.org/onlinedocs/gcc-2.95.3/g77_12.html	The GNU FORTRAN Language
14	www.acm.org/sigapl	ACM's Special Interest Group on APL and J
15	www.users.cloud9.net/~bradmcc/APL.html	A Resourceful Homepage on APL
16	allman.rhon.itam.mx/dcomp/awk.html	A Nice Introduction to the awk Language
17	www.gnu.org/software/gawk/gawk.html	The Web Page for GNU awk, gawk
18	www.tcl.tk	The tcl Developers Site
19	www.w3.org/MarkUp/	Homepage for HTML Activities

8.9 SUMMARY

LINUX and UNIX support many programming languages from low-level assembly languages to high-level visual and scripting langues. Some of the well-known high-level languages (both interpreted and compiled) that they support are C, C++, Pascal, Java, Javascript, FORTRAN, Perl, BASIC, Prolog, awk, bash, tcl, and LISP. A source program in a compiled language such as C, C++, or Java has to go through some kind of translation before it can be executed. This translation process, known as compilation, consists of compilation, assembly, and linking phases. A program in an interpreted language such as Perl is executed, one statement or command at a time, by a program called the interpreter for the language.

High-level languages are usually classified as imperative, functional, logic, and object-oriented. Each language class dictates a programming style. Two of the most popular programming paradigms are procedural and object-oriented. Most application software today is written in the object-oriented style of programming. The development time for object-oriented program is longer and they spread over many files. But the upshot is that object-oriented software is moduler and, therefore, easy to maintain.

A software product is developed in a sequence of phases, collectively known as a software engineering lifecycle. The phases of a typical life cycle are requirement analysis, specifications, planning, design, coding, testing, installation, and maintenance. Some of the famous software engineering life cycles are waterfall and spiral. The choice of a life cycle for a product depends on the nature and size of the product.

8.10 QUESTIONS AND PROBLEMS

1. What are the differences between compiled and interpreted languages? Give three examples of each.

2. Give one application area each for assembly and high-level languages.

3. What are the differences between the procedural and object-oriented programming styles of programming?

4. What is an object in an object-oriented program? How can an object communicate with another object in such a program?

5. Write the steps that a compiler performs on a source program in order to produce an executable file. State the purpose of each step. Your answer should be precise.

6. Write the steps that a C or C++ compiler performs on a source program in order to produce an executable file. State the purpose of each step. Your answer should be precise.

7. Write the operations that a C/C++ preprocessor performs on a source program before giving the (modified) program to the compiler.

8. Write the names of three commonly used software life cycles.

9. Write down the three steps of the program development process and their purpose.

10. Browse the Web resources listed in Table 8.1 to learn more about the various languages.

11. What is the difference between Java and Javascript? Be precise.

12. Search the java.sun.com Web site for a sample Java program, create the source file for the program, compile it, and run it. Write down the steps involved to complete this task.

13. Which of the following languages are supported by your LINUX/UNIX system: C, C++, Perl, tcl, awk, tk, bash, Pascal, Java, BASIC, FORTRAN, and LISP? What are the names of their compilers (or interperters), and where are the interpreters located in the LINUX/UNIX file system structure? What commands did you use to complete the given task?

## CHAPTER 9

Program Generation Tools

OBJECTIVES

- To describe how to generate source program files
- To discuss program indentation and the LINUX/UNIX tool for indenting
- To describe the compilation of C, C++, and Java programs
- To discuss some important features of the C/C++ compilers
- To introduce compilation and linking of programs in multiple files
- To list some important Web resources
- Commands and primitives covered: `gcc`, `g++`, `indent`, `java`, `javac`

9.1 INTRODUCTION

The program development process comprises three phases: code generation, static analysis, and dynamic analysis. The **code generation phase** consists of creating source code and generating the executable code for it. Hence, it involves tools for editing text files, indenting the source code properly, compiling the source code, compiling module-based software, creating libraries, managing the source code, and controlling revisions. The **static analysis phase** consists of verifying the source code for portability and measuring source code metrics (e.g., the structure of the source code, its size in lines of code, and number of function points). The **dynamic analysis phase** comprises debugging, tracing, testing, and monitoring the performance of the software, including testing it against product requirements. In this and the remaining chapters of the book, we discuss the LINUX and UNIX tools needed during a typical software development process.

In this chapter, we discuss the LINUX and UNIX tools for creating source program files, indenting the source code, and compiling C, C++, and Java source files to generate executable files. We also discuss many important features of the C/C++ compilers.

9.2 GENERATING PROGRAM SOURCE FILES

Any text editor can be used to generate program source files. The most frequently used LINUX and UNIX editors are vi, emacs, and xemacs. Altough not a native LINUX text editor, pico is also a fairly popular editor on LINUX and UNIX computers, specially among the student community. We discuss LINUX and UNIX text editors briefly in Appendix A.

9.3 INDENTING SOURCE CODE

Proper indentation of source code is an important part of good coding practice, primarily because it enhances the readability of the code. The best known indentation style for C was proposed by Brian Kernighan and Dennis Ritchie in *The C Programming Language,* the first book on the C language. This style is commonly known as the K&R (for Kernighan and Ritchie) indentation style. Most programmers who do not work in C aren't familiar with this style. You can use the LINUX `indent` command (UNIX `indent` is similar) to indent a C program properly. The following is a brief description of this command.

Syntax:

> **indent [options] [input-files]**
> **indent [options] [single-input-file] [-o output-file]**

Purpose: This command reads a syntactically correct program specified in 'input-file,' indents it according to some commonly accepted C program structure by inserting or deleting spaces, and saves the formatted program in 'output-file' if 'output-file' is specified in the command line. If the output file is not specified, the formatted version replaces the original version after saving the original version in a file that has the same name as 'input-file' and extension BAK.

Syntax:	**indent [options] [input-files]** **indent [options] [single-input-file] [-o output-file]** *(continued)*

Commonly Used Options / Features:

/**INDENT OFF**/ /**INDENT ON**/	The source code between these two comments is not formatted by indent. Note that *INDENT OFF* and *INDENT ON* are strings without spaces; you can use spaces before and after these strings.
-bad	Force blank lines after declarations
-bap	Force blank lines after function bodies
-bl	Format according to Pascal-like syntax
-bls	Put braces on the line after **struct** declaration lines
-kr	Format according to the Kernighan & Ritchie coding style
-orig	Format according to the Berkeley coding style
-st	Send formatted program to standard output

If no input files are specified in the command line or if '–' is specified as the input file, the **indent** command reads input from standard input. By default, the **indent** command formats a program according to the GNU style indentation and preserves all user new lines. In the following session, the C program code in the second.c file is indented by using various options. The **indent second.c** command saves the original file in second.c~ and puts the indented version in the file second.c. The default indentation style is shown as the output of the **more second.c** command. The **more second.c~** command is used to display the backup of the original file. Some implementations of the indent command use the .BAK extension in place of ~.

```
$ more second.c
main()
{
int i,j;
for (i=0,j=10; i < j; i++)
{
printf("LINUX Rules the Networking World!\n");
}
}
$ indent second.c
$ ls
second.c second.c~
```

```
$ more second.c
main ()
{
  int i, j;
  for (i = 0, j = 10; i < j; i++)
    {
       printf ("LINUX Rules the Networking World!\n");
    }
}
$ more second.c~
main()
{
int i,j;
for (i=0,j=10; i<j; i++)
{
printf("LINUX Rules the Networking World!\n");
}
}
$
```

You can send the indented program to standard output by using the −st option. The following session demonstrates the use of these options. In the first command, the program is formatted by using the default (GNU) indentation style and displayed on the screen. You can save the formatted version of the program in a file called second.output by using the `indent −st second.c > second.output` command, as shown. You can perform the same task by using the `indent second.c −o second.out` or `cat second.c | indent −o second.out` command.

```
$ indent −st second.c
main ()
{
  int i, j;
  for (i = 0, j = 10; i < j; i++)
    {
       printf ("LINUX Rules the Networking World!\n");
    }
}
$ indent −st second.c > second.output
$
```

The following session shows how the C program can be formatted according to the popular K&R (the **–kr** option) and Berkeley (the **–orig** option) coding styles. The **–bad** option is used in the second command to insert a blank line after variable declarations.

```
$ indent -kr -st second.c
main()
{
    int i, j;
    for (i = 0, j = 10; i < j; i++) {
        printf("LINUX Rules the Networking World!\n");
    }
}
$ indent -bad -kr -st second.c
main()
{

    int i, j;

    for (i = 0, j = 10; i < j; i++) {
        printf("LINUX Rules the Networking World!\n");
    }
}
$ indent -orig -st second.c
main()
{
    int                 i,
                        j;
    for (i = 0, j = 10; i < j; i++) {
        printf("LINUX Rules the Networking World!\n");
    }
}
$
```

When the C style is used for turning formatting off or on (as shown in the syntax box), the indent program does not look for the closing */. You can, therefore, use /**INDENT OFF* or /**INDENT ON* control strings to turn indentation off or on, respectively. The indentation can also be turned off and on by using the C++ comment style, //*INDENT OFF* and //*INDENT ON*.

The following In-Chapter Exercise is designed to give you practice in using the **indent** command to properly indent your C/C++ programs and make them more readable.

IN-CHAPTER EXERCISES

9.1   Create the second.c file shown in Section 9.3 and indent it according to the K&R and original Berkeley styles by using the **indent** command. If some command line option does not work on your system, use the **man indent** command to get information about the command options on your system.

9.4 COMPILING C/C++ PROGRAMS

The C++ language is a superset of the C language, i.e., it has all the features of C and more. The most commonly used C compiler for LINUX and UNIX is **gcc** (GNU C/C++ compiler). This compiler is written for ANSI C, the most recent standard for C language. The **gcc** compiler assumes that the preprocessed files are for C source code and assumes C style linking. (See Section 8.6 for preprocessing and linking.) The **cc** command on LINUX and UNIX systems is a symbolic link to **gcc**. All C++ compilers, such as **g++** (GNU compiler for C++), can also be used to compile C programs. The **g++** compiler invokes **gcc** with options necessary to make it recognize C++ source code. The **g++** compiler assumes that the preprocessed files are for C++ source code and assumes C++ style linking. We primarily discuss the **gcc** compiler because it is the most widely used C compiler on LINUX and UNIX platforms. Also, most of our example commands in this book use C program files but you could use C++ files instead without changing the effect of the commands. We discuss compilation of C++ programs with the **g++** compiler in briefly Section 9.5 below. By default, all C/C++ compilers store the executable code in the a.out file. Here is a brief description of the **gcc** command.

Syntax: **gcc [options] file-list**

Purpose: This command can be used to invoke the C compilation system. When executed, it preprocesses, compiles, assembles, and links to generate executable code. The executable code is placed in the a.out file by default. This command accepts several types of files and processes them according to the options specified in the command line. The files can be archive files (.a extension), C source files (.c extension), C source files (.C, .cc, or .cxx extension), assembler files (.s extension), preprocessed files (.i extension), or object files (.o extension). When a file extension is not recognizable, the command assumes the file to be an object or library/archive file. The files are specified in 'file-list'.

Syntax:	**gcc [options] file-list** *(continued)*

Commonly Used Options / Features:

–ansi	Enforce full ANSI conformance
–c	Suppress the linking phase and keep object files (with .o extension)
–Dmacro=[dfn]	Define 'macro' to be 'dfn'. Without the optional definition part, define 'macro' to be string 1
–E	Stop after the preprocessing stage and send the preprocessed file to stdout
–g	Create symbol table, profiling, and debugging inform tion for use with the **gdb** (GNU DeBugger)
–llib	Link to the 'lib' library
–mconfig	Optimize code for 'config' CPU ('config' can specify a wide variety of CPUs, including Intel 80386, 80486, Motorola 68K series, RS6000, AMD 29K series, and MIPS processors)
–o file	Create executable in 'file', instead of in the default file a.out
–O[level]	Optimize. You can specify 0-3 as 'level'; generally, the higher the number for 'level,' the higher the level of optimization. No optimization is done if 'level' is 0.
–pg	Provide profile information to be used with the profiling tool **gprof**
–S	Do not assemble or link the .c files and leave assembly versions in corresponding files with the .s extension
–v	Verbose mode: display commands as they are invoked
–w	Suppress warnings
–W	Give extra and more verbose warnings

The **gcc** command can be used with or without options; the order in which options are specified in the command line is not important. We describe some basic options here and some in the later sections of this chapter. One of the options commonly used, even by beginners, is **–o** for output. You can use this option to inform **gcc** that it should store the executable code in a particular file instead of in the default a.out file. This means that with the **–o** option you can store multiple executable files for the same or different source programs. It is important to realize that the name of the file to contain the executable code must follow the **–o** option, otherwise whatever file name follows this option will be overwritten!

In the following session, we show compilation of the C program in the first.c file, with and without the **–o** option. The `gcc first.c` command produces the executable code in the a.out file and the `gcc –o slogan first.c` command produces the executable code in the slogan file. The `ls` command is used to show the names of the executable files generated by the two **gcc** commands.

```
$ cat first.c
main ()
{
        printf("LINUX and UNIX Rule the Networking World!\n");
}
$ ls
first.c    second.c
$ gcc first.c
$ ls
a.out      first.c second.c
$ a.out
LINUX and UNIX Rule the Networking World!
$ gcc -o slogan first.c
$ ls
a.out      first.c second.c slogan
$ slogan
LINUX and UNIX Rule the Networking World!
$
```

In the following example, we use the **–v** options to show the steps that the compiler goes through to compile your program. The compilation steps described for the C/C++ programs outlined in Chapter 8—preprocessing, compiling, assembly, and linking—are shown here clearly. Note that the command output shows that GNU C Preprocessor (CPP) and GNU C compiler version 2.96 are used. The assembler used is version 2.11.90.9.8. The output also shows that **dynamic linking** is used by LINUX to generate the executable code.

```
$ gcc -v slogan.c -lm
Reading specs from /usr/lib/gcc-lib/i386-redhat-linux/2.96/specs
gcc version 2.96 20000731 (Red Hat Linux 7.1 2.96-98)
 /usr/lib/gcc-lib/i386-redhat-linux/2.96/cpp0 -lang-c -v -D__GNUC__=2 -D__GNUC_M
```

INOR__=96 -D__GNUC_PATCHLEVEL__=0 -D__ELF__ -Dunix -Dlinux -D__ELF__ -D__unix__

-D__linux__ -D__unix -D__linux -Asystem(posix) -D__NO_INLINE__ -Acpu(i386) -Amac

hine(i386) -Di386 -D__i386 -D__i386__ -D__tune_i386__ slogan.c /tmp/ccOM86nu.i

GNU CPP version 2.96 20000731 (Red Hat Linux 7.1 2.96-98) (cpplib) (i386 Linux/ELF)

ignoring nonexistent directory "/usr/i386-redhat-linux/include"

#include "..." search starts here:

#include <...> search starts here:

 /usr/local/include

 /usr/lib/gcc-lib/i386-redhat-linux/2.96/include

 /usr/include

End of search list.

 /usr/lib/gcc-lib/i386-redhat-linux/2.96/cc1 /tmp/ccOM86nu.i -quiet -dumpbase slogan.c -
    version -o /tmp/cc4ySmiQ.s

GNU C version 2.96 20000731 (Red Hat Linux 7.1 2.96-98) (i386-redhat-linux) comp

iled by GNU C version 2.96 20000731 (Red Hat Linux 7.1 2.96-98).

 as -V -Qy -o /tmp/ccwNbFBb.o /tmp/cc4ySmiQ.s

GNU assembler version 2.11.90.0.8 (i386-redhat-linux) using BFD version 2.11.90. 0.8

 /usr/lib/gcc-lib/i386-redhat-linux/2.96/collect2 -m elf_i386 -dynamic-linker /l

ib/ld-linux.so.2 /usr/lib/gcc-lib/i386-redhat-linux/2.96/../../../crt1.o /usr/li

b/gcc-lib/i386-redhat-linux/2.96/../../../crti.o /usr/lib/gcc-lib/i386-redhat-li

nux/2.96/crtbegin.o -L/usr/lib/gcc-lib/i386-redhat-linux/2.96 -L/usr/lib/gcc-lib

/i386-redhat-linux/2.96/../../.. /tmp/ccwNbFBb.o -lm -lgcc -lc -lgcc /usr/lib/gc

c-lib/i386-redhat-linux/2.96/crtend.o /usr/lib/gcc-lib/i386-redhat-linux/2.96/../../../crtn.o

$

The following In-Chapter Exercise is designed to give you practice using the **gcc** command with the **-v** option to help you appreciate its basic working.

IN-CHAPTER EXERCISES

9.2 Repeat the above sessions on your UNIX or LINUX system to explore how the **gcc** command works and to appreciate the various steps a compiler takes to generate executable code. What versions of the compiler and assembler does your system use?

9.4.1 COMPILING MULTIPLE SOURCE FILES

You can use the gcc command to compile and link multiple C source files and create an executable file, all in a single command line. For example, you can use the following command line to create the executable file called polish for the C source files driver.c, stack.c, and misc.c.

```
$ gcc driver.c stack.c misc.c -o polish
$
```

If one of the three source files is modified, you need to retype the entire command line, which creates two problems. First, even though only one needs recompilation, all three files are compiled into their object modules, which results in longer compilation time, particularly if the files are large. Second, retyping the entire line may not be a big problem when you're dealing with three files (as here), but you certainly won't like having to do it with a much larger number of files. Although with the ! operator (see Section 1.6.11) you don't need to retype the whole command, specifying different patterns with this operator to invoke multiple commands is still a time-consuming task. To avoid these problems, you should create object modules for all source files and then recompile only those modules that are updated. This is called **incremental recompilation**. All the object modules are then linked together to create a single executable file.

You can use the gcc command with the −c option to create object modules for the C source files. When you compile a program with the −c option, the compiler leaves an object file in your current directory and does not generate the executable file. The object file has the name of the source file and an .o extension. You can link multiple object files by using another gcc command. In the following session, we compile three source modules, driver.c, stack.c, and misc.c, separately to create their object files, and then use another gcc command to link them and create a single executable file, polish.

```
$ gcc -c driver.c
$ gcc -c stack.c
$ gcc -c misc.c
$ gcc misc.o stack.o driver.o -o polish
$ polish
[output of the program]
$
```

You can also compile multiple source files with the −c option and generate their object modules. In the first of the following two command lines we compile all three source files with a single compiler command to generate the object files. The second command line links the three object files and generates one executable file, polish.

```
$ gcc -c driver.c stack.c misc.c
$ gcc misc.o stack.o driver.o -o polish
$
```

Now, if you update one of the source files, you need to generate only the object file for that source file by using the **gcc -c** command. Then you link all the object files again (using the second of the **gcc** command lines) to generate the executable, as shown below. In this example, we assume that only misc.c was updated.

```
$ gcc -c misc.c
$ gcc misc.o stack.o driver.o -o polish
$
```

In the following In-Chapter Exercise, you will use the **gcc** compiler to create an executable file for a C source file.

IN-CHAPTER EXERCISES

9.3 Create executable code for the C program in a file called power.c and place it in a file called XpowerY. What command(s) did you use? Run XpowerY to confirm that the program works properly.

9.4.2 LINKING LIBRARIES

The C/C++ compilers on LINUX and UNIX systems link appropriate libraries with your program when you compile it; you do need to include (with **#include** directive of the preprocessor) a header file such as <string.h> for the string library in order for the libraries to be linked. Sometimes, however, you have to tell the compiler explicitly to link the needed libraries. You can do so by including the header file for the library in your program and using the **gcc** command with the **-l** option, immediately followed by the letters in the library name that follow the string lib and before the extension. You have to use a separate **-l** option for each library that you need to link. In the following session, we link the math library (/lib/libm.a) to the object code for the program in the power.c file. We used the first **gcc** command line to show the error message generated by the compiler if the math library is not linked even though we have included the <math.h> header file (located in the /usr/include directory). The message says that the symbol **pow** is not found in the file power.o (the file in which it is used). The name of the math library is libm.a, so we use the letter m (which follows the string lib and precedes the extension) with the **-l** option and recompile the program to store the executable code in the power file. The program compiles and runs properly now.

```
$ cat power.c
#include <math.h>

main()
{
        float    x,y;
```

```
        printf ("The program takes x and y from stdin and displays
  x^y.\n");
        printf ("Enter number x: ");
        scanf ("%f", &x);
        printf ("Enter number y: ");
        scanf ("%f", &y);
        printf ("x^y is: %6.3f\n", pow((double)x,(double)y));
}
$ gcc power.c -o power
/tmp/ccj67RX0.o: In function `main':
/tmp/ccj67RX0.o(.text+0x62): undefined reference to `pow'
collect2: ld returned 1 exit status
$ gcc power.c -lm -o power
$ power
The program takes x and y from stdin and displays x^y.
Enter number x: 9.82
Enter number y: 2.3
x^y is: 191.362
$
```

In the following example, we compile multiple C files and link the socket and math libraries to the object codes for the programs in any of the source files listed in the command line. The executable code is placed in the file client.

```
$ gcc client.c passiveTCP.c connectsock.c -o client -lsocket -lm
$
```

The order in which options are placed in a **gcc** command line has no significance. Thus the command line above is equivalent to the command line

```
$ gcc -o client client.c passiveTCP.c connectsock.c -lm -lsocket
$
```

In the following example, we show how you can compile and link a multithreaded code that uses the POSIX pthreads library; we also link the socket and math libraries, as in the previous example. We use the **ls** command to show the source files in our current directory. TCPmtechod.c contains the code for a multithreaded echo server. We use the **gcc -c *.c** command to generate the object modules for all C files. We then use the **gcc -o mtechod *.c -lsocket -lpthread -lm** command to link the pthread (/lib/libpthread.a) and math (/lib/libm.a) libraries to the object files and generate the executable code in mtechod.

```
$ ls

errexit.c  passivesock.c  passiveTCP.c  passiveUDP.c  TCPmtechod.c
$ gcc -c *.c
$ gcc -o mtechod *.o -lpthread -lm
$
```

The following In-Chapter Exercise is designed to give you practice in using the gcc command with the -l option to appreciate how it works.

9.4.3 OPTIMIZING EXECUTABLE CODE

You can reduce the size of your executable code and its execution time by optimizing it with the -O compiler option, as described in the syntax box for the gcc command. Optimization saves disk space because the program size is smaller and saves CPU (and/or I/O) time because the program takes less time to run. Sometimes, though, you trade one for the other. For example, with the -O2 option, you trade space for speed. If the executable is to be e-mailed, the space optimized version will take less time to travel on the network (or Internet) than the non-optimized version. Optimizing your code is not so important for rather small programs written as part of a typical programming course, but it is very important for production quality code that would be used many times. In the following session, we use the first two -O options to show reduction in the size of the executable code for a small size program. We use the wc -c command to display the sizes of executable codes in bytes. Note that with the -O0 option no optimization is performed and the minimum optimization (-O1 option) results in about 6% space saving.

```
$ gcc Huffman.c -o Huffman
$ gcc Huffman.c -O0 -o Huffman0
$ gcc Huffman.c -O1 -o Huffman1
$ wc -c Huffman Huffman?
   9182 Huffman
   9182 Huffman0
   8632 Huffman1
  26996 total
$
```

In the following In-Chapter Exercise, you will use a large C source file and optimize it with the **–O1** and **–O2** options of the **gcc** compiler to appreciate time and space optimization of C programs.

IN-CHAPTER EXERCISES

1.1 **9.5** Obtain a large C source file (from a book on the C language or the Internet) and generate the executable for the file by using no option, the **–O1** option, and the **–O2** option of the **gcc** compiler. Make sure that you use the **–o** option to store the executables in three different files (do not overwrite the a.out file). Then use the **ls –l** or **wc –c** command to see the differences in size among the three executable files.

9.4.4 DEFINING MACROS AT COMMAND LINE

A **macro** definition has the following form.

```
#define    name    text
```

The **text** part is the rest of the line, which can be broken into multiple lines by placing a \ at the end of each line. The preprocessor substitutes every subsequent occurrence of **name** with **text**. The scope of **name** is from the point of its definition to the end of the source file in which the definition is placed.

Most C/C++ compilers allow you to define macros at the command line. You can use the **gcc** or **g++** command with **–D** option to do so, as described in the syntax box for the **gcc** command. In the following compiler command, we define a macro (a symbolic constant) BUFSIZE to be 512.

```
$ gcc -DBUFSIZE=512 Huffman.c -o Huffman
$
```

When **gcc** processes the command line arguments, the preprocessor behaves as if the program in the Huffman.c file had the following macro definition in it.

```
#define BUFSIZE    512
```

This allows you to use BUFSIZE as a symbolic constant in your code, as in the statements below.

```
$ more Huffman.c
...
char buf[BUFSIZE];
...
while ((nr = read(fd, buf, BUFSIZE)) > 0)
...
$
```

More complex macro definitions can be passed on the command line by enclosing them in double quotes. In the following session, we use the **g++** command to pass the macro definitions for BUFSIZE and max on the command line. The output of the executable file shows that the use of these macros in the program works as if these macros were defined at the beginning of the test.c file with the **#define** directive. Note that we run the program with the ./a.out command and not a.out because on most LINUX and UNIX systems, the current directory is not in the search path (see Section 1.4.1); if you use a.out and the current directory is not in the search path, you'll get an error message like **bash: a.out: command not found**. If your search path does include the current dirctory, you can use the a.out command to run the executable.

```
$ more test.c
#include <stdio.h>

int main()
{
    printf ("%d\t%d\n",BUFSIZE,max(10,20));
}
$ g++ -DBUFSIZE=512 -D"max(A,B)=((A)>(B)?(A):(B))" test.c
$ ./a.out
512      20
$
```

One of the main advantages of using the **-D** option is that it allows you to place debugging statements in your program that execute depending on the value of a symbolic constant, say, DEBUG. So, you may have a statement like the following in your program.

```
if (DEBUG) {
    /* prorgam statements for displaying debugging information */
}
```

Now, if you specify the -DDEBUG=1 option in the compiler command, the condition for the **if** statement will be true and the code between the braces will execute. If you use the -DDEBUG=0 option, the condition for the **if** statement will be false and the code between the braces will not execute.

The disadvantage of using the **-D** option is that it results in lack of cohesion in the code. So the preferred way of using macros is to define them in your code, instead of passing them at the command line.

9.4.5 Turning Off Compilation, Assembly, or Linking Phase

You can use the **gcc** (or **g++**) command with the **-E** option to turn off the compilation phase. This allows you to display the preprocessed version of your C/C++ code. In the following session we use the first command line to save the preprocessed version of the test.c program in the test.i file. You can display the preprocessed version by using the second command line. We don't display the command output here because it is sparse and takes many pages. The third command line outputs the number of lines in the preprocessed version of the program: 2233 lines of preprocessed code for a 6-line C program!

```
$ gcc -E test.c > test.i
$ gcc -E test.i
[ preprocessed version of the code for the C code in test.c ]
$ gcc -E test.c | wc -l
   2233
$
```

You can suppress the assembly phase by using the **-S** option. With this option, the assembly code for the program is left in the file with the same name as the source file and the .s extension. Similarly, as discussed earlier, you can suppress the linking phase by using the -c option. This leaves the object code in the file with the same name as the source file and the **.o** extension. In both cases, you can save the assembly or object code in a different file by using the **-o** option.

In the following In-Chapter Exercise, you will use the **-D** and **-E** options of the **gcc** compiler to appreciate how you can define macros at command line and how you can suppress compilation, assembly, and linking phases when you compile C programs to generate their preprocessed versions only.

IN-CHAPTER EXERCISES

9.6   Repeat the compilation sessions in Sections 9.4.4 and 9.4.5 to appreciate how you can define macros at command line and how you can generate the preprocessed version of a C program, that is, how you can suppress the compilation, assembly, and linking phases.

9.5 COMPILING C++ PROGRAMS

In this section, we give a few simple examples of compiling C++ prorgams with the GNU g++ compiler. Our examples show pre– and post–ANSI-ISO standard versions of a simple program with input and output. There are two post-standard versions, one without namespace and one with namespace. The following session shows the source codes for the three program versions, and shows compilation and execution of the post-standard with namespace version. The other two versions can be compiled and run the same way.

```
$ more ex1.cpp
// Pre-Standard version with simple I/O

#include <iostream.h>

void main (void)
```

```
{
        int i;

        cout << "You entered : ";
        cin >> i;
        cout << "You entered : " << i << endl;
}
```
$ **more ex2.cpp**
```
// Post-Standard version without namespace
#include <iostream.h>

void main (void)
{
        int i;

        std::cout << "You entered : ";
        std::cin >> i;
        std::cout << "You entered : " << i << endl;
}
```
$ **more ex3.cpp**
```
// Post-Standard version with namespace
#include <iostream.h>

using namespace std;

void main (void)
{
        int i;

        cout << "You entered : ";
        cin >> i;
        cout << "You entered : " << i << endl;
}
```
$ **g++ ex3.cpp**
$ **./a.out**
```
Enter an integer : 2003
You entered : 2003
```
$

We've not given any description of the **g++** compiler options because they are the same as the options for the **gcc** compiler described in Section 9.4. If you are interested in learning more about **g++**, use the **man g++** command on your system or browse a relevant Web page from those given in Table 9.1.

9.6 COMPILING JAVA PROGRAMS

Java source code is compiled (translated) into Java bytecode and is interpreted by the Java Virtual Machine (also known as the Java Interpreter). The Java compiler on our LINUX system is called **javac** and the Java Virtual Machine is **java**. In the following session, we use the **javac** command to compile the Java program in the myHelloProg.java file. It produces the Java bytecode and stores it in the myHelloProg.class file, which is interpreted with the **java** command.

```
$ more myHelloProg.java
/**
 *   The Hello, World! Program — the Java version
 */
class myHelloProg {
    public static void main(String[] args) {
        System.out.println("Hello, World!");
    }
}
$ javac myHelloProg.java
$ ls -l
total 2
-rw------    1 sarwar  152     475 Feb 23 23:59 myHelloProg.class
-rw------    1 sarwar  152     179 Feb 23 22:14 myHelloProg.java
$ java myHelloProg
Hello, World!
$
```

If you have a problem using the **javac** compiler, include /usr/java/j2sdk1.4.0/bin in your shell's search path.

In the following In-Chapter Exercise, you will use the **g++** and **javac** compiler commands to compile simple C++ and Java programs on your UNIX or LINUX system.

IN-CHAPTER EXERCISES

9.7 Repeat the compilation sessions in Sections 9.5 and 9.6 on your UNIX or LINUX system to appreciate the basic working of these two compilers.

9.7 DISASTROUS COMPILER COMMANDS AND TYPICAL COMPILE TIME ERRORS

The two most disastrous compiler commands involve the use of the **–o** compiler option and the use of the output redirection operator (**>**). As stated previously, when you use the **–o** option of a compiler command, the name of the file that should contain the executable code must follow the option, as in **gcc sample.c –o sample**. If you want to save the executable in a file with the name of the source file but without the extension (.c, .cpp, etc.), as is the case in the above command, you must type your command very carefully. It is possible that in the flow of things you may type the name of the source file as the name of the executable file, as in **g++ sample.c –o sample.c**. If you did so, you would overwrite your source file with the executable code, which means that you've lost your source file forever!

A similar situation results when you use output or error redirection and type the name of the source file after the redirection operator, as in **gcc sample.c –o sample 2> sample.c**. In this case you would again lose your source file because the shell will truncate the sample.c file since you have indicated that **sample.c** should contain the error messages produced by **gcc**. Similarly, **gcc –E test.c > test.c** will have the same disastrous effect. In this case, you will end up with an empty test.c file.

There are many reasons the shell may not be able to start your compiler command. Some common reasons are no source file, bad pathname for the file, or no read permission on the file.

Many compile time errors are reported due to simple mistakes in your source code. Most compile time errors, especially for beginners, are the result of missing semicolons, quotes, parentheses, or braces. A missing semicolon in particular is sometimes difficult to locate. The best solution in such circumstances is probably to scan through your source code to locate statements that don't terminate with a semicolon, insert semicolons that are missing, and recompile the program.

9.8 COMPILING AND INTERPRETING PROGRAMS IN OTHER PROGRAMMING LANGUAGES

The LINUX and UNIX systems have compilers for many other languages such as **f77** for FORTRAN and **perlcc** for the front end of Perl. The GNU FORTRAN compiler is **g77**. Similarly, these systems have many interpreters such as **bash** for interpreting a bash script and **perl** for interpreting a perl script.

9.9 WEB RESOURCES

Table 9.1 lists useful Web sites for some C, C++, and Java compilers and compiling tools.

Table 9.1	Web Resources for Some Compilers and Compiling Tools	
Reference	**URL**	**Description**
1	gcc.gnu.org/	The home page for the gcc compiler
2	www.delorie.com/gnu/docs/gcc/g++.1.html	The manual page for GNU C++ compiler g++
3	www.cs.wm.edu/cspages/computing/tutorial/ gpp.html	A nice tutorial on g++
4	developer.java.sun.com/developer/onlineTraining/ Programming/BasicJava1/	Essentials of the Java Programming Language
5	java.sun.com/products/jdk/1.1/docs/tooldocs/ solaris/javac.html	Manual page for the `javac` compiler
6	fpt://ftp.ugcs.caltech.edu/pub/elef/autotools/ toolsmanual.html	A repository of tools for developing software with GNU

9.10 SUMMARY

The program development process comprises three phases: code generation, static analysis, and dynamic analysis. LINUX and UNIX systems have many program development tools, including text editors and compilers. We discussed some of the basic and most commonly used tools for generating program source files, indenting program source code, and compiling source program files to generate executable code. The discussion of tools focused on their use for developing production-quality C and C++ software. We also discussed the `indent` command for indenting (for legibility) C and C++ programs and the `gcc`, `g++`, and `javac` commands to compile C, C++, and Java programs, respectively. Some important features of the C/C++ compilers such as producing object files, linking libraries, and storing the executable file in a particular file, were discussed with examples. We also discuss some of the most disastrous compiler commands, typical compile time errors, and ways to resolve compile time errors.

9.11 QUESTIONS AND PROBLEMS

1. What are the three steps involved in the program development process?
2. What tools are available for code generation on LINUX and UNIX? What is the purpose of each tool?
3. Write down the command to indent a C program in the myProg.c file according to the K&R indentation style and save the indented program in the same source file.
4. What C/C++ compilers are available on your LINUX or UNIX system? How did you obtain your answer?

5. What do the following commands do on your UNIX or LINUX system? Where does the output of these commands go?

    a. `gcc myProg.c`

    b. `gcc myProg.c -o myProg`

    c. `gcc -o myProg myProg.c`

    d. `gcc myProg.c -o myProg.c`

    e. `gcc myProg.c -o myProg -lm -lsocket`

    f. `gcc -E myProg.c`

    g. `gcc -E myProg.c > myProg.i`

    h. `gcc -S -DSIZE=256 myProg.c`

    i. `gcc -S -DSIZE=256 myProg.c -o myProg`

6. Write down the command to compile a C++ program in the myLab1.C file and store the executable code in the file myLab1. The C++ program uses functions in the math library and uses the PROMPT macro as shown below. The macro definition is not written at the beginning of the program.

    `#define PROMPT "UNIX and LINUX Rules the Networking World!:>"`

7. Write down the compiler command that performs the task outlined in Problem 6 and produces the most optimized executable code.

8. For an Internet client software, the following C program modules were developed: main.c, connectTCP.c, connectsock.c, and misc.c. Give the compiler command to produce the executable code in the client file. Some of the library calls used in the software are in the socket and math libraries; the compiler does not implicitly link these libraries.

9. Give the compiler command for producing the object file for the myLab1.c program in the file myLab1.o.

10. Convert the C program in the power.c file (Section 9.4.2) into C++. Store the pre-standard, post-standard without namespace, and post-standard with namespace versions of the program in files named power1.cpp, power2.cpp, and power3.cpp. Generate executable code for the three files and store the code in power1, power2, and power3 files, respectively. Then run the three programs to see if they all work as expected. Write down the sequence of commands you used to complete the task.

11. Repeat Problem 10 but use Java instead of C++.

12. Show the steps involved for compiling and executing a Java program in the myLab1.java file. The main function is in the myLab1 class. State clearly the commands for the compilation and execution of this program. Name the file that contains the Java bytecode.

13. In section 9.7 we say that the execution of the `gcc -E test.c > test.c` command results in an empty .c file. Why?

Compiling and Linking Multimodule Software

OBJECTIVES

- To describe the advantages and disadvantages of multimodule software

- To discuss the make utility and its many features that allow easy management of multimodule software

- To list some important Web resources

- Commands and primitives covered: ;, *, \, $, ^, (), {}, [], $@, $?, $<, $^, cat -e, cat -t, grep, make, touch

10.1   INTRODUCTION

Most useful software is divided into multiple source files; each file is called a module. This multimodule structure has several advantages over a monolithic structure, where the entire program is stored in a single file. First, smaller program files are easier to manage and maintain, that is, they are less time-consuming to edit, compile, test, and debug. A modular structure also allows recompilation of only those source files that have been modified, rather than the entire software system. Furthermore, the multimodule structure supports information hiding, the key feature of object-oriented (OO) design and programming. This **information hiding** capability is especially important when programming in purely procedural languages, such as C, that don't have support for information hiding in them.

However, the multimodule implementation also has its disadvantages. First, you must know the files that constitute the entire system, the interdependencies of these files (i.e., which files need recompilation), and which files have been modified since you built the last executable system. Also, compiling multiple files to create an executable sometimes becomes a nuisance when you're dealing with multimodule C/C++ software, because you must type two long command lines: one to create object files for all C/C++ source files, and the other to link the object files to create one executable file. An easy solution is to create a simple shell script that writes both commands. The disadvantage of using a shell script is that, if even one source file (or a header file) is modified, all object files are recreated, most of them unnecessarily.

10.2   THE make UTILITY

LINUX and UNIX have a much more powerful tool, called **make**, that allows you to manage compilation and linking of multiple modules into an executable. It offers a powerful and flexible mechanism for building large-scale software products that supports consistent, streamlined updating. The **make** utility reads a specification file, called makefile, that describes how the modules of a software system depend on each other. The **make** utility uses this dependency specification in the makefile and modification times of various components to minimize the amount of recompilation. This utility is very useful when your software system consists of tens of files and several executable programs. In such a system, remembering and keeping track of all header, source, object, and executable files can be a nightmare. The **make** utility automatically triggers the execution of commands whenever certain files are older or younger than certain other files. You use **make** to ensure that you never forget to run the commands that have to be executed whenever you update some of your files. It is important to note that makefiles need to be modularized also, especially as the complexity of the system they monitor increases. We start with a brief description of the syntax and some of the commonly used options of the make utility and then describe in detail its most commonly used features.

Syntax: **make [options] [targets] [macro definitions]**

Purpose: This utility updates a file based on the dependency relationship stored in a file, called makefile or Makefile. 'Options', 'targets', and 'macro definitions' can be specified in any order.

make [options] [targets] [macro definitions] *(continued)*

Syntax:

Commonly Used Options / Features:

-d	Display debugging information
-f file	This option allows you to instruct the **make** utility to read inter dependency specification from 'file'; without this option, the file name is treated as makefile or Makefile. A file name '–' implies stdin
-h	Display a brief description of all options
-n	Do not run any **makefile** commands, just display them
-s	Run in silent mode, without displaying any messages

There are several versions and extensions of the **make** utility such as GNU make, imake, makedepend, mk, nmake, shape, and others. We discuss many of the features of the basic **make** utility in the remaining sections of this chapter.

10.2.1 MAKEFILE AND MAKE RULES

The **make** utility is based on interdependencies between files, on target files that need to be built (e.g., executable or object files), and on commands that are to be executed to build the target files. These interdependencies, targets, and commands are specified in a file, called **makefile**, as **make rules.** When **make** is run without a command line argument, it reads make rules from makefile. If the make rules are in a file other than makefile (or Makefile), you need to run the make command with the **–f** option, as in **make –f my.makefile**. The following is the syntax of a make rule.

Syntax:

target-list: dependency-list
<TAB> command-list

Here, 'target-list' is a list of target files separated by one or more spaces, 'dependency-list' (also known as prerequisites) is a list, separated by one or more spaces, of files that the target files depend on, and 'command-list' is a list, separated by the new line character, of commands that are executed to create the target files. Each command in the 'command-list' must start with the **<Tab>** character. In older versions of **make**, you were required to terminate a command list with a blank line but it is no more the case. However, you can terminate a command list with a blank line for backward compatibility. An alternative syntax for a make rule is **target-list: dependency-list; command-list** where 'command-list' is a series of commands separated by semicolons. No tabs should precede targets. You can continue a long line by terminating it with the backslash (\) character, as in

```
cd /home/sarwar/courses/bin ; rm file1 file2 \
lab2 lab13 \
prog1.c prog2.c prog5.c
```

which is equivalent to

```
cd /home/sarwar/courses/bin ; rm file1 file2 lab2 lab13 prog1.c prog2.c prog5.c
```

This feature is the only way in which you can use multiline shell commands such as

```
while [ ... ] do ... done
```

To use these in a makefile, use semicolons and backslashes to terminate commands between **do** and **done** to inform shell to suppress interpretation of new lines. Note that you cannot insert a space between the \ and new line characters. A comment line starts with the # character and **make** ignores blank lines.

You can use shell's file name pattern-matching characters ?, *, and [ ] in 'dependency-list' and 'command-list.' For example the **rm -f *.o** command can be specified in 'command-list' to force removal of all object files in the current directory.

The makefile consists of a list of make rules that describe the dependency relationships between files that are used to create an executable file. The **make** utility uses the rules in the makefile to determine which of the files in your program files need to be recompiled and relinked to re-create the executable. **make** recompiles a source file involved in the **build** (creation of the executable file) if the last modify timestamp (the last update time) on the file is more current than the timestamp on the executable file. Thus, for example, if you modify a header (.h) file, the **make** utility recompiles all those source files that include this header file provided that the header file is in the dependency list of the object files for these source files. The files that contain this header file must be specified in the corresponding makefile. We show several examples of such dependency in this chapter. The directory that contains the source files and the makefile is commonly called the **build directory.**

The following makefile can be used for the power program discussed in Section 9.4.2.

```
$ cat makefile
#  Sample makefile for the power program
#  Remember: each command line starts with a TAB
power: power.c
        gcc power.c -o power -lm
$
```

If the executable file power exists and the source file power.c hasn't been modified since the executable file was created, running **make** will give the message that the executable file is up to date for power.c. Therefore **make** has no need to recompile and relink power.c. At times you will need to force remaking of an executable because, for example, one of the system header files included in your source has changed and this header file is not specified in the dependency list of the object (or source) file. In order to force re-creation of the executable, you will need to change the last update time of your source file. One commonly used method for doing so is to use the **touch** command and rerun **make**. The **touch** commands updates the last modify time to the current time. The following session illustrates these points.

```
$ make
make: 'power' is up to date.
$ touch power.c
$ make
gcc power.c -o power -lm
$
```

When you use the **touch** command with one or more existing files as its argument, it sets the last update time of those files to the current time. When used with a nonexistent file as an argument, **touch** creates a zero-length file (empty file) with the name provided.

The following In-Chapter Exercise is designed to give you practice using the **make** command with makefiles for a simple, one-module C program.

IN-CHAPTER EXERCISES

10.1 Copy the power.c program in Chapter 9 and the makefile in this section. Then repeat the above session with **make**, **touch**, and **make** commands. Run the **ls −l** command to see whether the executable file power is created. Run the **power** program to ensure that it works properly.

10.2 Create the executable code for the C program in the power.c file and place it in a file called XpowerY. Use the **make** utility to perform this task by modifying the makefile given above. Run XpowerY to confirm that the program works properly.

10.2.2 MULTIMODULE SOFTWARE, DEPENDENCY TREES, AND MAKE

In order to show a next-level use of the **make** utility, we partition the **C** program in the power.c file from Chapter 9 into two files: power.c and compute.c. The following session shows the contents of these files. The compute.c file contains the **compute** function, which is called from the **main** function in power.c. To create an executable file called power, we can compile the two source files independently and then link them, as shown in the two **gcc** command lines at the end of the following session.

```
$ cat power.c
#include <stdio.h>

double compute(double x, double y);

main()
{
        float    x,y;

        printf ("The program takes x and y from stdin and displays x^y.\n");
```

```
        printf ("Enter number x: ");
        scanf ("%f", &x);
        printf ("Enter number y: ");
        scanf ("%f", &y);
        printf ("x^y is: %6.3f\n", compute(x,y));
}
$ cat compute.c
#include <math.h>

double compute (double x, double y)
{
        return (pow ((double) x, (double) y));
}
$ gcc -c compute.c power.c
$ gcc compute.o power.o -o power -lm
$
```

The following In-Chapter Exercise is designed to let you partition the C program in the power.c file into two modules, compute.c and power.c, as shown in the above session and use the **gcc** compiler to generate the executable in the power file.

IN-CHAPTER EXERCISE

10.3 Create the compute.c and power.c files as shown in the above session. Then use the **gcc** command to generate the executable in the power file, as shown in the above session. Run the power program to ensure that it works properly.

The dependency relationship between the two source files is quite simple in this case. To create the executable file power, we need two object modules: power.o and compute.o. If either of the two files power.c or compute.c is updated, the executable needs to be re-created. Figure 10.1 shows this first cut on the dependency relationship.

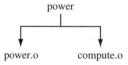

Figure 10.1 First cut on the make dependency tree

The **make** rule corresponding to this dependency relationship is therefore the following. Note that the math library (/lib/libm.a) has to be linked to the compute.o file because the compute function in the compute.c file uses the **pow** function in this library.

```
power: power.o compute.o

    gcc power.o compute.o -o power -lm
```

We also know that the object file power.o is built from the source file power.c and that the object file compute.o is built from the source file compute.c. Figure 10.2 shows the second cut on the dependency relationship.

Thus the make rules for creating the two object files are as follows.

```
power.o: power.c
        gcc -c power.c
compute.o: compute.c

        gcc -c compute.c
```

The following is the final `makefile`.

```
$ cat makefile
power: power.o compute.o
        gcc power.o compute.o -o power -lm
power.o: power.c
        gcc -c power.c
compute.o: compute.c
        gcc -c compute.c
$
```

The following is an execution of the **make** utility with the preceding makefile. In the absence of a command line argument, **make** makes the target file in the first rule in the makefile. Note the order in which the commands for the three make rules execute; this order is dictated by the structure

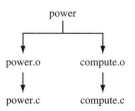

Figure 10.2 Second cut on the make dependency tree

of the dependency tree. The tree nodes are processed bottom up, level by level, starting with the parents of leaf nodes. Nodes at the same level are processed left to right. The command for generating the executable file, as expected, runs at the end.

```
$ make
gcc -c power.c
gcc -c compute.c
gcc power.o compute.o -o power -lm
$
```

In the following In-Chapter Exercise, you will use the **make** utility to create executable code from a C source code that is partitioned into two files.

IN-CHAPTER EXERCISE

10.4   Create the two source files power.c and compute.c shown above and follow the steps discussed to create the executable file power by using the **make** utility.

We now change the structure of our software and divide it into six files called main.c, compute.c, input.c, compute.h, input.h, and main.h. The contents of these files are shown in the following session. Note that the compute.h and input.h files contain declarations (prototypes) of the compute and input functions but not their definitions; the definitions are in the compute.c and input.c files. The main.h file contains two prompts to be displayed to the user.

```
$ cat compute.h
/* Declaration/Prototype of the "compute" function */
double compute(double, double);
$ cat input.h
/* Declaration/Prototype of the "input" function */
double input (char *);
$ cat main.h
/* Declaration of prompts to users */
const char *PROMPT1 = "Enter the value of x: "
const char *PROMPT2 = "Enter the value of y: "
$ cat compute.c
#include <math.h>
#include "compute.h"

double compute (double x, double y)
{
        return (pow ((double) x, (double) y));
```

```
}
$ cat input.c
#include "input.h"

double input(const char *s)
{
        float x;

        printf ("%s", s);
        scanf ("%f", &x);
        return (x);
}
$ cat main.c
#include <stdio.h>
#include "main.h"
#include "compute.h"
#include "input.h"

main()
{

        double x, y;

        printf ("The program takes x and y from stdin and displays x^y.\n");
        x = input(PROMPT1);
        y = input(PROMPT2);
        printf ("x^y is: %6.3f\n", compute(x,y));

}
$
```

To generate the executable for the software, you need to generate the object files for the three source files and link them into a single executable. The following commands are needed to accomplish this task. Note that, as before, you need to link the math library while linking the compute.o file to generate the executable in the power file.

```
$ gcc -c main.c input.c compute.c
$ gcc main.o input.o compute.o -o power -lm
$
```

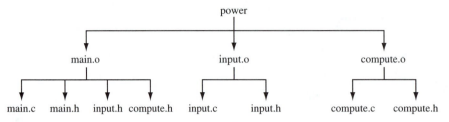

Figure 10.3 The make dependency tree for the sample C software

Figure 10.3 shows the dependency relationship between these files.
The makefile corresponding to this dependency relationship is

```
$ cat   makefile
power: main.o input.o compute.o
        gcc main.o input.o compute.o -o power -lm
main.o: main.c main.h input.h compute.h
        gcc -c main.c
input.o: input.c input.h
        gcc -c input.c
compute.o: compute.c compute.h
        gcc -c compute.c
$
```

Execution of the **make** command results in the execution of the commands associated with all targets in the makefile.

```
$ make
gcc -c main.c
gcc -c input.c
gcc -c compute.c
gcc main.o input.o compute.o -o power -lm
$
```

In the following In-Chapter Exercises, you will divide the program in the power.c and compute.c files into six modules as shown in the above session, create the makefile for the software, and create the executable in the power file. The purpose of these exercises is to let you appreciate how makefile can work with mutiple modules and to see how **make** automatically runs the commands necessary to generate the executable code when some modules are changed.

IN-CHAPTER EXERCISES

10.5   Create the main.c, input.c, compute.c, main.h, input.h, and compute.h files shown above and then use the **make** command to create the executable in the file power. Use the preceding makefile and the **make** utility without command line arguments to perform your task. Run the power program to ensure that it works properly.

10.6   Run the **make** command after running the **touch compute.c** command. Show the output of the **make** command. Does the output make sense to you? Now run the **touch main.h input.c** command, execute the **make** command, and show its output. What commands in the makefile are executed? Do you understand why they are executed? Finally, run the power program to ensure that it works as expected.

10.2.3 SUFFIX (DEFAULT) RULES

The make rules as shown in the preceding makefile contain some redundant commands. The **make** utility has many predefined make rules, also known as **suffix rules**, that allow the **make** utility to perform many tasks automatically. The suffix rules are based on the fact that C and FORTRAN compilers require their source files to have .c and .f suffixes, respectively. Similarly, assembly language and object files carry .s and .o suffixes, respectively. The make utility has built in rules for many other languages and for UNIX tools such as **SCCS**, **RCS**, **ar**, **lex**, and **yacc**. The **make -p** command displays the list of suffix rules. In order to build a target, make traverses a chain of dependencies in order to decide where to start building (or rebuilding). If an object file does not exist, make searches for a source file according to a precedence order. It first looks for a .c, .f, or .s file for building the object file. If make does not find one, it continues and looks for an SCCS file (with suffix .c~) and continues to search until it finds a source file. If it does not find a source file, make reports an exception.

The following are the definitions of the make rules for invoking a C compiler or assembler suffix rule.

```
SUFFIXES: .o .c .s
.c.o:
   $(CC) $(CFLAGS) -c $<
.s.o:
   $(AS) $(ASFLAGS) -o $@ $<
```

Here, $@ stands for the name of the current target (i.e., the target being built) and $< stands for the name of the current dependency (in the dependency list of the current target) that has changed more recently than the target (see Table 10.1 below in Section 10.2.5). **CC**, **CFLAGS**, **AS**, and **ASFLAGS** are macros; see Section 10.2.4 for further details. We show the use of suffix rules with a simple example.

The **make** utility has a predefined rule that invokes the **gcc –c xxx.c –o xxx.o** command for the rules whose targets are .o files, as in

```
xxx.o: xxx.c zzz.h

        gcc -c xxx.c
```

Furthermore, the **make** utility recognizes that the name of an object file is usually the name of the source file. This capability is known as a **standard dependency,** and because of it you can leave **xxx.c** from the dependency list corresponding to the target **xxx.o**. Note how important it is to follow standard naming of files. The following makefile therefore works as well as the one given previously.

$ **cat makefile**

```
power: main.o input.o compute.o
          gcc main.o input.o compute.o -o power -lm
main.o: main.h input.h compute.h
input.o: input.h
compute.o: compute.h
$
```

Running the **make** command with this makefile produces the following result, which is the same as produced by the **make** command when executed with the makefile that does not take advantage of any suffix rules.

$ **make**
```
gcc     -c main.c -o main.o
gcc     -c input.c -o input.o
gcc     -c compute.c -o compute.o
gcc main.o input.o compute.o -o power -lm
$
```

10.2.4 MACRO SUPPORT OF THE make UTILITY

The **make** utility supports simple macros that allow simple text substitution. You must define the macros before using them; they are usually placed at the top of the makefile. A macro definition can have one of the following two forms.

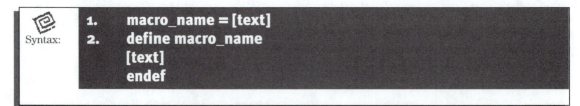

Syntax:
1. **macro_name = [text]**
2. **define macro_name**
   [text]
   endef

With this rule in place, 'text' is substituted for every occurrence of $(macro_name) or ${macro_name} in the rest of the makefile. For single-character macros, no parentheses or braces are needed. Once a macro has been defined, you can use it in subsequent macro definitions. The following are legal definitions of and references to macros. Note that parentheses or braces are not used around G in $G because it is a single-character macro.

```
G = gcc
NAME = Tom
ABC = memo.${NAME}
...
$G -o power power.c -lm

...
```

The make utility has some built-in macros, such as **CFLAGS**, that are set to default values and are used by the built-in rules, such as execution of the **gcc $(CFLAGS) -c xxx.c -o xxx.o** command for a predefined rule, as described previously. The default value of the **CFLAGS** macro is usually **-O** (for optimization), but it can be changed to any other flag for the **gcc** compiler. On our system **CFLAGS** is set to null—no options. The **make** utility uses several other built-in macros for the built-in rules.

The following makefile shows the use of **user-defined macros** and some useful make rules that can be invoked at the command line by specifying their targets as command line arguments of **make**. It also shows that the commands for make rules are not always compiler or linker commands; they can be any shell commands.

```
$ cat makefile
CC = gcc
OPTIONS = -O3
OBJECTS = main.o input.o compute.o
SOURCES = main.c input.c compute.c
HEADERS = main.h input.h compute.h
power: $(OBJECTS)
        $(CC) $(OPTIONS) -o power $(OBJECTS) -lm
main.o: main.h input.h compute.h
input.o: input.h
compute.o: compute.h
power.tar: makefile $(HEADERS) $(SOURCES)
        tar -cvf power.tar makefile $(HEADERS) $(SOURCES)
clean:
        rm *.o
$
```

When the **make** command is executed without arguments, the commands for the last two targets (**power.tar** and **clean**) are not executed, because these targets do not depend on anything and nothing depends on them. You can invoke the commands associated with these targets by passing the targets as parameters to the **make** command. The advantage of putting these rules in the **makefile** is that you don't have to remember which files to archive (by using the **tar** command in this case) and which to remove once the final executable has been created. The **make clean** command invokes the **rm *.o** command to remove all object files that are created in the process of building the executable for the software. The following session shows the output of **make** when executed with two targets as command line arguments. The **tar** archive is placed in the power.tar file.

```
$ make power.tar clean
tar -cvf power.tar makefile main.h input.h compute.h main.c input.c compute.c
makefile
main.h
input.h
compute.h
main.c
input.c
compute.c
rm *.o
$
```

The following In-Chapter Exercise is designed to have you appreciate the use of macros in a makefile.

IN-CHAPTER EXERCISE

10.7 Create the above makefile and run the makefile without a command line argument. Show the output of the **make** command. Run the power program to ensure that it works as expected. Then run the **make clean power.tar** command to remove the object files from your build directory and create a **tar** archive for your project files.

10.2.5 BUILT-IN MACROS

The **make** utility has several built-in (internal) macros that you can use for brevity. Table 10.1 describes some of the commonly used internal macros and their meanings.

Table 10.1	Built-in (Internal) Macros in the make utility and their meanings
Internal Macro	**Meaning**
$@	The name of the current target. When used in make rules for making libraries, it stands for the library name.
$?	The list of dependencies (i.e., the files that a target depends on) that have changed more recently than the current target.
$<	The name of the current dependency that has been modified more recently than the current target.
$^	A space-separated list of all dependencies without duplications.

We update our makefile to incorporate the use of some of these internal macros. The updated makefile and some sample runs of the **make** command are shown in the following session. Note that when a command in the command list for a target is preceded by @, the command is not echoed when the **make** utility is executing (i.e., building the target). You can display these commands (and other makefile commands) by executing the **make –n** command. In the session that follows, we have also used an alternative syntax for the definition of the **CC** macro. The command for the clean target has been changed to force the removal of the executable file power, any core file, and all object files.

```
$ cat makefile
# Updated makefile that uses some built-in macros and
# @-preceded commands
define CC
    gcc
endef
OPTIONS = -O3
OBJECTS = main.o input.o compute.o
SOURCES = main.c input.c compute.c
HEADERS = main.h input.h compute.h
complete: power
        @echo "Build complete"
power: $(OBJECTS)
        $(CC) $(OPTIONS) —o $@ $^ -lm
        @echo "The executable is in the 'power' file."
main.o: main.h input.h compute.h
```

```
compute.o: compute.h
input.o: input.h
power.tar: makefile $(HEADERS) $(SOURCES)
        tar -cvf $@ $^
clean:
        rm -f *.o core power
```

$ **make**

```
gcc    -c main.c -o main.o
gcc    -c input.c -o input.o
gcc    -c compute.c -o compute.o
gcc -O3 -o power main.o input.o compute.o -lm
The executable is in the 'power' file.
Build complete
```

$ **make power.tar clean**

```
tar -cvf power.tar makefile main.h input.h compute.h main.c input.c compute.c
makefile
main.h
input.h
compute.h
main.c
input.c
compute.c
rm -f *.o core power
```

$

The following In-Chapter Exercise is designed to have you appreciate the use of commonly used built-in macros in a makefile.

IN-CHAPTER EXERCISE

10.8 Repeat the preceding session to appreciate how some of the commonly used built-in macros can be used in a makefile.

10.2.6 DUMMY TARGETS

In a makefile you can have targets that are files that don't exist and that you have no intention to create. These targets, known as dummy targets, allow you to force an event, which would not take place in the normal chain of events as defined by the make rules. You can use this feature with convenient names to perform some useful activities. Since dummy targets (or prerequisites) are not actual files, **make** uses somewhat arbitrary rules for them. Here are the rules followed by **make** for dummy targets and prerequisites.

1. If a dummy target is used as a prerequisite, it must appear as a target somewhere in the makefile.
2. A dummy target always causes the associated commands to execute (it is always out of date).
3. A dummy prerequisite is always newer than the target associated with it and always causes the target to be rebuilt.

In Section 10.2.4, we used the dummy targets **clean** and **power.tar** to force make to remove all the object files in the build directory and to create tar archives of all the source files and the makefile, respectively.

In a client-server based software, we can use a dummy target to build both the client and server executables. In the following makefile, we use the dummy target **install** (any name can be used) for this purpose. We can build the client executable only by using the **make client** command. Similarly, the target server can be built by using the **make server** command. Without the dummy target **install**, only the first target, **client**, would be built.

```
$ more makefile

install: client server

client: client.o miscc.o rcopyc.o

        gcc client.o miscc.o rcopyc.o -lnsl -o client

client.o: client.c netc.h rcopy.h

        gcc -c client.c

miscc.o: miscc.c

        gcc -c miscc.c

rcopyc.o: rcopyc.c rcopy.h

        gcc -c rcopyc.c

server: server.o miscs.o rcopys.o

        gcc server.o rcopys.o miscs.o -lnsl -o server

server.o: server.c nets.h miscs.h

        gcc -c server.c
```

```
miscs.o: miscs.c

        gcc -c miscs.c

rcopys.o: rcopys.c

        gcc -c rcopys.c
$
```

We enhance this makefile to install the client and server software in an install directory, called /home/sarwar/courses/bin. Note that whereas the **cp** and **rm** commands can be on separate lines as shown or on the same line (with a semicolon between them), the **cd** and **chmod** commands have to be on the same line since they must execute in the same shell process. We also include a dummy target **uninstall** to be able to uninstall the software. In this case, the **cd** and **rm** commands must be on the same line so that they run under the same shell process. Here is the enhanced version.

```
$ cat makefile

INSTALLDIR = /home/sarwar/courses/bin

install: client server

        cp -f $^ ${INSTALLDIR}

        rm -f *.o $^

        cd ${INSTALLDIR}; chmod 755 $^

uninstall:

        cd ${INSTALLDIR}; rm client server

client: client.o miscc.o rcopyc.o

        gcc client.o miscc.o rcopyc.o -lnsl -o client

client.o: client.c netc.h rcopy.h

        gcc -c client.c

...

$
```

In the following session, we use the **make install** command (we could have used the **make** command only) with this makefile for installing the software in the install directory /home/sarwar/courses/bin. The **ls -l ~/courses/bin** command shows that the software has been installed properly. The **make uninstall** command is used to uninstall the software.

```
$ make install

gcc -c client.c

gcc -c miscc.c

gcc -c rcopyc.c

gcc client.o miscc.o rcopyc.o -lnsl -o client

gcc -c server.c

gcc -c miscs.c

gcc -c rcopys.c

gcc server.o rcopys.o miscs.o -lnsl -o server

cp -f client server /home/sarwar/courses/bin

rm -f *.o client server

cd /home/sarwar/courses/bin; chmod 755 client server
$ ls -l ~/courses/bin

total 17

-rwxr-xr-x     1 sarwar     152          7823 Nov 22 23:42 client

-rwxr-xr-x     1 sarwar     152          8599 Nov 22 23:42 server
$ make uninstall

cd /home/sarwar/courses/bin; rm client server
$ ls -l ~/courses/bin

total 0
$
```

The following In-Chapter Exercise is designed to help you appreciate the use of dummy targets in a makefile.

IN-CHAPTER EXERCISE

10.9   Run the `make clean power.tar` command with the makefile that you created for In-Chapter Exercise 10.7. What does the command do? Show command output.

10.2.7 SPECIAL TARGETS

The **make** utility has some predefined targets that are treated by it in a special way. These targets are known as **special targets.** Some of these targets are briefly described in Table 10.2.

Except for the `.PHONY` target, all other special targets are global, i.e., they apply to the entire build.

In some of the previous sections, we used the following **make** rule to clean up all the object modules from the build directory.

```
clean:

    rm *.o
```

If the directory does not have a file called clean, you can invoke the **make clean** command for cleaning up the build directory without any problem. If a file called clean does exist in your build directory, invocation of the command will result in the message **make: 'clean' is up to date.**, and the command will not execute.

Table 10.2	Some Special Targets and Their Purposes
Special Target	**Purpose**
`.DEFAULTS`	If make cannot find any `makefile` entry or suffix rules for building a target, it executes the commands associated with the target.
`.IGNORE`	make ignores error codes and continues to build if the `makefile` contains this target on a line by itself; normally, make stops if a command exists abnormally. make with option −i does the same thing.
`.PHONY`	Allows you to specify a target that is not a file so you can instruct make to invoke a sequence of commands from the `makefile` even if a file with the name of the target exists in your current directory.
`.SILENT`	make executes the commands without displaying them. make with option −s does the same thing. As discussed in Section 10.2.5, you can execute a particular command silently by putting an @ sign before the command.
`.SUFFIXES`	The prerequisites (suffixes) specified for this target can become associated with the suffix rules. If no prerequisites are associated with this target, the existing suffix list is removed.

```
$ touch clean
$ make clean
make: 'clean' is up to date.
$
```

You can use a special target, called `.PHONY`, to overcome this problem. In the example that follows, the dependency for `.PHONY` is `clean` and there is no command list. Here are the updated lines along with the invocation of the rule for cleaning.

```
$ more makefile
...
.PHONY: clean
clean:
        rm -f *.o core power
$ touch clean
$ make clean
rm -f *.o core power
$
```

The following In-Chapter Exercise is designed to help you appreciate the use of special targets in a `makefile`.

IN-CHAPTER EXERCISE

10.10   Create a file called clean in your build directory and run the **make clean** command. Does the command clean your build directory as expected? What does the output mean to you? In the makefile for In-Chapter Exercise 10.7, add the following line before the line that contains the dummy target **clean**.

.PHONY: clean

Rerun **make clean**. Does the command work this time? Why does the command work as expected this time?

10.2.8 COMMON SYNTAX ERRORS AND THEIR CURES

Not starting a command with a tab character is probably the most common mistake while creating a makefile. It is not possible to distinguish visually a tab character from a sequence of space characters. The **make** utility error message for this mistake is not useful, as shown in the following session.

```
$ make
makefile:4: *** missing separator.   Stop.
$
```

The **make** utility also offers no option that can be used to display tags (or their absence) in front of a command. However, you can use the **cat** command with the **-t** option to display a tab character in your makefile as ^I. In the session that follows, we use this command to display the makefile for the above **make** command.

```
$ cat -t makefile
#   Sample makefile for the power program
#   Remember: each command line starts with a TAB
power:   power.c
         gcc power.c -o power -lm
$
```

Note the absence of ^I (the tab character) before the **gcc** command. We insert the tab character before the **gcc** command, redisplay the makefile with the **cat -t** command, and execute the **make** command to generate the executable file without a problem, as shown below.

```
$ cat -t makefile
#   Sample makefile for the power program
#   Remember: each command line starts with a TAB
power:   power.c
^Igcc power.c -o power -lm
$ make
gcc power.c -o power -lm
$
```

Since you need to physically examine the output of the **cat -t makefile** command, a better choice would be to use the **grep '^ '** **makefile** to output only those lines that start with a space instead of a tab.

The second most common mistake is to insert spaces between \ (for line continuation) and the new line character. You can use the **cat -e** makefile command to display new line characters in the makefile as $. Again, since you need to physically examine the output of the **cat -e** makefile, a better choice would be to use the **grep '\\[ ]$'** makefile command to display the incorrect lines in makefile.

The following In-Chapter Exercise will help you practice identifying commands in a makefile that don't start with a tab.

IN-CHAPTER EXERCISE

10.11 Replace the initial tabs with spaces in a few commands in the makefile for In-Chapter Exercise 10.8. Run the **make** command without a command line argument. What happens? **make** should report an error message. Run the **cat –t makefile** and **grep '^ '** makefile commands to identify lines without tab characters. Replace spaces with tabs in the lines that you modified and rerun the **cat –t makefile** and **grep '^ '** makefile commands to ensure that you have tabs at the required places. Rerun make to see if it executes properly and produces the executable code as expected.

10.2.9 COMMAND-LINE USAGE AND DEBUGGING

You can run the **make** command with many options, as shown in the beginning of Section 10.2. The **–f** option allows you to specify a makefile with a nonstandard name. For example, you can use the following command to inform **make** that the make rules are in prog1.makefile and that it should generate the target **client1**.

```
$ make -f prog1.makefile client1
...
$
```

You can use the **make –f –** command to have the **make** utility read input from stdin. This syntax allows the use of the **make** utility in a pipeline. If the input comes from the keyboard, the input must teminate with **<Ctrl-D>** on a new line.

By default, **make** displays on stdout each command that it executes. You can use the **–n** option to display the sequence of commands that would be executed if make were to run, without executing the commands. Saving the output of the **make –n** command in a script file before building software allows you to be able to debug the makefile and complete the build manually.

10.3 WEB RESOURCES

Table 10.3 lists useful Web sites for **make** and other similar utilities.

Table 10.3	Web Resources for make and Similar Build Tools	
Reference	**URL**	**Description**
1	www.gnu.org/software/make/make.html	The home page for GNU make
2	www.tru64unix.compaq.com/demos/ ossc-v51a/html/gnusites.htm	Web page for well- known GNU sites
3	www.xfree86.org/4.2.0/makedepend.1.html	Manual page for makedepend
4	jakarta.apache.org/ant/	The Jakarta Project. This Web page describes Apache Ant, a Java-based build tool like the make utility
5	www.bell-labs.com/project/nmake/	Main Web site for nmake
6	www.chmi.cz/meteo/ov/lace/aladin_lace/ MaKpage/MK.html	Main Web site for mk

10.4   SUMMARY

Most useful software has multiple modules. The LINUX and UNIX **make** utility allows you to handle multimodule software in a manner that minimizes the compilation and build times. It does its work based on a set of rules, called make rules, stored in a specification file, known as the makefile. A make rule contains a list of targets, lists of their prerequisites, and a list of commands to be executed to generate the list of targets. The **make** utility has a number of built-in make rules, also known as suffix rules, which can be used to simplify the makefile. The **make** utility also supports the use of macros and has many built-in macros that can be used for making the **make** rules shorter and easier to read. The make utility also has support for debugging the makefile.

10.5   QUESTIONS AND PROBLEMS

1. Describe how the **make** utility decides what targets to build.
2. For the makefile in Section 10.2.6, write down the targets and their prerequisites. If the dummy target **install** is removed, what targets will be built by the **make** command when it is run without an argument?
3. Draw the dependency tree for the makefile in Section 10.2.6.
4. The execution of the **make** command for a makefile resulted in the error message: **makefile:4: *** missing separator. Stop**. What is the cause of this error message? How did you obtain your answer?
5. Give the **make** rule for printing all the C source files in the build directory on the hp313 printer. Use shell's filename pattern-matching character * whenever possible.
6. Draw the dependency tree for the following makefile. With this makefile, show the result of execution of the **make** utility.

```
build: spiderc spiderg
spiderc: process.o commandline.o
   gcc process.o commandline.o -o spiderc
spiderg: process.o graphical.o
   gcc process.o graphical.o -o spiderg
process.o: process.c process.h
   gcc -c process.c -lnsl
commandline.o: commandline.c commandline.h
   gcc -c commandline.c
graphical.o: graphical.c graphical.h
   gcc -o graphical.c
```

7. For the makefile in Problem 6, list all the targets and the commands needed to generate them. Identify dummy targets and explain why they are named as they are.

8. Give the command line for creating the graphical version of the spider, **spiderg**, with the makefile in Problem 6.

9. What are dummy and special targets? What are they used for? Give an example makefile that illustrates the use of both types of targets.

10. Give the command line for generating the sequence of commands executed for the above makefile and saving them in a file called spider.script.

11. The **make** command runs in verbose mode by default, i.e., it displays the list of commands executed as it builds a software. Suppose that you want to run the **make** command in silent mode. What are the two ways to perform this task?

12. Consider the following makefile and answer the questions that follow.

```
CC = gcc
OPTIONS = -ansi
CLIENT = pclient.o myinet.o
SERVER = pserver.o myinet.o
all: client server
client: $(CLIENT)
    $(CC) $(OPTIONS) -o pclient $(CLIENT) -lsocket -lnsl -lposix4
server: $(SERVER)
    $(CC) $(OPTIONS) -o pserver $(SERVER) -lsocket -lnsl -lposix4
pclient.o: pclient.c myinet.h ipc.h
    $(CC) $(OPTIONS) -c pclient.c
pserver.o: pserver.c myinet.h ipc.h
    $(CC) $(OPTIONS) -c pserver.c
myinet.o: myinet.c myinet.h
    $(CC) $(OPTIONS) -c myinet.c
.PHONY: clean
clean:
    rm -f $(CLIENT) $(SERVER)[end scr]
```

a. List all the macros, dummy targets, and special targets in the makefile.

b. If the **make** command is executed without a command line argument, what executable(s) will it build? Why?

c. If the **make all** command is run, what executable(s) will it build? Why?

d. Draw the dependency tree for the makefile.

e. What command will you use to display the sequence of commands that would be executed if **make** were to run, without executing the commands? Show a sample run of your command.

f. What command will you run to display lines in the makefile that don't start with a tab? Show a sample run of your command.

## CHAPTER 11

Developing, Using, and Debugging Libraries

OBJECTIVES

- To describe what libraries are and how they can be used

- To discuss how libraries can be developed, manipulated, installed, and used

- To describe briefly the structure of an executable binary file in LINUX and UNIX

- To discuss how the symbol table for a library, object, or executable file can be displayed and studied

- To list useful Web resources

- Commands and primitives covered: `ar, gcc, nm, ranlib`

11.1   INTRODUCTION

The LINUX and UNIX operating systems allow you to archive (bundle) object files into a single library file. In other words, they allow you to use the name of one file instead of the names of a number of object files in a compiler command or a makefile and allow you to use the same function in more than one program. The LINUX and UNIX systems have many prepackaged libraries for C, C++, and many other languages. These libraries contain the object modules for many functions to perform commonly used operations for I/O, character handling, string processing, mathematical functions, and interprocess communication. Some of the commonly used C library functions are `printf`, `malloc`, `free`, `strcmp`, `srand`, `rand`, `pow`, and `gethostbyname`. The use of library calls makes a programmer's job easier because she does not have to write functions for performing these tasks. The libraries in LINUX and UNIX are located in the /lib and /usr/lib directories. You can handle library tasks such as creating and modifying libraries with the LINUX and UNIX tools `ar` and `ranlib`. You can use the `nm` utility to display the symbol table for an executable binary, object, or library file. This information gives you ample information to be able to debug these files.

11.2   USING LIBRARIES

A typical LINUX or UNIX system contains libraries for C, C++, and FORTRAN. The archive files for one of these languages can be used by applications developed in that language. This allows software developers to use the prewritten and pretested functions in their software. The /lib and /usr/lib directories in LINUX and UNIX contain libraries. Most language libraries are located in the /usr/lib directory, such as the standard C library (/usr/lib/libc.a) and standard C++ library (/usr/lib/libstdc++.a). The *.a suffix is reserved for libraries of object files.

The header file for a library contains declarations for the resources (e.g., functions and macros) defined in the library. There are two types of header files: public and private. A public header declares resources that are available to other programs and a private header file declares resources that are meant to be used by the library code only. In order to make a library public, you should install it in the /usr/lib directory and place its public header file in the /usr/include directory. In order to use a standard library function in your program, you must include the header file for the library in your prorgam with the preprocessor directive `#include` as in

```
#include <stdlib.h>
```

When the preprocessor encounters this directive, it searches the /usr/include file for the stdio.h header file.

A private header file can be included in a program by placing the pathname for the header file in quotes, as in

```
#include "localheaderfile.h"
```

In this case, the preprocessor searches your current directory to locate the `localheaderfile.h` file. For a directive like

```
#include "~/include/localheaderfile.h"
```

the preprocessor searches the localheaderfile.h in your ~/include directory.

You can use prewritten functions in standard language libraries by including the header file corresponding to the library functions used. You don't need to explicitly link the library with the −l compiler option. For example, you can use the C standard library function printf() in your program by including the header file /usr/include/stdio.h in the program with the #include <stdio.h> directive. The C standard library, /usr/lib/libc.a, is automatically linked by the C compiler such as gcc. Most of the facilities of the C programming language that are not part of the language itself, such as I/O and dynamic memory allocation/deallocation, are defined by the /usr/lib/liba.c library. Many header files such as stdio.h, stdlib.h, and ctype.h declare parts of this library. Similarly, most of the facilities of the C++ programming language are defined by the /usr/lib/libstdc++.a library. If you want to use the GNU features in your C++ programs, you need to use the /usr/libg++.a library.

Many of the C/C++ library functions that you may use in your programs are not part of the standard libraries. For example, the mathematical functions are not part of the C or C++ standard libraries. Instead, they are defined by the math library (/usr/lib/libm.a). If you want to use a math function from this library, in addition to including the /usr/include/math.h header file in your program file with the #include <math.h> directive, you must also explicitly link this library with the −lm compiler option. Note that you specify the substring between lib and .a with the −l compiler option, hence −lm for linking the math library (libm.a). Similarly, you need to explicitly link the libsocket.a, libnsl.a, and libg++.a libraries, with the linker options −lsocket, -lnsl, and −lg++, respectively. Failure to explicitly link these libraries will result in compile time errors.

The following program shows use of the standard C library functions printf() and scanf() and the math library function pow(). We've included the header file /usr/include/stdio.h for the standard C library (libc.a) and the header file /usr/include/math.h for the math library (libm.a). For compiling this program, we explicitly link the math library with the −lm compiler option. Note that we don't need to use the −lc option explicitly because the standard C library is automatically linked by the linking stage of the compiler.

```
$ cat power.c
#include <stdio.h>
#include <math.h>

main()

{

        float   x,y;
        printf ("The program takes x and y from stdin and displays x^y.\n");
        printf ("Enter number x: ");
        scanf ("%f", &x);
        printf ("Enter number y: ");
        scanf ("%f", &y);
        printf ("x^y is: %6.3f\n", pow((double)x,(double)y));
```

```
}
$ gcc -o power power.c -lm
$ power
The program takes x and y from stdin and displays x^y.
Enter number x: 9.82
Enter number y: 2.3
x^y is: 191.362
$
```

Some common programming errors related to libraries are

■ Failure to include header file for a library

■ Failure to explicitly link a library that is not automatically linked by the compiler

■ Using the wrong version of a library

■ Linking incompatible libraries

11.3 THE ar UTILITY

The ar utility, also called **librarian,** allows you to perform various library-related tasks such as creating, modifying, and extracting modules from archives. The following is a brief description of this utility.

Syntax:

ar key archive-name [file-list]

Purpose: This utility allows creation and manipulation of archives. For example, it can be used to create an archive of the object files in 'file-list' and store it in the file called 'archive-name'

Commonly used keys:

d	Delete a file from an archive
q	Append a file at an existing archive
r	Create a new archive or overwrite an existing archive
t	Display the table of contents of an archive
s	Force generation of the archive symbol table
x	Extract one or more files from an archive and store them in your current working directory
v	Generate a verbose output

The archive name must end with the .a extension. Once an archive file has been created for a set of object modules, the modules can be accessed by the C compiler and the LINUX/UNIX linker (**ld**) by specifying the archive file as an argument. (The **ld** command can be used to link object files and libraries explicitly.) The compiler or the linker automatically links the object modules needed from the archive.

A key is like an option for a command. However, unlike with most LINUX/UNIX commands, with the **ar** command you don't have to place a hyphen (**–**) before a key, but you can use the hyphen if you choose to. In our examples of the **ar** command, we do not insert a hyphen before a key.

In the sessions throughout this chapter, we use the multimodule program developed in Chapter 10. We show it again here for your reference. We assume that object files input.o and compute.o have been created with the compiler command **gcc –c main.c input.c compute.c**.

```
$ cat compute.h
/* Declaration/Prototype of the "compute" function */
double compute(double, double);
$ cat input.h
/* Declaration/Prototype of the "input" function */
double input (char *);
$ cat main.h
/* Declaration of prompts to users */
const char *PROMPT1 = "Enter the value of x: "
const char *PROMPT2 = "Enter the value of y: "
$ cat compute.c
#include <math.h>
#include "compute.h"

double compute (double x, double y)
{
        return (pow ((double) x, (double) y));

}
$ cat input.c
#include "input.h"

double input(const char *s)
{
        float x;
        printf ("%s", s);
```

```
        scanf ("%f", &x);
        return (x);
}
$ cat main.c

#include <stdio.h>

#include "main.h"

#include "compute.h"

#include "input.h"

main()
{
        double x, y;

        printf ("The program takes x and y from stdin and displays x^y.\n");
        x = input(PROMPT1);
        y = input(PROMPT2);
        printf ("x^y is: %6.3f\n", compute(x,y));

}
$
```

In the following In-Chapter Exercise, you will create object modules for C source files using the gcc compiler.

IN-CHAPTER EXERCISE

11.1   Create the object modules for the C source files input.c and compute.c with the **gcc** compiler. What command(s) did you use to perform the task?

11.3.1 CREATING OR APPENDING TO AN ARCHIVE

You can create an archive by using the **ar** command with the **r** key. The following command line creates an archive of the input.o and compute.o files in libmath.a. Note that we have not used **-r**, although we could have.

```
$ ar r libmath.a input.o compute.o
$
```

If libmath.a exists, the command line overwrites it with the new archive. Once the archive has been created in your current directory, you can link it to the main.c file by using the following compiler command. Note that **gcc** links the object modules input.o and compute.o in the libmath.a library to main.o. We must use the **-lm** option to link the math library libm.a because of the **pow** function used in compute.o.

```
$ gcc main.c libmath.a -o power -lm
$
```

You can use the **q** key to append the object modules at the end of an existing archive. Thus, in the following example, the object modules input.o and compute.o are appended at the end of the existing archive libmath.a. If the mathlib.a archive doesn't exist, it is created.

```
$ ar q libmath.a input.o compute.o
$
```

Once you have created an archive of some object modules, you can remove the original modules, as in

```
$ rm compute.o input.o
$
```

If you want to archive all of the object files in your current directory in the libnew.a archive, you can use the following command. You can also use `` `ls *.o` `` instead of *.o.

```
$ ar r libnew.a *.o
$
```

The command substitution is used to generate names of all the object files in the current directory.

In the following In-Chapter Exercise, you will use the ar r command to create a library archive and use the archive in a compiler command.

IN-CHAPTER EXERCISE

11.2   Create the library archive libmath.a of the object files input.o and compute.o created in In-Chapter Exercise 11.1. Then use the **gcc** compiler to generate the executable file power for main.c and the object modules in the libmath.a library and run the executable to ensure that it works as expected. Write down the commands you used to complete the task.

11.3.2 Displaying the Table of Contents

You can display the table of contents of an archive by using the **ar** command with the **t** key. The following command displays the table of contents of the libmath.a archive. You can run the **ar** command in verbose mode as in **ar vt libmath.a**.

```
$ ar t libmath.a
input.o
compute.o
$
```

11.3.3 DELETING OBJECT MODULES FROM AN ARCHIVE

You can delete one or more object modules from an archive by using the **ar** command with the **d** key. In the following session, the first **ar** command deletes the object module input.o from the libmath.a archive, and the second displays the new table of contents (confirming the removal of object module input.o from the archive).

```
$ ar d libmath.a input.o
$ ar t libmath.a
compute.o
$
```

In the following In-Chapter Exercise, you will use the **ar t** and **ar d** commands to appreciate how they work.

IN-CHAPTER EXERCISE

11.3 Use the **ar t** command to display the table of contents of the libmath.a library, then use the **ar d** command to delete compute.o module from the library. Use the **ar t** command again to confirm that the compute.o module has been removed from the archive.

11.3.4 EXTRACTING OBJECT MODULES FROM AN ARCHIVE

You can extract one or more object modules from an archive by using the **ar** command with the **x** key. The following command line can be used to extract the object module compute.o from the libmath.a archive and put it in your current directory.

```
$ ar x libmath.a compute.o
$
```

In the following In-Chapter Exercise, you will use the **ar x** command to examine how it works.

IN-CHAPTER EXERCISE

11.4 Use the **ar x** command to extract the input.o module from the libmath.a archive. Where is id the input.o module placed? Is this module still in the libmath.a library? How did you obtain your answer?

So far we have shown the use of the **ar** command from the command line, but you can also run this command as part of a makefile so that an archive of the object files of a software product is created after the executable file has been created. Doing so allows future use of any general-purpose object modules (one or more functions in these modules) created as part of the software. You would put an archiving command in the command list for a target to be invoked as an argument of make, such as we have done for 'bundle' in the makefile below.

To show the use of the **ar** command in a makefile, we enhance the makefile from Section 10.2.5 so that the compute.o and input.o object modules are appended to the libmath.a library if the **make bundle** command is executed after the final executable has been built. The following session shows the resultant makefile and sample runs of the **make** command, first to create the executable and second to create the archive.

```
$ more makefile
# Updated makefile that uses some built-in macros and
# @-preceded commands. It also archives some of the
# newly generated object modules in a library.

CC = gcc
OPTIONS = -O3
OBJECTS = main.o input.o compute.o
SOURCES = main.c input.c compute.c
HEADERS = main.h input.h compute.h
ARCHIVE = compute.o input.o
LIBRARY = libmath.a
AR_KEYS = qv

complete: power
        @echo "The build is complete"
power: $(OBJECTS)
        $(CC) $(OPTIONS) —o $@ $^ -lm
        @echo "The executable is in the 'power' file."
        @echo
main.o: main.h input.h compute.h
compute.o: compute.h
input.o: input.h
buldle: @echo "Archiving object modules ..."
        ar $(AR_KEYS) $(LIBRARY) $(ARCHIVE)
        @echo
        @echo "Archiving is complete."
        @echo
power.tar: makefile $(HEADERS) $(SOURCES)
```

```
        tar -cvf $@ $^
.PHONY: clean
clean:
        rm -f *.o core power
$ make
gcc     -c main.c -o main.o
gcc     -c input.c -o input.o
gcc     -c compute.c -o compute.o
gcc -O3 -o power main.o input.o compute.o -lm
The executable is in the 'power' file.

The build is complete
$ make bundle
Archiving object modules ...
ar qv libmath.a compute.o input.o
a - compute.o
a - input.o

Archiving is complete.
$
```

11.3.5 ORDERING ARCHIVES

The object files in an archive file aren't maintained in any particular order; the order is dependent on the order in which the modules were inserted in the archive. The `ranlib` utility can be used to add a table of contents to one or more archives that are passed as its parameters. This utility performs the same task as the `ar` command with the **s** key. An archive with a table of contents is necessary for the linking phase and allows functions in the archive to call each other, regardless of their location in the archive. The following is a brief description of the `ranlib` command.

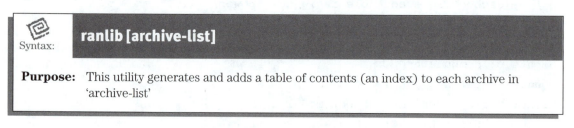

Syntax: **ranlib [archive-list]**

Purpose: This utility generates and adds a table of contents (an index) to each archive in 'archive-list'

The following `ranlib` command adds a table of contents to the libmath.a archive. The `ar s libmath.a` command can also be used to perform the same task.

```
$ ranlib libmath.a
$
```

The `ranlib -v` command displays the version number of `ranlib`.

In the following In-Chapter Exercise, you will use the `ranlib` and `ar s` commands to appreciate how they work.

IN-CHAPTER EXERCISE

11.5 Use the `ranlib` and `ar s` commands (one by one) to add a table of contents to the libmath.a library.

11.3.6 INSTALLING LIBRARIES

Once a library archive has been created and a table of contents has been added to it, you can install the library to make it publically available. In order to do so, you need to take two steps:

1. Create a header file for the library and place it in the /usr/include directory. This header file contains declarations for the resources (macros and functions) in the library. For our libmath.a library, the header file will be /usr/include/mymath.h (remember that the header file math.h is for the math library libm.a).

2. Install (place) the library archive in the /usr/lib directory. In our case, the library will be /usr/lib/libmath.a

Once library (libmath.a in our case) has been installed, you can use any of its functions in a program by including its header file (<mymath.h>) in the program and compiling it with the `-lmath` option.

11.4 THE nm UTILITY

You can use the **nm** utility to display the symbol table (i.e., names, types, sizes, entry points, etc.) of a library, object, or executable file. It displays as its output one line for each identifier, such as a function or variable name, in the file, informing you about its attributes. The information displayed by the **nm** utility is useful for debugging libraries and executables files. Here is a brief description of this utility.

Syntax: **nm [options] [file-list]**

Purpose: Display the symbol table of the executable, object, or library files in 'file-list'; if no object file is given, use the a.out file

<table>
<tr><td rowspan="2">Syntax:</td><td>**nm [options] [file-list]** *(continued)*</td></tr>
</table>

Commonly Used Options / Features:

−D	Display dynamic symbols only (useful when working with dynamic libraries)
−V	Display the version number of **nm** on standard error
−f format	Display output in 'format,' which can be **bsd**, **sysv**, or **posix**; default is **bsd**
−g	Display information about external (global) symbols only
−l	For each symbol, find and display the file name and line number
−n, −v	Sort external symbols by address
−u	Display only the undefined symbols, those external to each object module
−W	Give extra and more verbose warnings

If no symbolic information is available for a file, the **nm** utility reports that fact. If the symbolic information is available for the files in the command line, for each file or every member of an archive, the **nm** utility sends at least the following information to stdout: the address of each symbol, its value, and its type. Depending on the options used in the command line, the name of the library or object and symbol's size (if, for example, a symbol is a variable) may also be part of the output.

The type of a symbol is indicated by a letter; uppercase letters are used for global symbols and lowercase letters are used for local symbols. The letter informs you about the segment in which the symbol is located. The binary image of a program in LINUX includes four important segments: text/code, data, stack, and heap. The text segment contains the program code, the data segment contains the data variable (initialized or uninitialized), the stack segment contains the **activation records** (also known as **stack frames**) for function calls, and the heap segment contains the memory space that is allocated and deallocated dynamically (with calls like **malloc()** and **free()**). The data segment is subdivided into two parts; one for initialized variables and the other for uninitialized variables. The part containing uninitialized variables is commonly known as **bss.** Table 11.1 shows the most commonly displayed type letters and their meanings; for brevity, we've shown the uppercase letters only.

Table 11.1	Type Letters Used in the Output of the **nm** Utility
Type Letter	**Meaning**
A	Global absolute symbol
B	Global symbol in the uninitialized data segment (bss)
D	Global symbol in the initialized data segment
F	File symbol
T	Global symbol in the text (code) segment—with respect to your program, these are mostly function names
U	Undefined symbol, an external symbol (usually a library function)

In the sections that follow, we show the use of the **nm** utility with a few commonly used options.

11.4.1 DISPLAYING LIBRARY INFORMATION

In the following session, we use the **nm –V** command to display the version of the **nm** command. The **nm –l /usr/lib/libc.a | more** command is used to display the symbol table information for the standard C library. The output, among other things, informs us about the library that contains the character-related functions/macros such as **isdigit**, as well as some external functions such as **__ctype_tolower**.

```
$ nm –V
GNU nm 2.9.1
Copyright 1997 Free Software Foundation, Inc.
This program is free software; you may redistribute it under the terms of
the GNU General Public License.  This program has absolutely no warranty.
$ nm –l /usr/lib/libc.a | more
...
ctype.o:
         U __ctype_b     (null):0
         U __ctype_tolower      (null):0
         U __ctype_toupper      (null):0
00000000 t gcc2_compiled.
00000000 T isalnum
00000018 T isalpha
00000034 T iscntrl
0000004c T isdigit
00000084 T isgraph
00000068 T islower
000000a0 T isprint
000000bc T ispunct
000000d4 T isspace
000000f0 T isupper
0000010c T isxdigit
0000010c T isxdigit
00000128 T tolower
00000148 T toupper
...
$
```

In the following example, we use the **-f** and **-l** options to display the symbol table for the bugged.o file with line numbers in the System V format. The output shows the absolute pathname of the C source file and the line number where a symbol occurs. The line numbers are listed after the file names, as in get_input on line 31 in the bugged.c file. The class **U** means that it is an undefined symbol, usually an external variable, a library function, or a function in another object module, such as **getchar** and **malloc** in the following output.

```
$ nm -f sysv -l bugged.o
```

Symbols from bugged.o:

Name Section	Value	Class	Type	Size	Line
get_input	|000000b0|	T |	|	|	|
/home/faculty/sarwar/linuxtools/chapters/ch12/bugged.c:31					
getchar	|	| U |	|	|	|
/home/faculty/sarwar/linuxtools/chapters/ch12/bugged.c:37					
main	|00000010|	T |	|	|	|
/home/faculty/sarwar/linuxtools/chapters/ch12/bugged.c:13					
malloc	|	| U |	|	|	|
/home/faculty/sarwar/linuxtools/chapters/ch12/bugged.c:34					
mcount	|	| U |	|	|	|
/home/faculty/sarwar/linuxtools/chapters/ch12/bugged.c:13					
null_function1	|00000070|	T |	|	|	|
/home/faculty/sarwar/linuxtools/chapters/ch12/bugged.c:25					
null_function2	|00000090|	T |	|	|	|
/home/faculty/sarwar/linuxtools/chapters/ch12/bugged.c:28					
printf	|	| U |	|	|	|
/home/faculty/sarwar/linuxtools/chapters/ch12/bugged.c:19					

```
$
```

In the following In-Chapter Exercise, you will use the **nm** command to display the table of contents of a library of object modules.

IN-CHAPTER EXERCISE

11.6 Use the **nm** command to display the table of contents of the libmath.a library archive created in In-Chapter Exercise 11.2. Identify the library symbols in the output. What are these symbols for?

In the following example, we display the symbol table for the executable file nmexample for the C program file nmexample.c. The output of the first **nm** command shows that **main** and **foo** are the two functions in this file at offsets 08048390 and 0804833d0, respectively. With this information, we can determine that the size of the main function is 64 bytes. With additional information given in the output, we can also determine that the size of the foo function is 92 bytes. The output also shows that the global variables j and c are in the initialized data segment and the global variable *i* is in **bss** (the uninitialized data segment). The output of the second **nm** command shows that the static local variable *whereisit* is in the initialized data segment as a local initialized variable (type **d**) and the *andthis* variable is in the uninitialized data segment as a local uninitialized variable (type **b**). Notice that in the output of **nm −n** command, the symbols that end with the extension .4 are local initialized static variables and the ones with extension .5 are local uninitialized static variables. Similarly, the global variable **s** is located in the uninitialized data segment as a global variable and the global variable *ip* is located in the initialized data segment as a global variable.

```
$ more nmexample.c
#define SIZE         512

int i;
int j = SIZE;
char c = 'A';
static char *s;
static int *ip=&j;

int main(void)
{
        int k = 10;

        i = foo (j, k);
        printf ("%i\n", i);
        exit (0);

}

int foo (int x, int y)
{
        static int whereisit = 100;
        static int andthis;

        whereisit += (x + y);
        return (whereisit);
```

```
}
$ gcc -o nmexample nmexample.c
$ nm -ng nmexample | more
         U __deregister_frame_info@@GLIBC_2.0
         U __gmon_start__
         U __libc_start_main@@GLIBC_2.0
         U __register_frame_info@@GLIBC_2.0
         U _fp_hw
         U exit@@GLIBC_2.0
         U printf@@GLIBC_2.0
080482bc ? _init
08048350 T _start
08048400 T main
08048450 T foo
080484ac A _etext
080484ac ? _fini
080484c8 R _IO_stdin_used
080494d0 D __data_start
080494d0 W data_start
080494dc D j
080494e0 D c
08049500 ? _GLOBAL_OFFSET_TABLE_
08049524 ? _DYNAMIC
080495c4 A __bss_start
080495c4 A _edata
080495e4 B i
080495e8 A _end
$ nm -n nmexample | more
...
080494d0 W data_start
080494d4 d p.2
080494d8 d completed.3
080494dc d force_to_data
080494dc D j
080494e0 D c
080494e4 d ip
```

```
080494e8 d whereisit.4
080494ec ? __EH_FRAME_BEGIN__
080494ec ? __FRAME_END__
080494ec d force_to_data
080494f0 ? __CTOR_LIST__
080494f4 ? __CTOR_END__
080494f8 ? __DTOR_LIST__
080494fc ? __DTOR_END__
08049500 ? _GLOBAL_OFFSET_TABLE_
08049524 ? _DYNAMIC
080495c4 A __bss_start
080495c4 A _edata
080495c4 b object.8
080495dc b andthis.5
080495e0 b s
080495e4 B i
080495e8 A _end
...
$
```

11.5 WEB RESOURCES

Table 11.2 lists useful Web sites related to libraries.

Table 11.2	Web Resources for gdb, ddd, and GNU Tools for Sofware Testing	
Reference	**URL**	**Description**
1	www.opengroup.org/onlinepubs/007908799/xcu/ar.html	The manual page for the ar utility
2	www.npaci.edu/MTA/tera-cgi/man.cgi	Manpage viewer: a Web page for UNIX/LINUX manual pages
3	www.opengroup.org/onlinepubs/007908799/xcu/nm.html	The manual page for the nm utility

11.6 SUMMARY

The LINUX and UNIX operating systems allow you to archive (bundle) object files into a single library file. In other words, they allow you to use the name of one file instead of the names of a number of object files in a makefile and allow function-level software reuse of C programs. The UNIX and LINUX systems have many prepackaged libraries for C, C++, and other languages. These libraries contain the object modules for many functions to perform commonly used operations for I/O, character handling, string processing, mathematical functions, and interprocess communication. Some of the commonly used C library functions are `printf`, `malloc`, `free`, `strcmp`, `srand`, `rand`, `pow`, and `gethostbyname`. The use of library calls makes a programmer's job easier because she does not have to write functions for performing these tasks. The C libraries in LINUX and UNIX are located in the /usr/lib directory. In order to use a library function, you must include a header file that declares the library resources (e.g., macros and functions). Although many libraries are automatically linked to your code by the linking phase of the compiler, others need to be explicitly linked with the `-l` compiler option. For example, the standard C and C++ libraries libc.a and libstdc++.a are automatically linked to your program but math, socket, and GNU C++ libraries (libm.a, libsocket.a, and libg++.a, respectively), are not. In order for a program that uses a math library function to work correctly, you must include the <math.h> header file and compile it with the `-lm` option.

You can use the `ar` utility to create, display, and manipulate libraries. After creating a library archive with the `ar` utility, you must add a table of contents to it with the `ranlib` command. Some UNIX systems don't require the use of `ranlib` command because the `ar` command on these systems adds the table of contents. Once a library has been created and a table of contents has been added to it, you can install the library by placing a header file for it in the /usr/include directory and placing the library archive in the /usr/lib directory. The header file contains declarations for the resouces (macros and functions) contained in the library file. Once a new library has been installed, it can be used like any other library, except that you need to explicitly link it.

The `nm` utility allows you to display the symbol table of a library, object, or executable file. The output of the `nm` command gives you ample information for debugging.

11.7 QUESTIONS AND PROBLEMS

1. What is a library file? Where are the C language libraries located in LINUX and UNIX? Give examples of three C libraries.
2. Name two libraries that don't require explicit linking and four that do.
3. What steps are required to use functions for the standard C, standard C++, and the math library? Use an example C/C++ program to illustrate your answer.
4. What LINUX and UNIX utilities can be used for creating and manipulating libraries?
5. Suppose that you wrote some C functions to perform commonly used miscellaneous tasks and stored their object codes in the mysocketlib.o and myoutput.o files. Archive these modules in the ~/lib/mylib.a library file. Write down the command line for performing this task.
6. Suppose that you created an object file myinput.o. Give the command line for appending this file in the ~/lib/mylib.a file.
7. Give the command line for displaying the table of contents of your library file ~/lib/mylib.a.
8. Run this command on your system and show its output.
9. Delete the myoutput.o file from your library file. Show your command line for doing so. Confirm the deletion of the file by displaying the new table of contents of the file. Show your session for performing these tasks.

10. What is the purpose of the **nm** utility?

11. Compile the following code in an executable file, myhello. Use the **nm** utility to display the symbol table for this file. Show the output of your command and identify the text, uninitialized data, and initialized data segments in it.

```
#define SIZE          512


int i;
int j = SIZE;
static char *greetings="Hello, world!\n";


int main(void)
{
        foobar();
        exit (0);
}


void foobar (void)
{
        static int i;
        static int *ip = &i;


        printf ("%s", greetings);
}
```

12. What are the sizes of main and foobar functions in Question 10 in bytes? Explain how you obtained your answer. Show all your work.

13. Where are the global and local static variables in the program in Question 10 allocated space in your executable file? Write down the offsets and types (with type letters) of these variables.

14. Use the **nm** command to determine the number of times the **strcmp** call is used in the libstdc++.a library.

## CHAPTER 12

Source Code Debugging

OBJECTIVES

- To describe briefly what is meant by source code debugging and software testing
- To discuss the various debugging approaches
- To discuss features of GNU gdb for debugging C, C++, and Java programs
- To discuss briefly how to debug a process with gdb
- To describe briefly how to use gdb to debug a crashed program with a core file
- To explain briefly how to use gdb under the Emacs editor
- To list useful Web resources
- Commands and primitives covered: gdb

12.1   INTRODUCTION

Dynamic analysis of a program involves analyzing the program during run time. This phase consists of debugging, tracing, and monitoring performance of the software, including testing it against product requirements. In this chapter, we discuss debugging C, C++, and Java programs under UNIX and LINUX.

There are times when your program compiles flawlessly but does not behave properly when you run it—it either crashes or produces wrong output for simple input. This means that your program is syntactically correct but has some logic errors. Such programs are commonly known as "buggy" programs. You need to find the problematic code (the "bug") in your program and make appropriate changes in it, so that the program will work correctly. Identifying the causes of problems in a program as it runs is known as **debugging.** To be a successful programmer, you must be proficient in debugging. Identifying the problem code is the most difficult and time-consuming part of the debugging process. Once you know the problem, you can make the necessary changes in your code to make it work correctly. To isolate the bad code, you need to examine the logic of your program. Several techniques will help you find the bugs in your code, but the proper and efficient way to do so is to use a tool that runs your program and allows you to interact with it and trace its execution. Such a program is called a **debugger.** Several debuggers are available on LINUX and UNIX systems, the most popular of which is GNU gdb. In this chapter we discuss some of the most useful features of gdb.

Before proceeding further we would like you to appreciate the difference between debugging and testing. In debugging, you start with a non-working program (that either crashes or doesn't produce expected output even for the simplest input) and you take various actions to make it work for simple input data. In **testing,** you start with a working program and run it against a set of input data (expected and unexpected) to ensure that it produces expected output. Toward the end of the chapter we touch on some of the important elements of testing.

12.2   SOURCE CODE DEBUGGING

Debugging software is a time-consuming and difficult task. It consists of monitoring the internal working of your code, examining the values of program variables and values returned by functions, and executing functions with specific input parameters. Two approaches can be used for this purpose.

12.2.1   USING printf OR cout

Many C/C++ programmers tend to use **printf** or **cout** statements at appropriate places in their programs to display the values of program variables to help them find the origin of a bug. This technique is simple and convenient, and it works well for small programs. However, for large software, where an error may be hidden deep in a function call hierarchy, this technique takes a lot of time in editing, including adding and removing **printf** or **cout** statements in the source file. In addition, every time you insert or delete an output statement, you must recompile and relink your code, which is quite inconvenient. Also, this technique does not identify the source of a fatal error such as "segmentation fault." We recommend that you don't make a habit of using this approach for debugging your programs. Of course, under some circumstances, using **printf** and **cout** may be your best option. For example, if you are trying to debug a multithreaded software, running your program through a debugger changes the program so much that locating the error will become extremely difficult.

12.2.2 USING A DEBUGGING TOOL

The proper method of debugging a program is to use a tool known as **symbolic debugger.** The use of such a tool can save you much time and frustration during the debugging process. Many debugging tools are available on LINUX and UNIX. Most of these tools are text-based, but some also have front-end GUIs available. Using these tools through a GUI interface makes the debugging experience more palatable. Typical facilities available in a symbolic debugger include

- running programs
- setting break points
- single stepping
- listing source code
- editing source code
- accessing and modifying variables
- tracing program execution
- displaying activation records (also known as stack frames) on the program stack
- searching for functions, variables, and objects
- displaying values of variables or expressions

The standard debugger on LINUX and UNIX systems is `gdb` (GNU DeBugger), which can be used for debugging C, C++, Java, and Modula-2 programs. Here we discuss primarily its features for debugging C and C++ programs only, but do give a session for debugging Java programs as well.

12.3 THE DEBUGGING PROCESS

Debugging programs with a symbolic debugger involves many steps. We outline these steps for a general debugger here and describe them in detail for `gdb` in the remaining sections of this chapter. The general steps are

1. Recompile your program with an option that generates extra debugging information in the executable code to be used by the debugger.
2. Start the debugger.
3. Run your program inside the debugger.
4. Obtain the run-time information necessary to identify the buggy code. This information can be obtained by setting break points, single-stepping through your code, searching for identifiers, and displaying the program source.
5. Identify the bad code.
6. Make corrections in the source to remedy the problem.
7. Recompile and rerun the code to confirm its correct working.
8. Feel lucky and be happy!

12.4 **THE GNU DEBUGGER** gdb

GNU debugger **gdb** is a text-based debugger. It does have GUI front-ends such as **xxgdb** and **ddd**, but here we describe only the text-based version. You can invoke **gdb** by using the **gdb** command. Once it starts running, **gdb** reads commands from the keyboard to perform various tasks and quits when you give it the **quit** command. The following is a detailed description of the **gdb** command.

Syntax: | **gdb [options] [execprog [core | PID]]**

Purpose: Allows execution of a program 'execprog' to be traced, to determine what goes on inside it, helping you identify the location of a bug in the program. You can also specify a core file or the PID of a running program.

Commonly Used Options / Features:

-c core	Use 'core' as the core file to examine
-h	List command options with brief explanations
-n	Do not execute commands in the ~/.gdbinit file after processing all command line options
-q	Do not display the introductory and copyright messages
-s file	Use symbol table from the 'file' file

During startup, **gdb** searches for ~/.gdbinit file and executes the commands in it. You can use the **-n** option to ask **gdb** to ignore this file.

During a typical session, you need to use only a small set of **gdb** commands. Table 12.1 lists some of the commonly used commands and their brief descriptions. Short command names can be used for most of these commands, such as **b** for **break** and **bt** for **backtrace**.

Table 12.1	Commonly Used gdb Commands and Their Brief Descriptions
Command	**Description**
break [[file:]line|func]	Set break point at line number 'line' or function 'func' in 'file.' Without an argument, set break point at the next instruction
backtrace [n]	Display trace of all stack frames; or n frames (innermost n frames for n>0 and outermost n frames for n<0) clear
[[file:]line|func]	Delete break point at line number 'line' or function 'func' in 'file.' Without an argument, delete break point at the next instruction.
continue [count]	Continue the execution of the program being debugged, after a breakpoint or a signal. If proceeding from a breakpoint, the 'count' number is used to ignore that breakpoint (count -1) times.
finish	Execute program until the selected stack frame returns
frame [n]	Without an argument, select the current (topmost) stack frame. With an argument, select stack frame n or stack frame at address n.

Table 12.1	Commonly Used gdb Commands and Their Brief Descriptions *(continued)*
Command	**Description**
help [class|cmd]	Without an argument, list classes of commands. With a class argument, display one-line descriptions for commands in 'class.' With a command argument, display the command description
info break	Display currently defined break points
info func	Display names and types of defined functions
info frame [addr]	Describe the selected stack frame or stack frame at address 'addr'
info locals	Display local variables in the current stack frame
info var	Display names and types of global variables
list	Display the next 10 lines of the source program
list -	Display the previous 10 lines of the source program
list a,b	Display source program lines a through b
list [func]	Display lines in the function 'func'
next [count]	Execute the next source program statement and step over any function call; repeat 'count' times if specified
nexti [count]	Same as next, except that machine instruction is executed
print [/f] [expr]	Display the value of the expression 'expr' according to the format specified with f (e.g., x for hex, d for decimal, o for octal, and t for binary)
run [args]	Run the program with arguments in 'args' (if the program requires command line arguments)
step [count]	Execute the next source program instruction and step inside any function call; repeat 'count' times if specified
stepi [count]	Same as step, except that machine instruction is executed
whatis [expr]	Show the data type of the expression 'expr'
x expr	Display the contents of memory location identified by 'expr'

12.4.1 USING gdb WITH C/C++ PROGRAMS

As outlined in Section 12.3 above, the first step in debugging a program is to compile it with a compiler option that includes the debugging information in the executable program. You then run the executable program under the debugger and obtain the required run-time data by using various debugger commands to perform operations such as setting break points, single stepping through the program execution, displaying stack frames, and displaying values of variables at different places in your program. This helps you indentify the bad code in your program. You then correct the code to remove the problem. The debugged code is recompiled and tested for its expected (correct) behavior. In this section we use a buggy C program and take you through the above steps to debug the program.

In order to debug a C/C++ program with **gdb** (or any other debugger), you must compile it with the **-g** compiler option to include the symbol table information in the executable file. If you are using make to build your executable, set the **CFLAGS** macro to −g in your makefile, delete all object files (or touch all source files), and rebuild the executable file. We use the C program in the bugged.c file to show various features of **gdb**. The program prompts you for keyboard input, displays the input, and exits. We demonstrate the use of several features of **gdb**, including displaying the stack trace, setting break points, single-stepping through your code, and displaying the values variables. The following session shows the program code, its compilation without the −g option, and its execution.

```
$ nl -ba bugged.c
     1   /*
     2    *  Sample C program bugged with a simple, yet nasty error
     3    */
     4
     5   #include <stdio.h>
     6
     7   #define PROMPT   "Enter a string: "
     8   #define SIZE     255
     9
    10   char *get_input(char *);
    11
    12   int main ()
    13   {
    14       char *input;
    15       int i=10;
    16
    17       input = get_input(PROMPT);
    18       (void) printf("You entered: %s.\n", input);
    19       (void) printf("The end of buggy code!\n");
    20       return(0);
    21   }
    22
    23       char *get_input(char *prompt)
    24   {
    25       char *str;
    26       int i=20;
    27
    28       (void) printf("%s", prompt);
    29       for (*str = getchar(); *str != '\n'; *str = getchar())
```

```
30              str++;
31          *str = '\0'; /* string terminator */
32          return(str);
33   }
34
```

`$ gcc bugged.c -o bugged`

`$ bugged`

`Enter a string: Hello, World!`

`Segmentation fault`

`$`

Note that the program prompts you for input and faults without echoing what you enter from the keyboard. That happens frequently in C/C++ programming, particularly with programmers who are new to C/C++ or aren't careful about initializing pointer variables in their programs and rely on the compiler. It's time to use **gdb**!

In the following In-Chapter Exercise, you will create the bugged.c file, compile it to create the executable in the bugged file, and run the executable.

IN-CHAPTER EXERCISE

12.1   Repeat the above session, creating the bugged.c file, compile the file to create executable in the bugged file, and run the executable.

ENTERING THE gdb ENVIRONMENT

As we've mentioned before, in order to enter the **gdb** environment, you must compile your C/C++ program with the **-g** compiler option. This option creates an executable file that contains the symbol table and debugging, relocation, and profiling information for your program. After the code compiles successfully, you can then use the **gdb** command to debug your code, as in the following session. Note that we ran the **gdb -q** command to prevent the introductory message from being displayed. (**gdb**) is the prompt for the **gdb** debugger.

`$ gcc -g bugged.c -o bugged`

`$ gdb -q bugged`

`(gdb)`

Once you are inside the **gdb** environment, you can run many commands to monitor the execution of your code. You can use the **help** command to get information about the **gdb** commands. Without an argument, the **help** command displays a list of the classes of the **gdb** commands. You can get information about the commands in any class by passing the class name as an argument to the **help** command. In the following session, the `help` command shows the names of classes of all **gdb** commands, and the `help running` command displays a brief description of the commands for running the program. The `help tracepoints` command displays a brief description of the commands that can be used for tracing program execution without stopping the program. Finally, the `help trace` command displays a brief description of the **trace** command.

```
(gdb) help
List of classes of commands:

aliases — Aliases of other commands
breakpoints — Making program stop at certain points
data — Examining data
files — Specifying and examining files
internals — Maintenance commands
obscure — Obscure features
running — Running the program
stack — Examining the stack
status — Status inquiries
support — Support facilities
tracepoints — Tracing of program execution without stopping the program
user-defined — User-defined commands

Type "help" followed by a class name for a list of commands in that class.
Type "help" followed by command name for full documentation.
Command name abbreviations are allowed if unambiguous.
(gdb) help running
Running the program.

List of commands:

attach — Attach to a process or file outside of GDB
continue — Continue program being debugged
detach — Detach a process or file previously attached
finish — Execute until selected stack frame returns
go — Usage: go <location>
handle — Specify how to handle a signal
info handle — What debugger does when program gets various signals
```

jump — Continue program being debugged at specified line or address

kill — Kill execution of program being debugged

next — Step program

nexti — Step one instruction

run — Start debugged program

set args — Set argument list to give program being debugged when it is started

set environment — Set environment variable value to give the program

set follow-fork-mode — Set debugger response to a program call of fork or vfork

set scheduler-locking — Set mode for locking scheduler during execution

show args — Show argument list to give program being debugged when it is started

show follow-fork-mode — Show debugger response to a program call of fork or vfork

show scheduler-locking — Show mode for locking scheduler during execution

signal — Continue program giving it signal specified by the argument

step — Step program until it reaches a different source line

stepi — Step one instruction exactly

target — Connect to a target machine or process

thread — Use this command to switch between threads

thread apply — Apply a command to a list of threads

apply all — Apply a command to all threads

tty — Set terminal for future runs of program being debugged

unset environment — Cancel environment variable VAR for the program

until — Execute until the program reaches a source line greater than the current

Type "help" followed by command name for full documentation.

Command name abbreviations are allowed if unambiguous.

(gdb) **help tracepoints**

Tracing of program execution without stopping the program.

List of commands:

actions — Specify the actions to be taken at a tracepoint

collect — Specify one or more data items to be collected at a tracepoint

delete tracepoints — Delete specified tracepoints

disable tracepoints — Disable specified tracepoints

enable tracepoints — Enable specified tracepoints

end — Ends a list of commands or actions

passcount — Set the passcount for a tracepoint

save-tracepoints — Save current tracepoint definitions as a script

tdump — Print everything collected at the current tracepoint

tfind — Select a trace frame

tfind end — Synonym for 'none'

tfind line — Select a trace frame by source line

tfind none — De-select any trace frame and resume 'live' debugging

tfind outside — Select a trace frame whose PC is outside the given range

tfind pc — Select a trace frame by PC

tfind range — Select a trace frame whose PC is in the given range

tfind start — Select the first trace frame in the trace buffer

tfind tracepoint — Select a trace frame by tracepoint number

trace — Set a tracepoint at a specified line or function or address

tstart — Start trace data collection

tstatus — Display the status of the current trace data collection

tstop — Stop trace data collection

while-stepping — Specify single-stepping behavior at a tracepoint

Type "help" followed by command name for full documentation.

Command name abbreviations are allowed if unambiguous.

(gdb) **help trace**

Set a tracepoint at a specified line or function or address.

Argument may be a line number, function name, or '*' plus an address.

For a line number or function, trace at the start of its code.

If an address is specified, trace at that exact address.

Do "help tracepoints" for info on other tracepoint commands.

(gdb)

In addition to the **gdb**-specific commands, **gdb** also allows you to execute all shell commands.

In the following In-Chapter Exercise, you will start learning the basics of **gdb** by creating the executable for the bugged.c program, starting the debugger, and using the **help** command to learn about a few debugger commands.

IN-CHAPTER EXERCISE

12.2   Use the **gcc –o buggy –g bugged.c** command to create the executable for the bugged.c program for debugging purposes in the file buggy. Run the **gdb buggy** command to start the debugger for the buggy program. Read the introductory message if you like. Then use the **help** command to learn about the various **gdb** commands.

Executing a Program

You can run your program inside the **gdb** environment by using the **run** command. The following command executes the program bugged. The program prompts you for input. When you enter the input (**Hello, world!** in this case), and hit **<Enter>**, the program fails when it tries to execute the **for** statement at line 29 in the get_input() function. The error message is cryptic for beginners and those who aren't familiar with LINUX jargon. All the error message says is that a signal of type SIGSEGV was received by the program when it was executing the **for** statement that uses the C library call **getchar()**. We must step through the program execution to determine where the failure occurs.

```
$ gdb bugged
GNU gdb Red Hat Linux 7.x (5.0rh-15) (MI_OUT)
Copyright 2001 Free Software Foundation, Inc.
GDB is free software, covered by the GNU General Public License, and you are
welcome to change it and/or distribute copies of it under certain conditions.
Type "show copying" to see the conditions.
There is absolutely no warranty for GDB.  Type "show warranty" for details.
This GDB was configured as "i386-redhat-linux"...
(gdb) run
Starting program: /home1/msarwar/linuxtools/bugged
Enter a string: Hello, world!

Program received signal SIGSEGV, Segmentation fault.
0x08048511 in get_input (prompt=0x80485b8 "Enter a string: ") at bugged.c:29
29              for (*str = getchar(); *str != '\n'; *str = getchar())
(gdb)
```

Tracing Program Execution

To find out what went wrong, we need to narrow down what part of the code may be causing the problem. We do so by first backtracing the program with the **where** command (we could've used the **backtrace** command). This command prints the current location within the program and a stack trace that shows how the current location was reached. The following snapshot shows that the program was at location (memory address) 0x08048511 in the get_input () function (line 29 in the program) when the program received the SIGSEGV signal. It also informs that the function call sequence is main() → get_input() and shows us that the top of the program stack contains the activation record for the getchar() function.

```
(gdb) where
#0  0x08048511 in get_input (prompt=0x80485b8 "Enter a string: ")
    at bugged.c:29
```

```
#1   0x080484aa in main () at bugged.c:17
#2   0x40047507 in __libc_start_main (main=0x8048490 <main>, argc=1,
     ubp_av=0xbffffcc4, init=0x8048308 <_init>, fini=0x8048590 <_fini>,
     rtld_fini=0x4000dc14 <_dl_fini>, stack_end=0xbffffcbc)
     at ../sysdeps/generic/libc-start.c:129
(gdb)
```

The output of the **nl -ba bugged.c** command, given at the beginning of Section 12.4.1, shows that the code on line 29 has two assignment statements and one comparison statement. In all three statements, we dereference the pointer variable *str*. Two statements use the getchar() library function. This library function has been in use for many years and is well tested. Thus, the problem must be with the use of the pointer variable *str*. We pursue the use of the pointer variable *str* further in a later section.

You can switch to the stack frame of another function in your current function call sequence with the **frame** command. Once in the context of a function, you can display the values of variables in it with the **print** command. In the following session, we display the value of the variable *i* in the current context (the get_input() function), switch to the context of the get_input() function (frame 1), and display the value of the variable

```
(gdb) print i
$1 = 20
(gdb) frame 1
#1   0x080484aa in main () at bugged.c:17
17             input = get_input(PROMPT);
(gdb) print i
$2 = 10
(gdb)
```

SETTING BREAK POINTS

Before you can display the value of a variable or monitor closely the execution of a piece of code, you have to execute the program without interruption until control reaches the statement or function that you want to study more closely. The process of stopping a program this way is known as setting **break points.** You can set break points in **gdb** by using the **break** command. In our **gdb** session, we set a break point at the call to the get_input () function in the main () function and run the program again, as shown.

```
(gdb) break 17
Breakpoint 1 at 0x804849d: file bugged.c, line 17.
(gdb) run
```

The program being debugged has been started already.
Start it from the beginning? (y or n) **y**

Starting program: /home1/msarwar/linuxtools/bugged

Breakpoint 1, main () at bugged.c:17
17   input = get_input(PROMPT);
(gdb)

SINGLE-STEPPING THROUGH YOUR PROGRAM

Always set your break points in a way that allows you to view the execution of all or part of your code statement by statement. The process of tracing program execution statement by statement is known as **single-stepping** through your program. Single-stepping, combined with tracing variables, allows you to study program execution closely. Single-stepping can be done by using the **step** command. This command executes the next source line, stepping into a function if necessary. The **next** command can be used to do this, but it executes a function in its entirety. In the following session, the **step** command is used to single-step through the code after a break point is set at source line 17. We use the **continue** command to continue program execution. When we enter the keyboard input, the error message appears again. The hexadecimal number to the left of the last line (second line of the error message) contains the memory address (0x08048511) of the statement in the getchar( ) function that causes the exception. You can use the **x** command to display the contents of this memory location. The output of the **x** command shows that the problem occurs at the 50th byte in the get_input( ) function. We still don't know the reason for the failure.

```
(gdb) step
get_input (prompt=0x80485b8 "Enter a string: ") at bugged.c:25
25          char *str=0;
(gdb) step
26          int i=20;
(gdb) step
28          (void) printf("%s", prompt);
(gdb) step
printf (format=0x80485f3 "%s") at printf.c:32
32      printf.c: No such file or directory.
        in printf.c
(gdb) step
33      in printf.c
```

```
(gdb) step
_IO_vfprintf (s=0x4015f180, format=0x80485f3 "%s", ap=0xbffffc24)
    at vfprintf.c:236
236     vfprintf.c: No such file or directory.
        in vfprintf.c
...

(gdb) continue

Continuing.
Enter a string: Hello, world!

Program received signal SIGSEGV, Segmentation fault.

0x08048511 in get_input (prompt=0x80485b8 "Enter a string: ") at bugged.c:29

29          for (*str = getchar(); *str != '\n'; *str = getchar())

(gdb) x 0x08048511

0x8048511 <get_input+49>:       0x8b901088
(gdb)
```

DISPLAYING THE VALUE OF A VARIABLE OR EXPRESSION

In order to determine the cause of program failure, we need to examine the value of the variable str involved in the for loop. To do so, we need to rerun the program so that it stops before the first execution of the for loop. Remember that we've already set a break point for this purpose. At the break point, we use the print command to display the value of the pointer variable str and find out that this variable points to memory location 0 (i.e., the memory location with address 0) as we would expect. str is pointing to a region in the memory that does not belong to our program's address space, because on most systems the lower memory region/area is used for storing part of the operating system kernel code. In fact, it points to a memory location that belongs to the operating system.

```
(gdb) delete
Delete all breakpoints? (y or n) y
(gdb) run
The program being debugged has been started already.
Start it from the beginning? (y or n) y

Starting program: /home1/msarwar/linuxtools/bugged
```

Enter a string: **Hello, world!**

```
Program received signal SIGSEGV, Segmentation fault.
0x08048511 in get_input (prompt=0x80485b8 "Enter a string: ") at bugged.c:29
29              for (*str = getchar(); *str != '\n'; *str = getchar())
(gdb) print str
$3 = 0x0

(gdb)
```

LISTING PROGRAM CODE

Now that we know that the *str* variable is not initialized properly, we display the program code to see what it is initialized to. We use the **list** command to display all or part of our source code. This command can be used to display a range of lines or functions. In the following session, we use the **help** command to find out how to use the **list** command, then display the get_input function to see initialization of the *str* variable.

```
(gdb) help list
List specified function or line.
With no argument, lists ten more lines after or around previous listing.
"list -" lists the ten lines before a previous ten-line listing.
One argument specifies a line, and ten lines are listed around that line.
Two arguments with comma between specify starting and ending lines to
list.
Lines can be specified in these ways:
  LINENUM, to list around that line in current file,
  FILE:LINENUM, to list around that line in that file,
  FUNCTION, to list around beginning of that function,
  FILE:FUNCTION, to distinguish among like-named static functions.
  *ADDRESS, to list around the line containing that address.
With two args if one is empty it stands for ten lines away from the other
  arg.
(gdb) list get_input,
24      {
25              char *str=0;
26              int i=20;
27
28              (void) printf("%s", prompt);
29              for (*str = getchar(); *str != '\n'; *str = getchar())
```

```
30              str++;
31          *str = '\0'; /* string terminator */
32          return(str);
}
(gdb)
```

FIXING THE BUG

From the listing of the get_input function, we find out that *str* is a local variable that is never initialized. Its value is 0x0 (in hexadecimal)—it points to memory location 0. The lower memory locations are used to store part of the LINUX operating system. With the `*str=getchar();` statement, our program tries to write to a location that is outside its process address space (i.e., a location that doesn't belong to it). This attempt is a clear violation that results in the program receiving a signal SIGSEGV, causing premature program termination and the error message `Segmentation fault`. Figure 12.1 illustrates the segmentation violation.

To fix the bug, all you need to do is initialize the *str* pointer to a memory space that has been allocated to the program. We use the malloc() library call for this purpose. The revised get_input function is shown in the following session, along with the compilation and proper execution of the program.

```
$ cat bugged.c
/*
 * Sample C program — the working version
 */
#define PROMPT "Enter a string: "
```

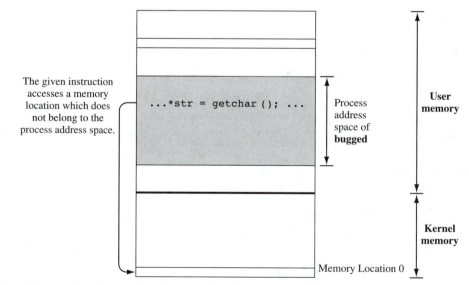

Figure 12.1 The memory (segmentation) access violation causing program

```
#define SIZE 255
char *get_input(char *);
int main ()
{
    char *input;
    int i=10;

    input = get_input(PROMPT);
    (void) printf("You entered: %s.\n", input);
    (void) printf("The end of buggy code!\n");
    return(0);
}
char *get_input(char *prompt)
{
    char *str, *temp;
    int i=20;

    str = (char *) malloc (SIZE * (sizeof (char)));
    temp = str;
    (void) printf("%s", prompt);
    for (*str = getchar(); *str != '\n'; *str = getchar())
        str++;
    *str = '\0'; /* string terminator */
    return(temp);
}
```

```
$ gcc bugged.c -o working
$ working
Enter a string: Hello, world!
You entered: Hello, world!.
The end of buggy code!
$
```

Leaving gdb and Wrapping Up

You can use the **quit** command to leave **gdb** and return to your shell.

```
(gdb) quit
$
```

Once your code has been debugged, you can decrease the size of the executbale binary file and release some disk space by removing from it the information generated by the **−g** option of the C compiler. You can do so by using the **strip** command. The information stripped from the file contains the symbol table and the relocation, debugging, and profiling information. In the following session we show the long list for the bugged file before and after execution of the **strip** command. Note that the size of the file has decreased from 21,906 bytes to 3,508 bytes, saving more than 84% disk space. Alternatively, you can use other options to recompile the source to generate an optimized executable.

```
$ ls -l bugged
-rwxrwxr-x    1 sarwar  152       21906 Mar 28 16:14 bugged
$ strip bugged
$ ls -l bugged
-rwxrwxr-x    1 sarwar  152        3508 Mar 28 16:35 bugged
$
```

In the following In-Chapter Exercise, you will make extensive use of **gdb** to understand its various features and the **strip** command to strip off the symbol table of the executable in the file buggy.

IN-CHAPTER EXERCISE

12.3 On the file buggy, go through all the **gdb** commands discussed in this section since In-Chapter Exercise 12.2 to appreciate how **gdb** works. If some of the commands used in this section don't work on your system, use the **help** command to list the **gdb** commands and use those that are available in your version of **gdb**. Note that since your executable code is called buggy, you will type buggy wherever bugged appears in the above sessions.

12.5 DEBUGGING A PROCESS

You can debug a running process with **gdb** by running the following command syntax

```
gdb executable_name PID
```

where executable_name is the pathname of the executing program and PID is its process ID. **gdb** looks for a "core" file with the name PID. If it finds one, it attaches the core file with the executable proram and allows us to debug it. If it doesn't find one, it assumes that PID is the process ID of the program that was run with the pathname executable_name and tries to attach to it. In the following session, we run the bugged program in background. The PID of the process is 3574. We then attach **gdb** to this process with the **gdb −q bugged 3574** command. After quitting **gdb**, we run the **ps** command to show that the bugged process was still running.

```
$ gcc -g bugged.c -o bugged
$ bugged&
[1] 3574
$ gdb -q bugged 3574
/home1/msarwar/linuxtools/3574: No such file or directory.
Attaching to program: /home1/msarwar/linuxtools/buggy, process 3574
Reading symbols from /lib/i686/libc.so.6...done.
Loaded symbols for /lib/i686/libc.so.6
Reading symbols from /lib/ld-linux.so.2...done.
Loaded symbols for /lib/ld-linux.so.2
0x08048444 in main () at buggy.c:11
11              for (i=0; i<=10; )
(gdb) where
#0  0x08048444 in main () at buggy.c:11
#1  0x40047507 in __libc_start_main (main=0x8048430 <main>, argc=1,
    ubp_av=0xbffffce4, init=0x80482bc <_init>, fini=0x8048490 <_fini>,
    rtld_fini=0x4000dc14 <_dl_fini>, stack_end=0xbffffcdc)
    at ../sysdeps/generic/libc-start.c:129
(gdb) break main
Breakpoint 1 at 0x8048436: file buggy.c, line 11.
(gdb) print i
$1 = 0
(gdb) quit
The program is running.  Quit anyway (and detach it)? (y or n) y
Detaching from program: /home1/msarwar/linuxtools/buggy, process 3574
$ ps
  PID TTY          TIME CMD
 3190 pts/10    00:00:00 bash
 3574 pts/10    00:00:14 buggy
 3598 pts/10    00:00:00 ps
$
```

It is important to note that once a process has been attached to **gdb**, you can execute commands such as **where** and **print** but you cannot run commands that imply execution of a statement such as **step** and **next**. You can attach a process with a **gdb** session by using the **gdb** command **attach**.

In the following In-Chapter Exercise, you will learn how to debug a process.

IN-CHAPTER EXERCISE

12.4 Run the `gcc -g bugged.c -o buggy` command. The executable code to be debugged is in the file buggy. Run the buggy program with the `buggy&` command to make it a background process. Start debugging this process with the `gdb` command as shown above and repeat the rest of the debug session.

12.6 RUNNING A CRASHED PROGRAM WITH A CORE FILE

If a program crash is difficult to reproduce, we cannot debug the program with the normal use of `gdb`; the exact circumstances that caused the crash cannot be reproduced as the program runs under `gdb`. If a crash produces a core file, we can debug the executable with `gdb` by using this core file.

A core file contains the memory image of a process before it terminated. The default action of some signals is to create a core file and terminate the process that receives the signal. SIGSEGV and SIGBUS are two common reasons for the creation of a core file. If the process executable that crashed contained debug info (i.e., it was compiled with the `-g` compiler option), it contains the stack trace, values of variables, and other run-time information about the process. If the size of the core file was not limited by the shell process under which the executable was run, we can debug a process using its core file.

We can use the following command line for debugging a program with a core file. Note that if the core file is not in the current directory, you will need to provide the pathname for the core file in the command line. If the core file's name is not core, then use the actual name of the core file.

```
gdb executable_name core
```

Once in the `gdb` environment, you can run the `gdb` commands such as **where** and **print**. You cannot use the commands that imply execution of a statement such as **step** or **next**.

12.7 DEBUGGING JAVA PROGRAMS WITH gdb

The more recent versions of `gdb` allow you to debug Java programs compiled with the GNU `gcj` compiler (see Web references 6 and 7 in Table 12.2). Since the Java run-time environment uses the SIGPWR and SIGXCPU signals for garbage collection, you need to inform `gdb` to ignore them by using the following `handle` command.

```
handle SIGPWR nostop noprint
handle SIGXCPU nostop noprint
```

You can run these commands after starting your **gdb** session or by putting them in your ~/.gdbinit file. In our sample session below, we run these handle commands after starting **gdb**. You can use the **info signals** command to display a table of signals and the **gdb** action for each.

As with the C/C++ programs, you must compile your Java programs with the **−g** compiler option so that the executable code contains the necessary debugging information. Below we show a short **gdb** session for debugging a Java program.

```
$ javac gdbDemo.java
$ gcj -g -main=gdbDemo gdbDemo.class -o gdbDemo
$ gdb -q gdbDemo

(gdb) handle SIGPWR nostop noprint
Signal Stop    Print    Pass to program   Description
SIGPWR No      No       Yes                   Power fail/restart
(gdb) handle SIGXCPU nostop noprint
Signal Stop    Print    Pass to program   Description
SIGPWR No      No       Yes                   CPU time limit exceeded
(gdb)
[ gdb commands for setting break points, running the program,
  singlestepping, etc. ]
(gdb) quit
$
```

You can examine the state of Java threads and move from one thread to another with the **info thread** and **thread** commands. The **info thread** command gives you information about all currently executing threads and the **thread** command allows you to switch from the current thread to another thread. For example, the **thread 3** command lets you switch from your current thread to the third thread.

There are native Java debuggers like **JSwat** that are quite a bit nicer than **gdb** for debugging Java programs. See Web reference 5 in Table 12.2 .

In the following In-Chapter Exercise, you will learn how to debug a Java program.

IN-CHAPTER EXERCISE

12.5   Repeat the above session on a Java program of your own to understand how a Java program can be debugged. If your program has multiple threads, use the **info** and **thread** commands to get information about the currently executing thread and to switch from the current thread to another thread. Read Web reference 7 in Table 12.2 to learn more about debugging Java programs with **gdb**.

12.8 USING gdb UNDER EMACS

You can use the `M-x gdb` command in Emacs to start a special interface that allows you to view and edit the source files you are debugging with `gdb`. You can pass the name of an executable file as an argument to this command. The command starts a new Emacs window running `gdb`. Input and output take place through the buffer of this Emacs process. Using `gdb` under the Emacs window is just like using `gdb` normally, except for the following two things:

1. `gdb` displays the program source code through the Emacs window.
2. All terminal I/O (i.e., `gdb` and program I/O) takes throught the Emacs buffer.

Once you have the Emacs interface window, you can perform the various debugging operations with the Emacs commands. For example, you can set a break point at the current line with the `C-c SPACE` command (pressing `<Ctrl-C>` followed by pressing the `<SPACE>` bar. If you set a break point and run the program with the approprite arguments, Emacs will split your screen into two halves with the `gdb` command line at the top and your program source code at the bottom. You can step through your code with the `M-s` (`step`) or `M-n` (`next`) command. You can finish the execution of the current function with the `C-c C-f` (`finish`) command. With the `M-c` (or `C-c C-p`) command you can continue the execution of the program. You can display a description of the various features of the `gdb` mode Emacs interface with the `C-h m` command. Finally, you can leave the `gdb` mode Emacs interface with the `C-c o` command.

12.9 SOFTWARE TESTING

As stated earlier, software testing means running a "working" program against a set of expected and unexpected input data to see if it produces expected output. The purpose of testing is to fail the program. Although a programmer is expected to test the software that he writes during the coding phase of a product, formal software testing is carried out in three phases: code inspection (also known as code walk-through), white-box/glass-box testing, and black-box testing. A detailed discussion on software testing is beyond the scope of this book but we give a brief overview of its three phases.

Once a software has been written and tested by the developer, one or more members of the software development team describe their code, line by line, to a team of inspectors who are usually from the software quality assurance group in the organization. The purpose of this activity is to find interface faults between functions and between modules. This activity is known as **code inspection.** The faults are logged for correction by the software development team and, depending on the number of faults in the software, a follow-up inspection may be necessary.

White-box testing finds interface faults by testing the software against well-thought-out test inputs, which are drawn up based on the structure of the code. Testers choose input data to invoke as many program statements in the software as possible. The percentage of program statements that can be invoked during this phase of testing is called **code coverage.** Ideally, you would like to have 100% code coverage but in practice code coverage is dictated by the critical nature of the software. Again, the faults found in the code are logged and corrected.

Finally, during **black-box testing,** the software is tested against its requirements. The test cases are, therefore, drawn up based on the requirements document. Ideally, you should test your programs against all possible inputs to ensure 100% working of your program under all circumstances. But testing a program against all possible inputs is usually neither possible nor necessary—not possible because, depending on the number of test inputs, the testing process may take an outrageously long time, and not necessary because some (or most) test inputs may be similar to others. To clarify this point, let's assume that you have a program called `square` that takes a positive integer as input and produces its square as output. Assuming an integer to be 32 bits wide, in order to fully test the program, you would need to test it against 4 billion (2^{32}) possible input values! The good news is that testing the square program against just a few inputs (for example, a few values on the two boundaries and a few in the middle of the range) is sufficient. A popular technique that allows you to choose a representative set of black-box test cases is known as **equivalence class testing**.

There are many tools that allow you to automate software testing. One such tool for UNIX and LINUX platforms is `DejaGNU`. Browse the Web page for reference 8 in Table 12.2 for information on this tool.

12.10 WEB RESOURCES

Table 12.2 lists useful Web sites for `gdb` and other GNU tools for program development and testing.

Table 12.1	Web Resources for `gdb`, `ddd`, and GNU Tools for Software Testing	
Reference	**URL**	**Description**
1	www.gnu.org/software/gdb/gdb.html	The home page for `gdb`: the GNU project debugger
2	www.gnu.org/manual/gdb-5.1.1/ html_chapter/gdb_toc.html	Debugging with `gdb` version 5.1.1
3	www.gnu.org/software/ddd www.gnu.org/manual/ddd	The home pages for GNU `ddd`, a graphical front end for `gdb` and other command-line debuggers
4	fpt://ftp.ugcs.caltech.edu/pub/elef/ autotools/toolsmanual.html	A repository of tools for developing software with GNU
5	www.bluemarsh.com/java/jswat	A Web site for a standalone Java debugger `jswat`
6	gcc.gnu.org/java	Home page for the GNU compiler for Java, `gcj`
7	www.redhat.com/devnet/articles/gcj.pdf	A technical paper on using `gcj` to compile Java code into native machine code
8	www.gnu.org/software/dejagnu/ dejagnu.html	GNU home page for DejaGnu, a framework for testing programs

12.11 SUMMARY

The run-time errors in a program can be best identified with a program called a symbolic debugger. GNU gdb is a text-based debugger in UNIX and LINUX for debugging C, C++, Java, and Modula-2 programs. To be able to debug a program with **gdb**, you first generate the executable for your program by compiling it with the **-g** option and then run the **gdb [executable]** command (**executable** is the name of the file containing your executable program). **gdb** allows you to perform many tasks that help you debug your program such as running programs, setting break points, single stepping, listing source code, editing source code, accessing and modifying variables, tracing program execution, displaying activation records (stack frames) on the program stack, searching for functions, variables, and objects, and displaying values of variables or expressions. Having identified bugs in your program, you can make the necessary changes to get it to work correctly.

You can use **gdb** to debug a program with its core file and to attach to a process and debug it. You can invoke a special interface of Emacs that allows you to use **gdb** in Emacs and debug a program by using some Emacs commands. A popular graphical front-end for text-based debuggers such as **gdb** is GNU **ddd**.

12.12 QUESTIONS AND PROBLEMS

1. What is a bug in computer jargon? What is debugging?
2. What are the different approaches to debugging your programs? Which approach do you normally follow and why?
3. What is a symbolic debugger? What are some of the facilities provided by it to help you identify bad code in your program?
4. The C++ program in the buggy.c file compiles fine but gives a run-time error. List the steps to debug it using **gdb**.
5. The following code is meant to prompt you for integer input from the keyboard, read your input, and display it on the screen. The program compiles, but doesn't work properly. Use **gdb** to find the bugs in the program. What are they? Fix the bugs, recompile the program, and execute it to be sure that the corrected version works. Show the working version of the program.

```
#include <stdio.h>

#define PROMPT   "Enter an integer: "

void get_input(char *, int *);

void main ()
{
    int     *user_input;
    get_input(PROMPT, user_input);
    (void) printf("You entered: %d.\n", user_input);
}

void get_input(char *prompt, int *ival)
{

    (void) printf("%s", prompt);
    scanf ("%d", ival);

}
```

6. The Java program in buggy.java does not produce expected output. Write down the steps to debug it.

7. Suppose that you run a program called `Huffman`. The process ID of this running program is 2978. How can you debug this process with `gdb`? Give the command(s) for doing so.

8. How do you debug a program with a core file using `gdb`?

9. What is the difference between the `gdb` commands `step` and `next`? Give an example to explain your answer.

10. What is the difference between debugging and testing? Explain your answer and give an example.

CHAPTER 13

Software Profiling and Metrics

OBJECTIVES

- To describe what is meant by software profiling and metrics
- To discuss briefly commonly used metrics and their values
- To discuss how LINUX and UNIX tools, including profiling, can be used for measuring software metrics
- To list useful Web resources
- Commands and primitives covered: `gprof, ls -l, size, time, wc`

13.1   INTRODUCTION

A noted software engineer, Tom DeMarco, once said, "You cannot control what you cannot measure" [*Controlling Software Projects,* Yourdon Press, New York, 1982]. The purpose of software metrics is to collect and measure quantifiable attributes of software projects in order to better control their execution and to help in future projects. For example, software metrics enable us to assess the processes used in a project, the resources involved in it (such as programmer hours), and its cost.

Software profiling means determining certain parameters of your program when it executes. These parameters include the most time-consuming segment of the program, the execution frequency of each line (or function), and the **function call graph** for the program. The purpose of software profiling is to identify the segments of code in a program where the program spends most of its time when it executes. Such information allows you to enhance the performance of your program in a more informed and systematic manner. **Software metrics** are usually meant to determine software product properties such as the number of lines of code (LOC), size in bytes of the executable, software structure, time taken for testing, total number of defects found in the product, the number of function points (FPs) or object points (OPs) for your software, and the running time of the program.

In this chapter, we describe the GNU profiling tool on LINUX and UNIX, `gprof`, which can be used to produce an execution profile of C or C++ programs. We also use the `wc`, `ls -l`, and `size` commands to determine the LOC count for a program, the program's size in bytes, and the size of the various segments (code/text and data segments, for example) of an executable program. Finally, we show the use of the `time` command to determine the execution time of the program.

13.2   SOFTWARE METRICS AND THEIR PURPOSE

Many facets of metrics are used by software engineering practitioners, such as

- Software cost and effort estimation
- Software productivity metrics
- Software quality measures
- Software size and complexity metrics
- Software run-time performance

Some of these metrics can be measured directly and others are derived. The metrics that can be measured directly are called **direct metrics** and the ones that are derived are known as **indirect metrics.** Table 13.1 lists some of the commonly used direct and indirect metrics of the size and complexity of a software product, the effort needed for a software project, the performance of programmers and testers involved in the project, the quality of the product, and the run-time performance of the product.

Some of the metrics mentioned in Table 13.1 help us assess the performance of programmers and testers, some help us estimate the effort needed for future products, some help us plan future products better, and some help us assess the run-time performance of the software. Some of the measures that we discuss in this chapter are size of the source code, size of the executable code, running time of a program, complexity of the source code, and software profiling.

Table 13.1	Commonly Used Direct and Indirect Metrics		
Metric	**Unit**	**Metric**	**Unit**
Length of source code	Lines of code (LOC)	Programmer productivity	LOC/Person-month
Size of executable code	Bytes	Module defect density	Defect count/Module size (LOC)
Time taken for testing	Duration (hours, days, months, or years)	Effort	Person-months/project
Number of defects	Count value	Requirements stability	Number of initial require-ments/Total number of requirements
Dynamic structure of source code (profiling)	Profile output (e.g., call graph, number of calls per function, time spent per function)	System spoilage	Effort spent fixing faults/Total project effort
Running time	Time units (e.g., seconds)	Complexity of source code	Function points (FPs) or object Points (OPs)
Time taken by a programmer to complete a module or a product	Time units (e.g., seconds)		

Profiling information can be used to identify the most time-consuming segments of codes in your program in order to optimize them. During the planning phase of a software project, parameters such as LOC, FPs, or OPs (taken from previously completed similar projects) are commonly used in **software cost models** to estimate the effort (e.g., number of person-months) needed to complete the software project.

A detailed discussion of software metrics and techniques is beyond the scope of this book. The interested reader should refer to a book on software metrics or software engineering.

13.3 PROFILING C/C++ PROGRAMS

At times you may find that your C/C++ program doesn't run as fast as you expected. If you know how long a program spends in each function when it executes and where it spends most of its time, you will know which part of the program you should make more efficient. The 80-20 rule says that a program spends 80% of its time in executing 20% of the code. Software profiling allows you to identify this 20% of the code so that you don't waste time optimizing the 80% of the code that runs infrequently. Halving the execution time of this 20% of the code makes your program 40% faster, whereas halving the execution time of the rest of the code makes your program only 10% faster!

You can use the LINUX and UNIX tool `gprof` to display an execution profile of your program in terms of the functions used, the function call graph, the frequency of calls to functions, and percentage of the total execution time taken by each function. The `gprof` tool is quite effective in identifying expensive segments of your program because it identifies the functions that are causing bottlenecks in the software. You can use this information to improve the performance of these program segments by optimizing them. A brief description of the tool follows.

Syntax:

gprof [options] [executable-file [profile-data-files]]

Purpose: Display execution profile of the C/C++ program in 'executable-file' (or 'a.out' if none is specified) by using the profile data taken from the profile file 'profile-data-files' ('gmon.out' if none is specified)

Commonly used options/features:

`-b`	Do not display a description of each field in the profile
`-e` name	Do not display profile information for the routine 'name' and all its descendents; more than one `-e` option may be given in order to suppress display for multiple routines
`-E name`	Same function as the `-e` option; also excludes the time spent in the 'name' routine (and its descendents) when computing total and percentage times
`-f name`	Display profile information for the routine 'name' and all its descendents; more than one `-f` option may be given in order to display for multiple routines
`-F name`	Same function as the `-f` option; also uses only the time spent in the 'name' routine (and its descendents) when computing total and percentage times
`-z`	Display names of those routines that have zero usage

When you specify an object file as a parameter to the `gprof` command, it reads the given object and establishes the relation between its symbol table and the call graph profile in the gmon.out file. The output shows two types of profiles. The first, known as the **flat profile,** shows the amount of time your program spent in each function and how many times each function was called. This profile allows you to identify those functions in your program that take most of the program execution time. The second profile, known as the **call graph,** shows how much time was spent in each function and its descendents. It includes, for every function, the functions called by it, the functions that called it, and the call count. It also displays an estimate of the time (in milli- or microseconds) spent in each function, including each function's children (i.e., the functions it called). This profile helps you to identify functions which may not be very time consuming themselves but which call other functions that are costly. Having such information allows you to possibly eliminate the expensive function calls. If the parent of a function cannot be determined, the string <spontaneous> is displayed in the name field and all the other fields are blank. This sometimes happens for the main function.

13.3.1 STEPS FOR USING gprof

Before we discuss any example in detail, we outline the procedure for using **gprof** to generate the execution profile of a program. You can use the following steps to profile your program with **gprof**.

1. Get your program to work correctly. Remember that you profile a program to identify bottlenecks in it and to improve its performance, and not to debug it.

2. Compile your program for profiling by using the **-pg** (or **-p**) option of the compiler command (e.g., **gcc** or **g++**).

3. Run your program as it is meant to be run and let it terminate normally; terminating it with **<Ctrl-C>** or the **kill** command terminates it abnormally. If the program terminates normally, it will cause the profiling information to be generated and stored in the **gmon.out** file in a format that **gprof** understands.

4. Run the **gprof** command like **gprof executable [data-file]**. If the profile data is in the gmon.out file, you don't need to specify any data file in the command line. Since the output of the **gprof** command is all text, it can be viewed by any LINUX or UNIX text editor or with commands like **cat**, **more**, or **less**.

5. Study the output of the **gprof** command,—the profile of your program—to identify the bottlenecks in your program.

The following session shows the compilation of the gprofexample.c program, its execution to generate the gmon.out file, and the execution of the **gprof** command to save or display the profiling information. We've used the **-b** option with the **gprof** command in order to keep the output short. Without this option, every term used in the output is clearly described as part of the output. These terms and their meaning are described in Table 13.2.

```
$ gcc -pg gproexample.c -o gproexample
$ gprofexample
[ program output ]
$ ls -l gmon.out
-rw-------    1 sarwar    152        325 Mar 17 12:24 gmon.out
$ gprof gprofexample > gprofexample.profile
$ gprof -b gprofexample | more
Flat profile:
Each sample counts as 0.01 seconds.
```

% time	cumulative seconds	self seconds	calls	self ps/call	total ps/call	name
53.33	0.24	0.24	3000000	80000.00	80000.00	mygetpid
46.67	0.45	0.21				main
0.00	0.45	0.00	249	0.00	0.00	mysocket

```
                      Call graph

granularity: each sample hit covers 4 byte(s) for 2.22% of 0.45 seconds

index % time    self  children    called     name
                                                       <spontaneous>
[1]     100.0   0.21   0.24                   main [1]
                0.24   0.00 3000000/3000000       mygetpid [2]
                0.00   0.00     249/249          mysocket [3]
-----------------------------------------------
                0.24   0.00 3000000/3000000       main [1]
[2]      53.3   0.24   0.00 3000000           mygetpid [2]
-----------------------------------------------
                0.00   0.00     249/249           main [1]
[3]       0.0   0.00   0.00     249          mysocket [3]
-----------------------------------------------

Index by function name
   [1] main                 [2] mygetpid                 [3] mysocket
$
```

Table 13.2   Fields in the Output of the gprof Command and Their Meaning

Field	Meaning
	Flat Profile
% time	Percentage of the total running time used by a function
cumulative seconds	The number of seconds accounted for by a function and those listed above it
self seconds	The number of seconds accounted for by a function alone.
calls	Total number of times a function is called; blank for a function that is not profiled
self us/call	The average number of microseconds spent in a function and its descendents per call; blank for a function that is not profiled (the time could be in milli-, micro-, nano-, or pico seconds)
name	The name of the function; the index show the location of the function in the gprof listing
	Call Graph
index	A unique number given to every element of the table or list
% time	The percentage of the total time that was spent in a function and its children
self	The amount of time spent in a function
children	The amount of time spent by a function's children; a '+' followed by a number indicates that recursive calls were made to the function
called	Total number of times a function is called
name	Name of the current function

In the following In-Chapter Exercise, you will use the `gprof` command to appreciate how it works and what kind of output it generates.

IN-CHAPTER EXERCISE

13.1   Use the program in power.c from Chapter 12 power.c from Section 10.2.2 and profile it with the `gprof` command. Write down the series of commands used to accomplish the task.

13.3.2 ANALYZING THE OUTPUT OF `gprof`

As shown in the above preceding session, the default output of the `gprof` command consists of a flat profile and the call graph for the program under study. The flat profile shows the percentage of the total amount of time your program spends in each function, total time spent in each function (including the time spent in its descendents), time spent in itself, the number of calls made to each function, and the time taken by each function call in micro- or milli seconds. Note that the functions `mount` and `profil` are inserted in your code by `gprof` for collecting the profile data, and the amount of time taken by these functions indicates the overhead of profiling. Depending on the version of `gprof`, this information may or may not be displayed but should not be considered as part of your program's profile for the sake of analysis.

The call graph shows percentage of the total time taken by each function, the amount of time taken by each function and its children, the number of times each function is called by other functions (with the names of the caller functions), and the number of times it calls other functions (i.e., its children functions). The output is divided into one entry per function, and the information for each function is separated from the next by a dashed line.

In each entry, one line starts with an index number in square brackets. This line, known as the primary line, shows all the information about this function, its ancestors, and its descendents. The lines preceding the primary line for a function are for its caller functions and those that follow it represent its children (callee) functions.

The flat profile in the above example shows that the `mygetpid` function is called 3 million times and that each call takes 8000 pico seconds. The `mysocket` function is called 249 times and that time taken by each call takes less time is less than the granularity of the timer used by gprof to measure function execution times can measure. The call graph shows that the `mygetpid` and `mysocket` functions are called from the main function. These profiles inform us that the `mygetpid` function is the bottleneck.

The following example shows the profile for a larger program which displays the **Huffman codes** and other related information for the characters in a text file which is passed to the program as a command-line argument. The following session shows the execution of the Huffman program to display the Huffman tree, Huffman codes, average code length (ACL), and code efficiency against ASCII coding of the letters in a text file, called Data. An obvious observation is that `MakeListNode`, `MakeTreeNode`, `AddOrderedListNode`, and `DeleteFirstListNode` are some of the most heavily called functions. The call graph shows from where and how often various functions are called. It is easy to conclude that, in order to make it an efficient program, these functions must be made as efficient as possible.

```
$ gcc -p Huffman.c -o Huffman
$ Huffman Data
Char      Freq      Huffman Code
|         21        0001111110000
4         21        0001111110001
q         42        000111111001
&         42        011010100010
X         63        011010100011

...

t         10878     0101
e         12936     0111
          59934     11
ACL Huffman code: 4.560958 ascii: 8 efficiency: 0.570120
$ gprof -b | more
Flat profile:
Each sample counts as 0.01 seconds.
```

% time	cumulative seconds	self seconds	calls	self us/call	total us/call	name
100.00	0.03	0.03	1	30000.00	30000.00	getstatistics
0.00	0.03	0.00	241	0.00	0.00	MakeListNode
0.00	0.03	0.00	239	0.00	0.00	MakeTreeNode
0.00	0.03	0.00	159	0.00	0.00	AddOrderedListNode
0.00	0.03	0.00	158	0.00	0.00	DeleteFirstListNode
0.00	0.03	0.00	1	0.00	0.00	CopyList
0.00	0.03	0.00	1	0.00	0.00	HuffmanCode
0.00	0.03	0.00	1	0.00	0.00	MakeHuffmanTree
0.00	0.03	0.00	1	0.00	0.00	printresults

```
                              Call graph
granularity: each sample hit covers 4 byte(s) for 33.33% of 0.03 seconds
index % time    self  children    called     name
                0.03    0.00       1/1           main [2]
[1]    100.0    0.03    0.00       1         getstatistics [1]
                0.00    0.00      80/239          MakeTreeNode [4]
                0.00    0.00      80/159          AddOrderedListNode [5]
------------------------
                                              <spontaneous>
```

[2]	100.0	0.00	0.03		main [2]
		0.03	0.00	1/1	getstatistics [1]
		0.00	0.00	2/241	MakeListNode [3]
		0.00	0.00	1/1	CopyList [7]
		0.00	0.00	1/1	MakeHuffmanTree [9]
		0.00	0.00	1/1	HuffmanCode [8]
		0.00	0.00	1/1	printresults [10]
		0.00	0.00	2/241	main [2]
		0.00	0.00	80/241	CopyList [7]
		0.00	0.00	159/241	AddOrderedListNode [5]
[3]	0.0	0.00	0.00	241	MakeListNode [3]
		0.00	0.00	79/239	MakeHuffmanTree [9]
		0.00	0.00	80/239	getstatistics [1]
		0.00	0.00	80/239	CopyList [7]
[4]	0.0	0.00	0.00	239	MakeTreeNode [4]
		0.00	0.00	79/159	MakeHuffmanTree [9]
		0.00	0.00	80/159	getstatistics [1]
[5]	0.0	0.00	0.00	159	AddOrderedListNode [5]
		0.00	0.00	159/241	MakeListNode [3]
		0.00	0.00	158/158	MakeHuffmanTree [9]
[6]	0.0	0.00	0.00	158	DeleteFirstListNode [6]
		0.00	0.00	1/1	main [2]
[7]	0.0	0.00	0.00	1	CopyList [7]
		0.00	0.00	80/239	MakeTreeNode [4]
		0.00	0.00	80/241	MakeListNode [3]
				158	HuffmanCode [8]
		0.00	0.00	1/1	main [2]
		0.00	0.00	158/158	MakeHuffmanTree [9]
[6]	0.0	0.00	0.00	158	DeleteFirstListNode [6]

```
                      0.00      0.00         1/1                 main [2]
  [7]        0.0      0.00      0.00          1              CopyList [7]
                      0.00      0.00        80/239               MakeTreeNode [4]
                      0.00      0.00        80/241               MakeListNode [3]
-----------------------------------------
                                            158                  HuffmanCode [8]
                      0.00      0.00         1/1                 main [2]
  [8]        0.0      0.00      0.00        1+158           HuffmanCode [8]
                                            158                  HuffmanCode [8]
-----------------------------------------
                      0.00      0.00         1/1                 main [2]
  [9]        0.0      0.00      0.00          1              MakeHuffmanTree [9]
                      0.00      0.00       158/158               DeleteFirstListNode [6]
                      0.00      0.00        79/239               MakeTreeNode [4]
                      0.00      0.00        79/159               AddOrderedListNode [5]
-----------------------------------------
                      0.00      0.00         1/1                 main [2]
  [10]       0.0      0.00      0.00          1              printresults [10]
-----------------------------------------
```

Index by function name

    [5] AddOrderedListNode   [8] HuffmanCode   [4] MakeTreeNode

    [7] CopyList   [9] MakeHuffmanTree   [1] getstatistics

    [6] DeleteFirstListNode   [3] MakeListNode   [10] printresults

$

By using the information in the call graph, we can construct the a picture of the call graph, as shown in Figure 13.1. The arrow heads point to the called function. The integer numbers on an arc represent the number of times a function is called by another funciton. For example, the **MakeTreeNode** function is called 80 times by the **CopyList** function. Note that the **HuffmanCode** function makes 158 recursive calls to itself. Function call overhead includes construction and destruction of the **stack frame** (also known as **activation recored**) for the function to store function parameters, local variables, and return addresses. The space for stack frames is allocated on the program stack. Because of this overhead, recursive programs, though elegant in structure, are not considered good because a large number of recursive calls may cause the program stack to overflow and result in an abnormal termination of the program.

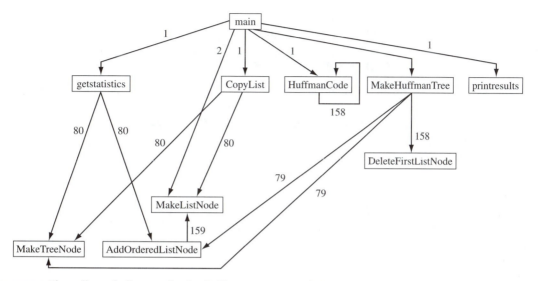

Figure 13.1 The call graph diagram for the Huffman program with the above

In the following In-Chapter Exercise, you will analyze the output of the **gprof** command and draw a call graph similar to the one in Figure 13.1.

IN-CHAPTER EXERCISE

13.2 Modify the program in power.c in Section 10.2.2 so that it prompts the user for input numbers 10 times (instead of once). Profile the resulting program. Does the profile make sense? Draw call graph for the program similar to the one given in Figure 13.1.

13.4 OPTIMIZING SOFTWARE

The profile information for a program identifies bottlenecks in a program. This information guides you to make informed decisions about the program segments that should be optimized for speeding up the program execution. Compiler technology today is quite advanced and good C/C++ compilers (such as gcc or g++) can perform many optimizations in your code when you compile your programs with the –O option. In particular, machine specific optimizations are best handled by compilers. Please refer to Section 9.4.3 where we discuss this issue in more detail.

13.5 SOFTWARE METRICS: SIZE AND RUNNING TIME

During the planning phase of a software project, parameters such as LOC, FPs, or OPs (from previously completed similar projects) are commonly used in software cost models to estimate the effort (e.g., number of person-months) needed to complete the software project. We can use the LINUX and UNIX command **wc** to measure LOC for a source program.

13.5.1 THE SIZE OF SOURCE AND EXECUTABLE PROGRAMS

In the following session, the first **wc** command shows that the LOC for the C program in the Huffman.c file is 281. The second **wc** command displays 1110 as the LOC parameter for a multimodule C software for the implementation of the binary search tree **abstract data type** in in the BST directory under your current directory.

```
$ wc -l Huffman.c
    281 Huffman.c
$ cd BST
$ wc -l *.[c,h]
    258 bst.c
     62 bst.h
    151 file.c
     26 file.h
    207 main.c
     21 main.h
    351 misc.c
     34 misc.h
   1110 total
$
```

You can estimate the FP or OP parameter for your program by careful analysis and some well-known methods. Further discussion of estimating FP and OP parameters is beyond the scope of this book. Interested readers can get more information about these methods by reading about software cost estimation in a textbook on software engineering.

There are two important software performance parameters, the size of the executable code and its running time. The size of the executable code can be measured with the **wc -c** (or **ls -l**) command. In the following example, the size of the executable code for the Huffman program is 9182 bytes.

```
$ wc -c Huffman

   9182 Huffman
$
```

You can use the **size** command to display the sizes of the various sections of an executable or binary code. Here is a brief description of the **size** command.

Syntax:

size [options] [objectfile-list]

Purpose: Displays the sizes of code, data, and uninitialized data (bss) sections of the object or executable files in 'objectfile-list' and their total sizes; if no file is specified as an argument, a.out is used

Note that the data section of an object or executable file contains space for initialized data items, and that **bss** contains space for uninitialized data items. In the following session, we use the `size` command, with and without arguments, to display the sizes of file a.out in our current directory and the sizes of various tools and commands discussed in this book, including the `size` command. As stated above, without an argument, the `size` command displays output for the ./a.out file in our current directory. Note the huge size of **gdb**.

```
$ size
   text    data     bss     dec     hex filename
   1380     280      32    1692     69c a.out
$ size /usr/bin/size
   text    data     bss     dec     hex filename
  13554     752     708   15014    3aa6 /usr/bin/size
$ size /usr/bin/ar /bin/bash /usr/bin/gcc /usr/bin/cvs /usr/bin/gdb
   text    data     bss     dec     hex filename
  35667     808     612   37087    90df /usr/bin/ar
 495971   22496   17392  535859   82d33 /bin/bash
  74533    2912    1144   78589   132fd /usr/bin/gcc
 539690    8032    3540  551262   8695e /usr/bin/cvs
1743831   34568   95460 1873859   1c97c3 /usr/bin/gdb
$
```

Note that the sum of the sizes of the three sections of an executable (or binary) file is not equal to its size displayed by the `wc` (or `ls -l`) command, as shown below. The sizes differ because an executable or object file has other sections, in addition to code, data, and bss.

```
$ wc -c  /usr/bin/ar /usr/bin/cvs /bin/bash
  37900 /usr/bin/ar
 549212 /usr/bin/cvs
```

```
 519964 /bin/bash
1107076 total
$
```

In the following In-Chapter Exercises, you will use the **wc**, **ls -l**, and **size** commands to appreciate how they work and the kind of output they generate.

IN-CHAPTER EXERCISES

13.3 Display the LOC attribute of the C source code in the power.c file. Show your command and its output.

13.4 Display the size of the executable for the power.c program in bytes. Show your command and its output.

13.5 Repeat the executions of the **size** commands in the above session. Are the sizes of different commands and tools the same on your system?

13.5.2 THE RUNNING TIME OF A PROGRAM

The run-time performance of a program or any shell command can be measured and displayed by using the **time** command. This command reports three times: elapsed time, system time, and user time in the format hours:minutes.seconds. Elapsed time is the actual time taken by the program to finish running, system time is the time taken by system activities while the program was executing, and user time is the time taken by execution of the program code. Because LINUX and UNIX are time-sharing systems, elapsed time is not always equal to the sum of system and user time, because many other users' processes may be running while your program executes, causing the elapsed time to be much greater than the sum of user and system times. Here is a brief description of the **time** command.

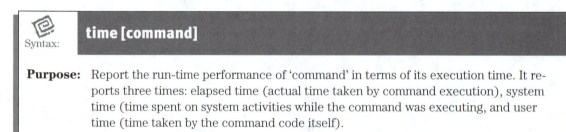

Syntax: **time [command]**

Purpose: Report the run-time performance of 'command' in terms of its execution time. It reports three times: elapsed time (actual time taken by command execution), system time (time spent on system activities while the command was executing, and user time (time taken by the command code itself).

The **time** command sends its output to stderr. So, if you want to redirect the output of the **time** command to a disk file, you must redirect its stderr (not its stdout) to the file.

There are two versions of the **time** command: the built-in command for the TC shell and the **/usr/bin/time** command. The output of the built-in **time** command is quite cryptic, whereas the output of the `/usr/bin/time` command is very readable. When the TC shell version of the `time` command is executed without a command argument, it reports the length of time the current TC shell has been running. The reported time includes the time taken by all its children, that is, all the commands that have run under the shell. The other version of the command doesn't have this feature.

The following `time` command, executed under the TC shell, reports how long the current shell has been running: 2 hours, 33 minutes, and 17 seconds. In the output, **u** represents user time and **s** represents system time. You can use the TC shell built-in time command in a shell script to time the shell script.

```
% time
2.0u 4.0s 2:33:17 0% 0+0k 0+0io 0pf+0w

%
```

The following command reports the time taken by the `find` command. For the sake of brevity, we have not displayed the error messages generated by the `find` command because of improper access privileges for certain directories. Note that the output contains additional information such as the number of page faults and swaps that occur while the `find` command executed. Discussion of that part of the output is beyond the scope of this book.

```
$ /usr/bin/time find /usr -name socket.h -print
0.87user 2.83system 0:03.71elapsed 99%CPU (0avgtext+0avgdata 0maxresident)k
0inputs+0outputs (110major+41minor)pagefaults 0swaps

$
```

As we've mentioned before, the sum of user and system times doesn't always equal elapsed time, especially if a program is idle and doesn't use the CPU for a while due to program I/O. In the example, however, the elapsed time is off by only .01 sec.

Because the `time` command can be used to measure the running time of any program, you can use it with an executable of your own—a binary image or a shell script. The following session shows the running time of the `Huffman` program when it is executed to generate the Huffman codes and other related information about the characters in the Data file. Note that the elapsed time equals the system time plus the user time, as the command was run late at night when the system was not running any other user processes.

```
$ /usr/bin/time Huffman Data
0.24user 0.01system 0:00.25elapsed 96%CPU (0avgtext+0avgdata 0maxresident)k
0inputs+0outputs (103major+21minor)pagefaults 0swaps

$
```

There are other ways of measuring the running time of a program that give you better precision, but using the `time` command is the easiest way, and is recommended for beginners. If you are an advanced user, you can use the **times** system call to measure the user and system times taken by a process and its children or the **getrusage** system call to measure the user and system times for a process. We encourage you to read the manual pages for these system calls with the **man 2 times** and **man 2 getrusage** commands.

In the following In-Chapter Exercises, you will use the **time** command to appreciate how it works and the kind of output it generates.

IN-CHAPTER EXERCISES

13.6 Run the **time** command. Show your **time** command and its output. If your current shell is not TC, first start a TC shell with the **tcsh** command. Use the TC shell for some time and then run the **time** command to determine how long you've running the TC shell for.

13.7 Use the time **find / -name foo -print 2> /dev/null** command to display the pathname for the foo file. Show the command output and identify the user, system, and elapsed times. Does the sum of user and system times equal the elapsed time? Why, or why not?

13.6 WEB RESOURCES

Table 13.3 lists useful Web sites for **gprof** and software metrics.

Table 13.3	Web Resources for gprof and Software Metrics	
Reference	**URL**	**Description**
1	www.gnu.org/manual/gprof-2.9.1/gprof.html	The home page for gprof: the GNU project profiler
2	sam.zoy.org/doc/programming/gprof.html	HOWTO: using gprof with multithreaded applications
3	user-mode-linux.sourceforge.net/gprof.html	Running gprof and gcov

13.7 SUMMARY

The purpose of software metrics is to collect and measure quantifiable attributes of software projects in order to have more control over their execution and help in future projects. For example, software metrics enable us to assess the processes used in a project, the resources involved in it (such as productivity of a programmer), and its cost.

Many facets of metrics are used by software engineers: software cost and effort, software productivity, software quality, software size and complexity, and software run-time performance. Some of these metrics can be measured directly, direct metrics, and some are derived, indirect metrics. Table 13.1 lists some of the commonly used metrics.

Software profiling allows you to identify bottlenecks in your software in order to optimize your code in terms of its running time. You can use the `gprof` command to generate and display the run-time profile for a C/C++ program. Software metrics such as LOC, FPs, and OPs can be used in software cost models to estimate the cost of a software project. You can use the `wc -l` command to display the LOC attribute of your source program. You can measure the size of a program with the `wc -c` or `ls -l` command. The `size` command allows you to display the sizes of code, text, and bss sections of object or executable files. A program's performance in terms of space and time can be measured with the `wc -c` and `time` commands.

13.8 QUESTIONS AND PROBLEMS

1. What is software profiling? Why is it useful?
2. What do we mean by software metrics? What are some of the commonly collected software metrics? Why are these metrics important?
3. Outline the procedure for profiling a C/C++ program in LINUX and UNIX.
4. What are is a flat profile? What is a call graph?
5. Profile one of your recently written C/C++ programs. Write down all the commands that you used to accomplish this task.
6. Identify the most time-consuming function in your the program you profiled in Problem 5. Do you think that this function is a bottleneck in your program? Why, or why not?
7. By using the call graph portion of the profile you created in Problem 5, draw a picture for the call graph (like the one in Figure 13.1). Identify the most called function and the number of times it is called. Which function calls the most number of functions in your program? How many functions does it call?
8. What would you do to improve the time and space performance of your program?
9. Display the LOC parameter for your program. Show the command and its output.
10. Display the size of your executable program. What command did you use?
11. Display the sizes of the text, data, and bss sections of your executable code. Does the sum of the sizes equal the output of the command that you used for Problem 10?
12. What are the sizes of the code, data, and bss sections of the `vi`, `find`, and `grep` commands? Show your command and its output.
13. Run your program and measure its execution time. Show your command line along with its output. What are the user, system, and elapsed times? What do they mean these times indicate? *Hint:* Read the manual page for the `time` command.
14. What does the `time bash` command line do when executed under the TC shell?
15. Give the command line to redirect the output of the `/usr/bin/time polish` command to a file called polish_output. Assume that you are using Bash.

Version Control with RCS and CVS

OBJECTIVES

- ■ To explain what is meant by version control
- ■ To discuss important features of the Revision Control System (RCS)
- ■ To describe important features of the Concurrent Versions System (CVS)
- ■ To list some important Web resources
- ■ Commands and primitives covered: `cat, cd, cp, ci, co, cvs` (and its commands), `echo, ls, rcs, rcsdiff, rcsmerge, rlog, source`

14.1 INTRODUCTION

Studies have shown that about two-thirds of the cost of a software product is spent on maintenance. As we have mentioned before, corrective maintenance and enhancement comprise the maintenance of a software product. In corrective maintenance, the errors and bugs found after installation are fixed. In enhancement, the product is enhanced to include more features, such as an improved user interface. Regardless of its type, maintenance means changing and/or revising the source code for the product and generating new executables. As you revise source code, you may need to undo changes made to it and go back to an earlier version of the software. Also, if you detect a bug in your software after it has been in use for a long time, you will wish to be able to retrieve earlier versions of the software to determine the change that induced the bug. Moreover, if a team of programmers is working on a piece of software, each team member should be able to check out and check in editable (modifiable) versions of the software. In the remainder of the chapter, we discuss the LINUX/UNIX tools that support such actions. We use the terms revision, version, release, and delta interchangeably.

Version control is the task of managing revisions to a software product. Typical software for version control allows you to

- Lock out other users from changing a file while one user is altering it (provide a checkout and checkin system of file access)
- Create different versions of a file
- Identify revisions to a file
- Store and retrieve different versions of a file
- Merge multiple versions of the same file to create a new "final" file
- Maintain a history of all versions of every file related to a product
- Access earlier versions of all the files of a product
- Limit access to a file to a subset of users on the system

Several LINUX/UNIX tools allow you to control versions of your files and almost all of them use the Revision Control System (RCS) as their engine. We discuss Revision Control System and Concurrent Versions System (CVS) in this chapter.

14.2 THE REVISION CONTROL SYSTEM (RCS)

The **Revision Control System (RCS)** was designed to perform all of the version control tasks. In RCS, version numbers start with 1.1. When you request a particular version of a file, RCS starts with the latest version and makes changes in it to re-create the requested version. The RCS way of creating a version is usually faster because most people work forward and create a newer version based on the current version, rather than on an older version. The version numbers in RCS are maintained in the format release.level.branch.sequence.

RCS maintains several versions of a file in a special rcs-format. You can't edit this file by using normal LINUX or UNIX editors such as **vi**, **vim**, or **emacs**. But, once this file has been created, you can access a version of your original file by using RCS-specific commands to create a new version (through checkout and checkin procedures), view the current editing activity on an RCS file, or view revisions made to the file. We describe the commands for performing the most common tasks. All the RCS utilities are in the /usr/bin directory. Add this directory to your search path (in the shell variable *PATH* or *path*) if it isn't already there.

14.2.1 WORKING WITH RCS

The first step to using RCS is to create a directory called **RCS** in the directory that contains the files you want to manage with RCS. This directory contains the revision control information on your files, including the latest version of each file, along with the information that can be used by RCS to create previous versions. An access list is maintained for every RCS file that contains the login names of the users who can access the file. Login names can be added to or deleted from the list.

14.2.2 CREATING AN RCS HISTORY FILE

The **ci** command is used to create and manage RCS history files. The following is a brief description of the utility.

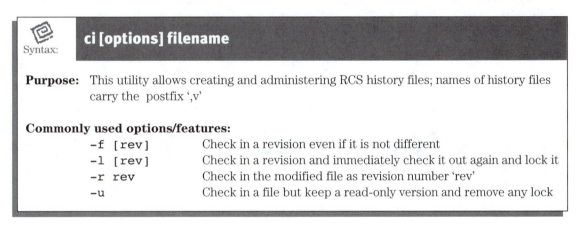

Syntax:

ci [options] filename

Purpose: This utility allows creating and administering RCS history files; names of history files carry the postfix ',v'

Commonly used options/features:

-f [rev]	Check in a revision even if it is not different
-l [rev]	Check in a revision and immediately check it out again and lock it
-r rev	Check in the modified file as revision number 'rev'
-u	Check in a file but keep a read-only version and remove any lock

Along with the access list, an RCS file contains multiple revisions of the text, a change log, descriptive text, and some control attributes such as file lock. In order for you to access a file, you must be its owner or the superuser, or your login name must be on the access list.

Once you have created an RCS history file, you can remove the original. From now on you will access the source file by using the RCS-specific commands, and these files work with RCS history files only. In the following session, we use the **ci** command to create (check in) an RCS history file called RCS/input.c,v. After depositing a new revision, **ci** prompts you for a log message that you can enter to summarize the change. This message must be terminated with a **<Ctrl-D>** or period (.) on a new line.

```
$ ci input.c
RCS/input.c,v <- input.c
enter description, terminated with single '.' or end of file:
NOTE: This is NOT the log message!
```

```
>> Initial version of the input.c file created by Syed Mansoor Sarwar
>> .
initial version: 1.1.
done
$
```

After creating the RCS/input.c,v file, the `ci` command removes the original file, input.c. You can use the **–u** option to check in a file and keep a read-only copy of the original in the current directory. In the following example, we check in the input.c file but keep a read-only copy, as shown by the output of the `ls –l input.c` command. The `ci` command did not prompt for a log message because the file was not changed. If the file is updated the check-in command prompts you for a log message, as shown later.

```
$ ci -u input.c
RCS/input.c,v <- input.c
Ci: RCS/input.c,v: no lock set by sarwar
$ ls -l input.c
-r--------    1 sarwar   faculty          137 Apr  1 11:03 input.c
$
```

In the following In-Chapter Exercise, you will use the `ci` command to create an RCS history file.

IN-CHAPTER EXERCISE

14.1   Create the RCS history file for input.c. What command(s) did you use? What is the pathname of the history file?

14.2.3 CHECKING OUT AN RCS FILE

The **co** utility is used to check out a file and store it in the corresponding working file. The following is a brief description of the utility.

Syntax: **co [options] file-list**

Purpose: This utility allows checking out of files in 'file-list' from the corresponding RCS history file, and storing them in the corresponding working files.

Commonly used options/features:

-l	Check out a file for editing in locked mode
-rver	Check out 'ver' version of the specified file
-u[ver]	Check out an unreserved (read-only) version of the specified file
-v	Display version number of RCS

Without any option, the **co** command checks out a read-only copy of the file. The **-l** option is used to check out a file for editing. The use of this option locks the file so that only one user can check it out for editing. You can use the following command to check out input.c for editing.

```
$ co -l input.c
RCS/input.c,v -> input.c
revision 1.1 (locked)
done
$
```

After you have finished editing input.c, you can check in its new version by using the **ci** command. In the following session, we check in a new version of input.c and keep a read-only copy of it in the current directory.

```
$ ci -u input.c
RCS/input.c,v <- input.c
new release: 1.2; previous revision: 1.1
enter log message, terminated with single '.' or end of file
>> Added a comment header to the file.
>> .
done
$
```

Note that the new version of input.c in RCS has the same release number (1) as the locked version but a new level number (2).

If a particular revision of a file has been checked out for editing, execution of a command for checking out the same version of the file results in an exception message that gives the user the opportunity to remove the checked-out version or exit. The following command line illustrates this point. We checked out version 1.1 of the input.c file before issuing the **co** command. The command prompts the user to remove the already checked-out version or abort checkout. In this case we just hit **<Enter>** at the prompt to abort checkout.

```
$ co -l input.c
RCS/input.c,v -> input.c
revision 1.1 (locked)
writable input.c exists; remove it? [ny](n):<Enter>
co checkout aborted
$
```

In the following In-Chapter Exercise, you will use the **co** and **ci** commands to practice checkin and checkout procedures under RCS.

IN-CHAPTER EXERCISE

14.2   Check out an editable copy of **input.c**, make changes to it, and check in the new version. Write the sequence of commands that you used to perform this task.

14.2.4 CREATING A NEW VERSION OF A FILE

If you want to retrieve a new version of a file, you must first create it. You can create a new version of a file by using the **ci** command with the **-r** option. In the following session, version 2.1 of the input.c file is created and stored in the RCS directory. Note that we use **-r2** as a shortcut for **-r2.1**.

```
$ ci -r2 input.c
RCS/input.c,v <- input.c
new revision: 2.1; previous revision 1.2
enter log message, terminated with single '.' or end of file
>> Just showing how a new version of a file can be created.
>> .
done
$
```

14.2.5 CHECKING OUT COPIES OF SPECIFIC VERSIONS

In RCS, you can check out an existing version of a file by using the **co** command with the **-r** option. If the checked-out version has the highest revision number, the new version generated at checkin time has the same release number with the level number (or sequence number if the file is a branch of a particular release) automatically incremented by 1. If the checked-out version isn't the latest, a branch of the file is generated.

In the following session, we check out version 1 of the input.c file for editing. By default, the **co** command always checks out the highest version of a release, or version 1.2 here. Note that we used the **ci -r** command in the previous section to create a new release (release 2) of this file. A higher release exists for the input.c file, so the **ci** command created a new branch at the checked-out level, resulting in version number 1.2.1.1.

```
$ co -l -r1 input.c
RCS/input.c,v -> input.c
revision 1.2 (locked)
done
$ vi input.c
```

```
... editing session ...
$ ci input.c
RCS/input.c,v <- input.c
new revision: 1.2.1.1; previous revision 1.2
enter log message, terminated with single '.' or end of file
>> Just showing how a branch of a file can be created.
>> .
done
$
```

To create a branch of an RCS file explicitly, we specify a version number with the branch number of the version in the `ci` command. In the following example, we create branch 1 of revision number 2.1 of input.c, resulting in the creation of version 2.1.1.1 of the file.

```
$ co -l input.c
RCS/input.c,v -> input.c
revision 2.1 (locked)
done
$ vi input.c
... editing session ...
$ ci -r2.1.1 input.c
RCS/input.c,v <- input.c
new revision: 2.1.1.1; previous revision 2.1
enter log message, terminated with single '.' or end of file
>> Just  showing  how a branch  of a file  can  be  created explicitly.
>> .
done
$
```

Figure 14.1 illustrates how revision numbers of the input.c file are related. From left to right, the first digit is the release number, the second digit is the level number, the third digit is the branch number, and the fourth digit is the sequence number.

In the following In-Chapter Exercise, you will use the `co` and `ci` commands to create specific versions of a file.

IN-CHAPTER EXERCISE

14.3 Create versions 1.2 and 2.1 of the input.c file. What command lines did you use?

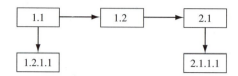

Figure 14.1 The version tree for `input.c`

14.2.6 ABANDONING CHANGES

If you've made changes to a file that didn't work out, you can undo the changes and uncheck out the file by using the **rcs** utility. The following is a brief description of the **rcs** utility.

Syntax:

rcs [options] file-list

Purpose: This utility allows control of RCS files, that is, it allows their attributes to be changed

Commonly used options/features:

`-alogins`	Add the login names in the comma-separated list 'logins' to the access list (i.e., allow the users in 'logins' to check out editable versions of the files specified in 'file-list' and check them back in)
`-e[logins]`	Remove the login names in the comma-separated list 'logins' from the access list (i.e., disallow the users in 'logins' to check out editable versions of files in 'file-list'
`-l[rev]`	Check out revision 'rev' of a file without overwriting it, i.e., lock revision 'rev'; use the latest revision of 'rev' if not specified
`-orange`	Remove versions of a file given 'range'; the range rev1:rev2 means revisions from 'rev1' to 'rev2'; :rev means from the beginning of the branch containing 'rev' up to (and including) 'rev'; rev: means revision from revisions 'rev' to the end of the branch containing 'rev'
`-u[rev]`	Unlock revision 'rev'; abandon changes made to the file and uncheck out the file

When you check out a file with the **co -l** command, it is locked and you can edit it and install changes made to the file by using the **ci** command. If the file is unlocked, the **ci** command does not install the changes made to the file. You can use the **rcs -u** command to unlock a file checked out for editing. Although a copy of the checked out file remains in your directory, any changes made to it before and after unlocking it cannot be installed in the RCS file. In order for you to be able to install changes made to the file, you must relock it or check it out again, overwriting the existing (unlocked) version. In the following session, we check out the input.c file by using the **co -l** command, save a backup copy of the file in input.c.bak, make changes to the checked out file, and unlock it with the **rcs -u input.c** command. We then use the **ci** command to install changes made to the file. Although the **ci** command does not tell us so, the changes made to the file are not installed. We confirm this by checking out the input.c file again and comparing it with the previously saved file input.c.bak.

```
$ co -l input.c
RCS/input.c,v  ->  input.c
revision 2.1 (locked)
done
$ cp input.c input.c.bak
$ vi input.c
...
$ rcs -u input.c
RCS file: RCS/input.c,v
2.1 unlocked
done
$ ci input.c
RCS/input.c,v  <-  input.c
ci: RCS/input.c,v: no lock set by sarwar
$ co -l input.c
RCS/input.c,v  ->  input.c
revision 2.1 (locked)
writable input.c exists; remove it? [ny](n): y
done
$ diff input.c input.c.bak
$
```

14.2.7 Locking a File Without Overwriting (Taking Care of a Mistake)

When you execute the **ci -u input.c** command, a read-only copy of input.c is left in your current directory. A word of caution: If you change permissions for input.c to make it writable and make changes to it, the changes cannot be installed in the RCS/filename,v file in the RCS database because you didn't properly check out an editable version of the file by using the **co -l input.c** command.

You can overcome this problem by locking input.c with the **rcs -l** command without checking it out from the RCS directory and overwriting the existing file (that you updated by mistake). This command, followed by the **ci -u input.c** command installs the changes in the RCS/input.c,v file and leaves a read-only copy in the current directory. This command creates a new version. The following session illustrates these points.

```
$ co -u input.c
RCS/input.c,v  ->  input.c
revision 1.2 (unlocked)
done
$ chmod 700 input.c
$ vi input.c
...
$ ci input.c
RCS/input.c,v  <-  input.c
ci no lock set by sarwar
$ rcs -l input.c
RCS file: RCS/input.c,v
1.2 locked
done
$ ci -u input.c
RCS/input.c,v  <-  input.c
new revision: 1.3; previous revision: 1.2
enter log message, terminated with single '.' or end of file
>> Demonstrated file locking.
>> .
done
$
```

14.2.8 REMOVING A VERSION

RCS allows you to remove any (including a nonleaf) version of a file by using the **rcs** command with the **–o** option. If the removed version is an intermediate version, the remaining versions are not renumbered. In the following session, we remove version 1.1 of input.c.

```
$ rcs -o1.1 input.c
RCS file: RCS/input.c,v
deleting revision 1.1
done
$
```

A range of versions can be deleted by specifying the range after the **–o** option. For example, the **rcs –o2.1:3.2 input.c** command deletes versions 2.1 through 3.2 of the input.c file. Similarly, the rcs −o:2.2 input.c command deletes versions 1.1 through 2.2 (including 2.2) of the input.c file and **rcs −o4.1: input.c** command deletes version 4.1 of the input.c file.

The following In-Chapter Exercise has been designed to enhance your understanding of the versions of a file in RCS. The exercise particularly asks you to use the **rcs −o** command to delete a version of a file.

IN-CHAPTER EXERCISE

14.4 Remove version 1.2 of input.c file just discussed in RCS. Give the command line for performing this task.

14.2.9 WORKING IN GROUPS

Working in groups is quite straightforward. All you need do is place the RCS subdirectory (or subdirectories) in a shared directory. You then run all RCS utilities by specifying the complete pathnames for the RCS files and editing files in your local directories. An alternative to creating a common shared directory is to maintain all RCS directories in one user's directory and create symbolic links (see Chapter 2) to this directory in the directories of the remaining members of the group. Of course, appropriate access privileges must be set for all components in the pathname for the RCS directory.

In the following session, we check out an editable version of the input.c file, assuming that the only RCS directory is in the /home/shared directory.

```
$ co −l /home/shared/RCS/input.c,v
RCS/input.c,v −> input.c
revision 2.1.1.1 (locked)
done
$
```

After making changes to the input.c file, we can check it back in using the following command. The −u option is used to keep a read-only copy in the current directory.

```
$ ci −u /home/shared/input.c
/home/shared/RCS/input.c,v <−− input.c
new revision: 2.1.1.2; previous revision 2.1.1.1
enter log message, terminated with single '.' or end of file
>> Illustrated working in groups.
>> .
done
$
```

The preceding command lines need long pathnames, so the users in the group may want to create one-line scripts to handle checkin and checkout procedures. The following are Bash scripts for the procedures **checkin** and **checkout**.

```
$ cat checkin
#!/bin/bash
# Check in command line; keep a read-only copy in the current
# directory
ci -u /home/shared/RCS/$1,v
$ cat checkout
# Check out command line; check out an editable copy of the file
co -l /home/shared/RCS/$1,v
$
```

After creating these scripts, you need to make them executable for yourself by using the **chmod u+x** command, as in

```
$ chmod u+x checkin checkout
$
```

Now you can use the **checkin input.c** command to check in the input.c file in the /home/shared/RCS directory and the **checkout input.c** command to check out an editable version of the input.c file from the /home/shared/RCS directory.

An alternative to creating script files **checkin** and **checkout** is for users in the group to create a symbolic link, called RCS, in the /home/shared/RCS directory and use short names (simple file names).

14.2.10 DISPLAYING THE HISTORY OF RCS FILES

You can use the **rlog** command to display the history of RCS files. The following is a brief description of the command.

Syntax: **rlog [options] file-list**

Purpose: Display history (log messages and other information) of RCS files in 'file-list'

Commonly used options/features:

-L	Display history of files that have been checked out for editing (i.e., files that have been locked)
-R	Display file names only
-l[users]	Display information about files locked by users whose login names are given in 'users,' a command-separated list of login names
-r[rev]	Display information about revisions given in 'rev,' a comma-separated list of revisions; rev1:rev2, :rev2, or rev1: can be used to specify a range of revisions

---

Without any option the `rlog` command displays the history of all the revisions that have been made to the files in 'file-list.' The following command displays the history of input.c file.

```
$ rlog input.c
RCS file: RCS/input.c,v
Working file: input.c
head: 2.1
branch:
locks: strict
access list:
symbolic names:
keyword substitution: kv
total revisions: 6;     selected revisions: 6
description:
The first version of the input.c file
-------------------------
revision 2.1
date: 2002/03/31 01:18:55;  author: sarwar; state: Exp; lines: +1 -0
branches: 2.1.1; 2.1.2;
Just showing how a new version of a file can be created.
-------------------------
revision 1.2
date: 2002/03/31 01:12:25;  author: sarwar; state: Exp; lines: +2 -0
branches: 1.2.1;
Added a comment header to the file.
-------------------------
revision 1.1
date: 2002/03/31 01:11:37;  author: sarwar; state: Exp;
Initial revision
-------------------------
revision 1.2.1.1
date: 2002/03/31 01:20:57;  author: sarwar; state: Exp; lines: +1 -0
Just showing how a branch of a file can be created.
-------------------------
revision 2.1.2.1
date: 2002/03/31 01:35:54;  author: sarwar; state: Exp; lines: +1 -0
*** empty log message ***
-------------------------
```

```
revision 2.1.1.1
date: 2002/03/31 01:33:46;   author: sarwar; state: Exp; lines: +2 -14
*** empty log message ***
=======================================================================
$
```

The following command line displays files that have been checked out by the user jonathan for editing. The files checked out as read-only are not included in this list.

```
$ rlog -L -R -ljonathan RCS/*
RCS/compute.c,v
RCS/input.c,v
$
```

In the following In-Chapter Exercise, you will display the checkin and checkout history of an RCS file by using the **rlog** command.

IN-CHAPTER EXERCISE

14.5 Execute the **rlog input.c** command on your system. What did it display? Does the output make sense?

14.2.11 BREAKING LOCKS

If you must update a file (perhaps to fix a bug in it) that has been checked out by another user in your group for editing, you can use the **rcs -u** command to uncheck out this file. Then check out an editable copy of the same file without overwriting the existing file, make appropriate changes to it, and check it back in. We show this sequence of events in the following session. The first **co** command checks out input.c. The second **co** command displays the message generated when the command is used to check out a file that has already been checked out. The **rcs -u input.c** command unchecks out the input.c file. The **rlog** command shows that input.c is no longer checked out. Once the file has been unlocked (unchecked out), the last three commands check out the input.c file, edit it, and check it back in (retaining a read-only version in the current directory).

```
$ co -l input.c
RCS/input.c,v  ->  input.c
revision 1.2 (locked)
done
$ co -l input.c
```

```
RCS/input.c,v  ->  input.c
revision 1.2 (locked)
writable input.c exists; remove it? [ny](n): n
co checkout aborted
$ rcs -u input.c
RCS file: RCS/input.c,v
1.3 unlocked
done
$ rlog -L -R -lsarwar input.c
$ co -l input.c
...
$ vi input.c
...
$ ci -u input.c
...
$
```

14.2.12 Displaying Differences Between Versions

You can use the `rcsdiff` command to display differences between different versions of a file. Without any argument, it displays differences between the current and last checked-in versions. The `rcsdiff` command calls the `diff` command to produce the difference output. You can use this utility to find differences between two or more revisions of a file before merging them. The following is a brief description of the utility.

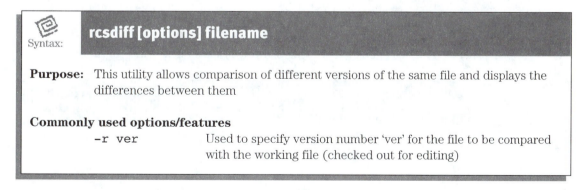

Syntax: **rcsdiff [options] filename**

Purpose: This utility allows comparison of different versions of the same file and displays the differences between them

Commonly used options/features

-r ver   Used to specify version number 'ver' for the file to be compared
                  with the working file (checked out for editing)

The following `rcsdiff` command line displays the differences between the latest revision and the last checked-out version of the input.c file. This command is useful for determining what changes have been made to input.c since the last checkin.

```
$ rcsdiff input.c
=============================================================
RCS file: RCS/input.c,v
retrieving version 2.1
diff -r2.1 input.c
[output of the above diff command]
$
```

You can explicitly name the two versions to be compared by using the −r option. The following command line displays the different output resulting from a comparison between versions 1.2 and 2.1 of input.c.

```
$ rcsdiff -r1.2 -r2.1 input.c
RCS file: RCS/input.c,v
retrieving revision 1.2
retrieving revision 2.1
diff -r1.2 -r2.1
1,2d0
< /* Just a test */
[remaining output of the above diff command]
$
```

14.2.13 MERGING VERSIONS

The **rcsmerge** command can be used to merge the differences between two versions of a file into the working file. These versions are the current version and a version specified in the command line, or the two versions specified in the command line. The following is a brief description of the utility.

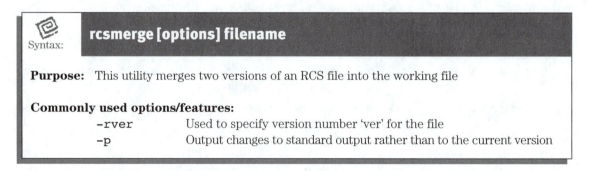

Syntax:

rcsmerge [options] filename

Purpose: This utility merges two versions of an RCS file into the working file

Commonly used options/features:

−rver	Used to specify version number 'ver' for the file
−p	Output changes to standard output rather than to the current version

If the currently checked-out version of input.c is 1.4 and you want to merge the changes made on version 1.1.1.2 into this file, you can run the following command. By default, the **rcsmerge** command overwrites the existing file with the merged file. You can use the **-p** option to redirect the merged version to stdout, which can then be redirected to another file. The use of **-p** option is highly recommended because the command sometimes doesn't work as you expect it to. If you don't use this option, the current version is changed and there is nothing to fall back on. In the following **rcsmerge** command we combine the currently checked-out version (1.4) and version 1.1.1.2 of the input.c file and store it in merged_input.c. With the **-p** option, you can remove the merged_input.c file and go back to input.c if necessary.

```
$ rcsmerge -r1.1.1.2 -p input.c > merged_input.c
RCS file: RCS/input.c,v
retrieving revision 1.1.1.2
retrieving revision 1.4
Merging differences between 1.1.1.2 and 1.4 into input.c; result to stdout
$
```

You can merge any two versions of an RCS file by specifying them in the command line. For example, the following **rcsmerge** command merges versions 1.2 and 3.2 of input.c and stores the merged version in the merged_input.c file.

```
$ rcsmerge -r1.2 -r3.2 -p input.c > merged_input.c
RCS file: RCS/input.c,v
retrieving revision 1.2
retrieving revision 3.2
Merging differences between 1.2 and 3.2 into input.c; result to stdout
$
```

You can use the following command to undo changes between revisions 1.2 and 2.1 in your currently checked out version of input.c. Note the order of revisions (later revision first).

```
$ rcsmerge -r2.1 -r1.2 input.c
RCS file: RCS/input.c,v
retrieving revision 2.1
retrieving revision 1.2
Merging differences between 2.1 and 1.2 into input.c
$
```

In the following In-Chapter Exercise, you will practice merging various versions of an RCS file.

IN-CHAPTER EXERCISE

14.6   Create a few new versions of file input.c and execute the **rcsmerge** command to merge them all into the merged input.c file.

14.2.14 LIMITING ACCESS RIGHTS TO RCS

Any user can check out an RCS file, provided that the user has appropriate permissions for the file and has access to the file's pathname. You can protect your RCS files by restricting access to one or more users by using the **–a** and **–e** options of the **rcs** command. As mentioned in the brief description of the **rcs** command, you can use the **–a** option to allow checkout rights on a file to one or more users. All other users are allowed to check out a read-only copy of the file. You can use the **–e** option to remove one or more users from the list. Multiple **–a** and **–e** options can be used in a command line.

In the following session, we demonstrate the use of both options. The first **rcs** command adds users matt, chang, and mona to the list of users allowed to check out an editable version of the input.c file and check it back in; no other user is allowed to perform these tasks. The second **rcs** command adds the user davis to the list of users who can access the file. The last **rcs** command denies chang the access right for editing input.c. The outputs of the **rlog** commands show the current access lists.

```
$ rcs -amatt,chang,mona input.c
RCS file: RCS/input.c,v
done
$ rcs -adavis input.c
RCS file: RCS/input.c,v
done
$ rlog -h RCS/input.c,v
RCS file: RCS/input.c,v
Working file: input.c
head: 2.1
branch:
locks: strict
access list:
        matt
        chang
        mona
        davis
symbolic names:
```

```
keyword substitution: kv
total revisions: 6
=============================================================
$ rcs -echang input.c
RCS file: RCS/input.c,v
done
$ rlog -h RCS/input.c,v
...
access list:
        matt
        mona
        davis
...

=============================================================
$
```

You can specify multiple **-e** or **-a** options with an **rcs** command line to allow or deny access to different users. In the following **rcs** command line, users sirini, chris, and kahn are allowed to access an editable version of the input.c file, but users liz and beena aren't.

```
$ rcs -asirini,chris -akahn -eliz -ebeena input.c
$
```

In the following In-Chapter Exercise, you will use the **rcs** command with **-a** and **-e** options to set different access rights for different users on an RCS file.

IN-CHAPTER EXERCISE

14.7 Give the command line that allows users osterberg, tom, and aziz editing rights to the RCS/input.c,v file and takes away the same rights from users debbie and sarah.

14.2.15 RCS SPECIAL CHARACTER SEQUENCES

You can place any of several special character sequences in the comment header of a source file. These character sequences are processed specially by RCS and are expanded to include information from the RCS log for the file. The general format for these special sequences is $string$. This sequence results in the expansion of **string** by RCS. This expansion takes place when you check a file into the RCS directory and is in place the next time you check out the file. Table 14.1 shows some of these sequences and their expanded values.

Table 14.1	RCS Special Character Sequences and Their Expanded Values
Character Sequence	**Replaced with**
$Author$	Author's login name
$Date$	Current date and time
$Header$	Full pathname of the RCS file in the repository, revision number, date and time of last change, author, and state.
Id	Like $Header$ but without the full pathname of the RCS file
$Name$	Name of the label (tag) if one exists, or blank if the file doesn't have a label
$RCSfile$	Name of the RCS file
$Revision$	The highest revision number
$Source$	Name of the source file

The comment header

```
/*
 * Author:      $Author$
 * Date:        $Date$
 * Module:      $RCSfile$
 * Revision:    $Revision$
 * Status:      $Id$
 */
```

in the **input.c** file expands to

```
/*
 * Author:      $Author: sarwar $
 * Date:        $Date: 2001/03/17 08:21:14 $
 * Module:      $RCSfile: input.c,v $
 * Revision:    $Revision: 2.2 $
 * Status:      $Id: input.c,v 2.2 2001/03/17 08:21:14 sarwar Exp $
 */
```

when the file is checked in.

The most commonly used sequence is **Id**, which is expanded by RCS to include the RCS file name, revision number, date, time, login name of the user making changes, and the RCS state of the file. If you want to put this information in an executable file, you need to include the following C/C++ statement in the source file.

```
static char rcsid[ ] = "$Id$";
```

This statement gets compiled into your C/C++ binary program. The statement can be local or global.

You can use the `ident` utility to display the expanded RCS special character sequences in a file. It works on both source and binary files. The following `ident` command displays the expanded forms of the special strings in the input.c file.

```
$ ident input.c
input.c:
      $Author: sarwar $
      $Date: 2002/03/31 08:21:14 $
      $RCSfile: input.c,v $
      $Revision: 2.2 $
      $Id: input.c,v 2.2 2002/03/31 08:21:14 sarwar Exp $
$
```

14.2.16 MISCELLANEOUS RCS UTILITIES

There are several other RCS utilities that an advanced user may need to learn. See the `man` page for the `rcs` command on your LINUX/UNIX system to learn what commands are available and to learn more about them.

14.2.17 USING RCS FROM WITHIN emacs

The **emacs** editor has a nice interface for version control under RCS and CVS. You can check in and check out files and run other RCS utilities from within the **emacs** editor. To do so, you need to run the editor in the Version Control mode (also known as the **VC** mode). The **VC** mode commands are **C–x v** followed by one character. The **C–x v v** command does the next right thing in most cases. For example, if a file is read-only, **C–x v v** will check it out for editing. If the file is an editable version, **C–x v v** will check the file in. The **C–x v u** command unchecks out the current file and reverts to the previous version. The **C–x v l** command shows the RCS history (version log) of the file. The **C–x v h** command inserts a special character sequence, the RCS ID header, at the current cursor position.

14.2.18 BEYOND RCS

Several freeware version control systems, mostly built on top of the RCS system, act as front ends to the RCS system. Many have been developed in-house by companies. One of the most popular of these systems is the standard version control system for LINUX and UNIX, called **Concurrent Versions System (CVS).** It is optimized to allow you to apply **RCS** commands to multiple files in various directories and allows concurrent file checkouts without locking the file. The latter feature is implemented by using **lazy locking,** which allows multiple users to check out for editing a file that has already been checked out, without having to break the lock. Although CVS was initially designed on top of RCS, it now has all the functionality of RCS built into it.

14.3   CONCURRENT VERSIONS SYSTEM (CVS)

The Concurrent Versions System is the LINUX and UNIX tool of choice for version control in a multi-developer, multidirectory environment. It allows you to perform many tasks that either cannot be performed or are tedious to perform with RCS. The following are some of the salient features of CVS.

1. It allows you to organize your sources in the form of a directory hierarchy, called a **module,** and check out the whole module for modification.

2. It allows multiple software developers in a team to check out and modify source modules concurrently. Under RCS, file modification operations are serialized by allowing only one developer to check out a file for editing (the file is "locked" by this developer); others can check out this file for read-only. CVS allows multiple developers to modify a file concurrently and it guarantees **conflict resolution** without loss of any changes to the file.

3. It allows you to tag a software release symbolically and check out this version at any point in time during the development and maintenance phases of the software by using this tag. It also allows you to check out a copy of any previous software release, regardless of the current state of the software. You can also check out a software release for a particular date.

We describe some of the basic features of CVS in this section.

14.3.1   THE CVS COMMAND SYNTAX

You need to use the **cvs** utility to interact with CVS. This utility is invoked with different commands to perform the various tasks involved in software revision control. Although **cvs** has a wealth of commands that you can use to perform many chores related to version control, we will focus on the basic commands that are commonly used in practice. The following is a brief description of the **cvs** command.

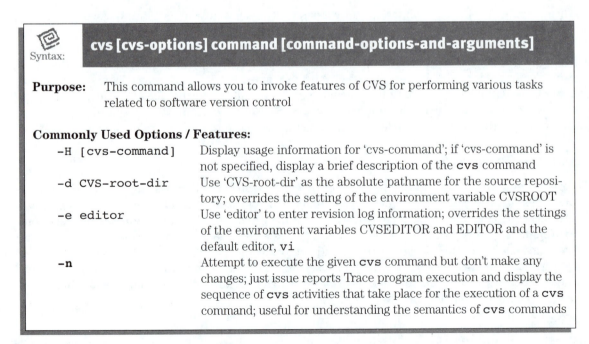

Syntax: **cvs [cvs-options] command [command-options-and-arguments]**

Purpose: This command allows you to invoke features of CVS for performing various tasks related to software version control

Commonly Used Options / Features:

`-H [cvs-command]`	Display usage information for 'cvs-command'; if 'cvs-command' is not specified, display a brief description of the **cvs** command
`-d CVS-root-dir`	Use 'CVS-root-dir' as the absolute pathname for the source repository; overrides the setting of the environment variable CVSROOT
`-e editor`	Use 'editor' to enter revision log information; overrides the settings of the environment variables CVSEDITOR and EDITOR and the default editor, **vi**
`-n`	Attempt to execute the given **cvs** command but don't make any changes; just issue reports Trace program execution and display the sequence of **cvs** activities that take place for the execution of a **cvs** command; useful for understanding the semantics of **cvs** commands

We discuss some of the more commonly used options and commands of the **cvs** command below.

14.3.2 DISPLAYING CVS HELP

You can use the **cvs -H** command to display a brief description of the **cvs** command. The **cvs * -H** command can be used to display the purpose of every **cvs** command. The following session shows sample runs of the two commands.

```
$ cvs -H
Usage: cvs [cvs-options] command [command-options-and-arguments]
  where cvs-options are -q, -n, etc.
    (specify —help-options for a list of options)
  where command is add, admin, etc.
    (specify —help-commands for a list of commands
     or —help-synonyms for a list of command synonyms)
  where command-options-and-arguments depend on the specific command
    (specify -H followed by a command name for command-specific help)
  Specify —help to receive this message

The Concurrent Versions System (CVS) is a tool for version control.
For CVS updates and additional information, see
    Cyclic Software at http://www.cyclic.com/ or
    Pascal Molli's CVS site at http://www.loria.fr/~molli/cvs-index.html
$ cvs * -H
CVS commands are:
        add         Add a new file/directory to the repository
        admin       Administration front end for rcs
        annotate    Show last revision where each line was modified
        checkout    Checkout sources for editing
        commit      Check files into the repository
        diff        Show differences between revisions
        edit        Get ready to edit a watched file
        editors     See who is editing a watched file
        export      Export sources from CVS, similar to checkout
        history     Show repository access history
        import      Import sources into CVS, using vendor branches
        init        Create a CVS repository if it doesn't exist
        log         Print out history information for files
        login       Prompt for password for authenticating server.
```

```
logout      Removes entry in .cvspass for remote repository.
rdiff       Create 'patch' format diffs between releases
release     Indicate that a Module is no longer in use
remove      Remove an entry from the repository
rtag        Add a symbolic tag to a module
status      Display status information on checked out files
tag         Add a symbolic tag to checked out version of files
unedit      Undo an edit command
update      Bring work tree in sync with repository
watch       Set watches
watchers    See who is watching a file
(Specify the —help option for a list of other help options)
$
```

You can get help about any CVS command by using the **cvs -H** command with the command name as its argument. In the following session, we display the help information for the **add** and **commit** commands.

```
$ cvs -H add
Usage: cvs add [-k rcs-kflag] [-m message] files...
        -k      Use "rcs-kflag" to add the file with the specified kflag.
        -m      Use "message" for the creation log.
(Specify the —help global option for a list of other help options)
$ cvs -H commit
Usage: cvs commit [-nRlf] [-m msg | -F logfile] [-r rev] files...
        -n      Do not run the module program (if any).
        -R      Process directories recursively.
        -l      Local directory only (not recursive).
        -f      Force the file to be committed; disables recursion.
        -F file Read the log message from file.
        -m msg  Log message.
        -r rev  Commit to this branch or trunk revision.
(Specify the —help global option for a list of other help options)
$
```

The following In-Chapter Exercises have been designed to give you practice in using the **cvs** command to display information about its various commands.

IN-CHAPTER EXERCISES

14.8 Repeat the sessions in this section on your computer. Log any differences between the outputs of the various commands.

14.9 Run the `cvs –H import` and `cvs –H checkout` commands to learn about the `import` and `checkout` commands.

14.3.3 CREATING A SOURCE REPOSITORY

The sources maintained by CVS are kept in a directory called the source repository. The source repository contains the RCS history (",v") files for the sources and a directory, called CVSROOT, that contains administrative files. You don't need to access files in the CVSROOT directory while performing simple, routine development tasks. Before you start using CVS, you need to set up the location of your source repository, create it, and move the source modules into it. In order to modify your source modules, you check them out into your work area, also known as the sandbox. After modifying your copies of the source modules in the sandbox, you check their updated versions back in to the source repository.

You can inform CVS of the location of your source repository in one of two ways. You can specify the pathname of the source repository as an argument to the **cvs –d** command or set up the environment variable, *CVSROOT*, to contain the absolute pathname of the source repository. Since the location of a source repository normally stays the same during the development of a product, setting it up in a system or shell startup file saves a lot of time. You can choose any name for your source repository but cvsroot is commonly used. For the examples in this book, we want to make the ~/cvsroot directory our source repository and set up the *CVSROOT* variable to this pathname in a startup file (.profile or ~/.bashrc for Bash and ~/.cshrc or ~/.tcshrc for TC shell). We also use the *CVSAREA* variable (a user-defined variable) to store the location of our CVS sandbox, where the checked out modules are to be stored for modification. In the following session, we show how to perform this task for Bash.

```
$ cat ~/.bashrc
...
CVSAREA=~/projects
CVSROOT=~/cvsroot
export CVSAREA CVSROOT
$ source ~/.bashrc
$ echo $CVSROOT
/home/faculty/sarwar/cvsroot
$
```

For the TC shell, you will insert the following lines in the ~/.tcshrc file.

```
setenv CVSAREA ~/projects
setenv CVSROOT ~/cvsroot]
```

Although we are using a subdirectory in our home directory as the source repository, in an actual development environment you would like it to be outside any team member's home directory.

After setting the environment variable, you need to create the source repository by using the **cvs init** command, as shown below.

```
$ cvs init
$
```

If the pathname in the *CVSROOT* variable is incorrect, you don't have the write permissions for the directory that contains the source repository (cvsroot), or you forgot to export the *CVSROOT* variable, the **cvs init** command terminates with an error message informing you of the problem. If you have not set up the *CVSROOT* variable, you can use the **cvs** command with the **−d** option to inform CVS of the location of the source repository, as shown below.

```
$ cvs −d ~/cvsroot init
$
```

After the **cvs init** command has executed successfully, a directory named CVSROOT is created in the source repository. This directory, created for every source repository, contains a set of administrative files used by CVS for maintaining various logs. The following session shows a snapshot of this directory.

```
$ cd
$ ls −l cvsroot
total 1
drwxrwxr−x    2 sarwar    faculty        1024 Apr 18 13:21 CVSROOT
$ cd cvsroot
$ ls CVSROOT
checkoutlist     config          editinfo     loginfo,v  notify,v   taginfo,v
checkoutlist,v   config,v        editinfo,v   modules    rcsinfo    verifymsg
commitinfo       cvswrappers     history      modules,v  rcsinfo,v  verifymsg,v
commitinfo,v     cvswrappers,v   loginfo      notify     taginfo
$
```

In the following In-Chapter Exercise you will practice how to create the **cvs** repository and **cvs** sandbox.

IN-CHAPTER EXERCISE

14.10   Set up your CVS source repository and sandbox to ~/cvsroot and ~/CVSAREA, respectively. Then run the **cvs init** command to create the CVS source repository.

14.3.4 IMPORTING SOURCES INTO THE REPOSITORY

After creating a repository, you need to import your project source files to it before managing them with CVS. You need to use the **cvs import** command for this purpose. The Syntax box below gives a brief description of the **cvs import** command.

Syntax: **cvs import [options] repository vendor-tag release-tag**

Purpose: This command imports new sources into the source repository or updates the repository by incorporating changes to the sources as a vendor branch

Commonly Used Options / Features:

–b branch	Set vendor branch ID to 'branch'
–d	Use file's modification time as the import time
–m message	Log the message 'message' we want the history files to show

---

In the following session, we change directory to project1, the directory that contains the source files that we would like to manage with CVS (i.e., our sandbox). We use the **ls** command to ensure that we are importing the correct files into the repository. The **cvs import** command is used to import these sources into the source repository. The **–m** option is used to supply to CVS a message that we would like to be displayed with the history files. Without this option, the **cvs import** command would put us in an editor to enter the message. The name of the editor to be invoked is taken from the environment variable *CVSEDITOR*. If this variable is not set, then the editor name is taken from the variable *EDITOR*. If neither variable is set, then the **vi** editor is invoked. The command line argument project1 is the name of the directory to contain your source files and the argument DemoCVS is the vendor tag. The last argument must be start.

```
$ cd $CVSAREA/project1
$ ls
compute.c  compute.h  input.c  input.h  main.c  main.h  makefile
$ cvs import -m "Imported Demo Sources" project1 DemoCVS start
N project1/compute.c
```

```
N project1/compute.h
N project1/input.c
N project1/input.h
N project1/main.c
N project1/main.h
N project1/makefile

No conflicts created by this import

$
```

After you have imported the source modules into the source repository, you should remove your original source modules so that you don't become confused with two sets of modules.

Having imported the sources into the source repository, you need to set appropriate access permissions for the source repository, the history files in CVSROOT directory in the source repository, and the project1 directory in the source repository. **CVS** creates all ",v" files as read-only and you should not change permissions of these files as they are to be checked in and out through the **cvs** utility. The subdirectories in the source repository must be writable by all members of your development group who have permission to modify files in these directories. A common way to accomplish this goal is to create a LINUX/UNIX user group consisting of the members of the development team and to make this group the owner of the source repository. For the sake of examples in this chapter, we set access privileges of the source repository to read/write for every member of our team.

In the following In-Chapter Exercise you will use the **cvs import** command to learn how to import the source files that you want to maintain under CVS in the CVS source repository.

IN-CHAPTER EXERCISE

14.11   Create a directory called project1 in your CVS sandbox and copy the source files into this directory. Then import the source files in this directory into your CVS repository.

14.3.5 Checking Out Source Files

After importing sources into the repository and setting appropriate permissions on them, you are ready to check out the source files. You should modify only the checked out modules and not the modules in the source repository. You can check out the source modules by using the **cvs checkout** command. This command allows you to check out any number of source files simultaneously. If you want to check out a module (the complete source tree) for a project, you need to specify the name of the directory in the CVS source repository that contains it. The following Syntax box contains a brief description of the **cvs checkout** command.

Syntax:

cvs checkout [options] modules

Purpose: This command checks out source 'modules' for editing

Commonly Used Options / Features:

`-D date`	Check out versions as of 'date'
`-P`	Prune empty directories
`-R`	Process directories recursively
`-d dir`	Check out module into the directory 'dir' instead of module name(s)
`-j ver`	Merge in changes made between the current version and version 'ver'
`-r ver`	Check out version 'ver' (a version number or tag)

In the following session, we check out the project1 module. The **cvs checkout project1** command creates the project1 directory in your current directory (your CVS work area) and populates it with the sources from the project1 directory in the source repository. The project1 directory in your work area also contains a directory called CVS. As shown below, the **CVS** directory contains three files, called Repository, Entries, and Root. These files contain information that CVS maintains about the checked out files. The CVS directory is used by the CVS system and you should not administer it.

```
$ cd $CVSAREA
$ cvs checkout project1
cvs checkout: Updating project1
U project1/compute.c
U project1/compute.h
U project1/input.h
U project1/main.c
U project1/main.h
U project1/makefile
$ cd project1
$ ls -l
total 8
-rw-r--r--    2 sarwar    faculty       512 Apr  6 15:22 CVS
```

```
-rw-r--r--     1 sarwar     faculty        128 Apr   6 15:15 compute.c
-rw-r--r--     1 sarwar     faculty         87 Apr   6 15:15 compute.h
-rw-r--r--     1 sarwar     faculty        351 Apr   6 15:15 input.c
-rw-r--r--     1 sarwar     faculty         76 Apr   6 15:15 input.h
-rw-r--r--     1 sarwar     faculty        297 Apr   6 15:15 main.c
-rw-r--r--     1 sarwar     faculty        121 Apr   6 15:15 main.h
-rw-r--r--     1 sarwar     faculty        489 Apr   6 15:15 makefile
$ cd CVS
$ ls -l
total 3
-rw-------  1 sarwar     faculty        313 Apr   6 15:22 Entries
-rw-------  1 sarwar     faculty          9 Apr   6 15:13 Repository
-rw-------  1 sarwar     faculty         47 Apr   6 15:13 Root
$ more Entries
/input.c/1.1.1.1/Sat Sep 14 22:15:58 2002//
/compute.c/1.1.1.1/Sat Sep 14 22:15:58 2002//
/compute.h/1.1.1.1/Sat Sep 14 22:15:58 2002//
/input.h/1.1.1.1/Sat Sep 14 22:15:59 2002//
/main.c/1.1.1.1/Sat Sep 14 22:15:59 2002//
/main.h/1.1.1.1/Sat Sep 14 22:15:59 2002//
/makefile/1.1.1.1/Sat Sep 14 22:15:59 2002//
$ more Repository
project1
$ more Root
/home/faculty/sarwar/cvsroot
$
```

In the following In-Chapter Exercise you will use the **cvs checkout** command to check out the source files from the CVS repository so you can work on them (i.e., edit them).

IN-CHAPTER EXERCISE

14.12   Use the **cvs checkout** command to check out all the files in the CVS repository into the project1 directory in your CVS sandbox. Then repeat the above session starting with the **cd project1** command to verify that everything appears the way it is explained above.

14.3.6 Making and Committing Changes to Source Files

You are now ready to make changes to the checked out module (project1 in our case) by using the editor of your choice. After making the necessary changes to the source files in your work area, you can apply the changes to the source repository with the **cvs commit** command. Here is a brief description of the **cvs commit** command.

Syntax: **cvs commit [options] file-list**

Purpose: This command checks in changes in the files in 'file-list' into the source repository

Commonly Used Options / Features:

-F file	Read the log message from 'file'
-R	Process directories recursively
-f	Force the files in 'file-list' to be committed; disables recursion
-m message	Log the message 'message'
-r ver	Commit to this version

In the following session, we modify the input.c file with the **vi** editor and apply these changes to the source repository with the **cvs commit** command. As with the **cvs import** command, if you don't use the **-m** option, CVS puts you in an editor to allow you log a message in the history file. The output of the **cvs commit** command shows that CVS produces version 1.2 of the input.c file.

```
$ vi input.c
...
$ cvs commit -m "Enhanced user interface" input.c
Checking in input.c;
/home/faculty/sarwar/cvsroot/project1/input.c,v <- input.c
new revision: 1.2; previous revision: 1.1
done
$
```

Since CVS allows multiple users to check out the same source files concurrently, conflicts may arise when you commit changes to a file that is being updated by other developers. CVS informs you of such circumstances so you can resolve the conflict. Suppose that you and some other member of your team have concurrently checked out the above source tree. If you try to install changes to a source file after the other member has already done so, CVS will inform you accordingly. The following session illustrates this point. The error message informs you that the changes that you are trying to install were made to an older version of the input.c file.

```
$ cvs commit -m "Testing concurrent checkout" input.c
cvs commit: Up-to-date check failed for 'input.c'
cvs [commit aborted]: correct above errors first!
$
```

You can solve this problem by updating your working copy of the input.c file with the newer version in the repository, making changes to the updated version, and then committing these changes. The **CVS** command **update** can be used to deal with concurrent checkouts and to merge a new source file in the CVS repository with an altered source file that you checked out prior to the newly installed changes to this source. If you try to update a source that you have not checked out, this command works like the **checkout** command.

In the following session, we use the **update** command to bring up to date the input.c file. The **update** command could not merge the repository version of input.c (version 1.2) with your version (updated copy of version 1.1) because your changes were made to the same sections of the file that a team member had changed and committed to the repository. In this case, CVS checks out a version of input.c that includes everything it had before (in version 1.1) as well as changes made to it by you and your team member who last installed changes. Your current version of the input.c file (that you could not commit) is saved in the .#input.c.1.1.1.1 file in your current directory, as shown by the **ls -a** command in the following session.

```
$ cvs update input.c
RCS file: /home/faculty/sarwar/cvsroot/project1/input.c,v
retrieving revision 1.1.1.1
retrieving revision 1.2
Merging differences between 1.1.1.1 and 1.2 into input.c
rcsmerge: warning: conflicts during merge
cvs update: conflicts found in input.c
C input.c
$ ls -a
.   ..   compute.c input.c main.c makefile
.#input.c.1.1.1.1 CVS compute.h input.h main.h
$
```

The **more** command below shows the version of input.c that has been checked out to you. The section of source between <<<<<<< and ======= is what was in your working input.c file, and the section of source between ======= and >>>>>>> is what was in the source repository. CVS informs you of the situation but leaves the conflict resolution up to you. You can edit this file to make appropriate changes and commit the final version of the file. In this case, we keep both changes and install them, as shown below. Note that a new version (1.3) of the input.c file is created in the source repository.

```
$ more input.c
...

<<<<<<< input.c
#include <string.h>
=======
#include <ctype.h>

>>>> 1.2
#include "input.h"
double input(char *s)
{
...
$ vi input.c
...

#include <string.h>
#include <ctype.h>

...
$ cvs commit -m "Final version" input.c
Checking in input.c;
/home/faculty/sarwar/cvsroot/project1/input.c,v <- input.c
new revision: 1.3; previous revision: 1.2
done
$
```

In the following In-Chapter Exercise you will edit one of the source files (input.c, for example) and learn how to commit changes to the source file in the repository. You will also learn how to commit changes to a file if it has been checked out concurrently.

IN-CHAPTER EXERCISE

14.13 Repeat the above session on your system using versions of input.c. This would allow you to learn how to commit changes to a file in the source repository, how to checkout a source file concurrently, and how to commit changes to a source file that has been checked out simultaneously.

14.3.7 Adding New Files and Directories to the Repository

You can use the **cvs add** command to add new files to a module in the source repository. Once the new files are in your CVS working directory, running the **cvs add** command marks them for inclusion in the source repository. You need to run the **cvs commit** command in order to make these files available to other users. In the following session, we add the misc.c file to the project1 module in the source repository and make it available to other users. As expected, the file is assigned version number 1.1.

```
$ cvs add misc.c
cvs add: scheduling file 'misc.c' for addition
cvs add: use 'cvs commit' to add this file permanently
$ cvs commit -m "A new file for the project1 module" misc.c
RCS file: /home/faculty/sarwar/cvsroot/project1/misc.c,v
done
Checking in misc.c;
/home/faculty/sarwar/cvsroot/project1/misc.c,v ← misc.c
initial revision: 1.1
done
$
```

You can add a directory to the source repository in a similar way. But once a directory has been added to the repository with the **cvs add** command, you don't need to commit it because directories are added in real time. In the following session, we add a directory called newproject to the repository.

```
$ mkdir newproject
$ cvs add newproject
Directory /home/faculty/sarwar/cvsroot/newproject added to the repository
$
```

The following In-Chapter Exercise has been designed to allow you to create a source repository in your CVS source repository.

IN-CHAPTER EXERCISE

14.14 Use the mkdir and **cvs add** commands to create a source repository called project2 in your CVS source repository. Write down the commands that you used to perform this task.

14.3.8 Removing Files and Directories from the Source Repository

You can use the **cvs remove** command to remove a file from a module in the source repository. Before marking the file for removal, you must remove it from your working directory with the **rm** command and then run the **cvs remove** command. Finally, you need to run the **cvs commit** command to remove the file from the source repository. In the following session, we remove the misc.c file from the project1 module in the source repository.

```
$ rm misc.c
$ cvs remove misc.c
cvs remove: scheduling 'misc.c' for removal
cvs remove: use 'cvs commit' to remove this file permanently
$ cvs commit -m "Testing file removal" misc.c
Removing misc.c;
/home/faculty/sarwar/cvsroot/project1/misc.c,v ← misc.c
new revision: delete; previous revision: 1.1
done
$
```

You can use the **–R** option with the **cvs** remove command to process directories recursively.

You can remove a directory from the source repository in real time, without needing a **commit** command. The following session shows how the newproject directory can be removed.

```
$ cvs remove newproject
$ cvs -rf newproject
$
```

In the following In-Chapter Exercise you will practice removing files and directories from the CVS source repository.

IN-CHAPTER EXERCISE

14.15 Use the command sequences in the above sessions to remove the input.c file from the project1 and project2 directories in the source repository. Write down the command sequences that you used for this purpose.

14.3.9 FREEZING AND EXTRACTING A VERSION

You can use the **cvs rtag** (or **cvs tag**) command to tag or label the files in a module in the source repository. This allows you to freeze a release of the product while allowing continued development for the next release. You would usually use this command if you're about to make significant changes to a module (or files), if you have already done so, or if you are ready to release the module in its present state. You can recreate a tagged release even if the product has been changed since the tagged version.

Syntax: **cvs rtag [options] label module-list**

Purpose: This command adds a symbolic 'label' to the modules in 'module-list'

Commonly Used Options / Features:

-D	Use existing date as the tag
-F	Move the tag if it already exists
-R	Process directories recursively
-b	Make the tag a "branch" tag to allow concurrent development
-d	Delete the given tag
-r ver	Assign 'ver' as the tag

In the following session, we freeze project1 with a label Release_0_1.

```
$ cvs rtag Release_0_1 project1
cvs rtag: Tagging project1
$
```

You can extract a frozen version of a module, by using its label, with the **cvs export** command. Here is a brief description of the **cvs export** command.

Syntax: **cvs export [options] module**

Purpose: This command exports sources in 'module' with a particular tag

Commonly Used Options / Features:

-D date	Export version of the 'date' date
-d dir	Export into the 'dir' directory instead of into the module name
-r ver	Export sources with 'rev' as tag

In the following session, we extract the Release_0_1 release of project1.

```
$ cvs export -r Release_0_1 project1
cvs export: Updating project1
U project1/compute.c
...
$
```

You can use the **–d** option to check out the unfrozen release in a directory with a name other than the name of the module being unfrozen. The **cvs export -r Release_0_1 -d prj1R1 project1** command extracts the Release_0_1 release of the project1 module and puts the files in the prj1R1 directory instead of the project1 directory.

In the following In-Chapter Exercise you will practice removing files and directories from the CVS source repository.

IN-CHAPTER EXERCISE

14.16   Use the command sequences in the above sessions to freeze a version of a project, Release_1_2, for project2. Then use the **cvs export** command to extract release Release_1_2 from the project2 repository. Write down the commands that you used for this purpose.

14.3.10 DISPLAYING DIFFERENCES

You can use the **cvs diff** command to display the differences between files in the sandbox and in the source repository, or between two versions of a file in the repository. You can use this command with **more** and with any of the options for the **rcsdiff** commands. A popular option is **–c**, for displaying the "context" difference. For example, if you have checked out the input.c file, the **cvs diff –c** displays the differences between the input.c file in the sandbox and its version in the source repository.

14.3.11 DISPLAYING THE LOG HISTORY

You can use the **cvs log** command to display the complete history of a file, including any comments added by the developers while committing changes to the file. The **cvs log input.c** commands displays the log for the input.c file. You can display the log of all the files in a module (directory), get into the module with the **cd** command, and run the **cvs log | more** command.

14.3.12 CVS SPECIAL CHARACTER SEQUENCES

Like in RCS, with CVS you can place any of several special character sequences in the comment header of a source file. These character sequences are processed specially by CVS and are expanded to include information from the CVS log for the file. The general format for these special sequences is

$string$. This sequence results in the expansion of **string** by CVS. This expansion takes place when you check a file into the CVS directory and is in place the next time you check out the file. Table 14.2 shows some of these sequences and their expanded values.

The comment header

```
/*
 * Author:      $Author$
 * Date:        $Date$
 * Module:      $RCSfile$
 * Revision:    $Revision$
 * Status:      $Id$
 */
```

in the **input.c** file expands to

```
/*
 * Author:      $Author: sarwar $
 * Date:        $Date: 2002/04/08 10:11:41 $
 * Module:      $RCSfile: input.c,v $
 * Revision:    $Revision: 2.2.1 $
 * Status:      $Id: input.c,v 2.2.1 2002/04/08 10:11:41 sarwar Exp $
 */
```

when the file is checked in.

Table 14.2	CVS Special Character Sequences and Their Expanded Values
Character Sequence	**Replaced with**
$Author$	Author's login name
$Date$	Current date and time
$Header$	Full pathname of the RCS file in the repository, revision number, date and time of last change, author, and state.
Id	Like $Header$ but without the full pathname of the RCS file
Log	CVS log message
$Name$	Name of the label (tag) if one exists, or blank if the file doesn't have a label
$RCSfile$	Name of the RCS file in the source repository
$Revision$	The highest revision number
$Source$	Full pathname of the RCS ",v" file in the source repository

The most commonly used sequence is `$Id$`, which is expanded by CVS to include the RCS file name (not its full pathname), revision number, date, time, login name of the user making changes, and the RCS state of the file. If you want to put this information in an executable file, you need to include the following C/C++ statement in the source file.

```
static char rcsid[ ] = "$Id$";
```

This statement gets compiled into your C/C++ binary program. The statement can be local or global.

You can use the **ident** utility to display the expanded CVS special character sequences in a file. It works on both source and binary files. The following **ident** command displays the expanded forms of the special strings in the input.c file.

```
$ ident input.c
input.c:
     $Author: sarwar $
     $Date: 2002/04/08 10:11:41 $
     $RCSfile: input.c,v $
     $Revision: 2.2.1 $
     $Id: input.c,v 2.2 2002/04/08 10:11:41 sarwar Exp $

$
```

In the following In-Chapter Exercise you will use some of the special character sequences to appreciate their meaning.

IN-CHAPTER EXERCISE

14.17 Use the some of the special character sequences in one of your source files in the sandbox and display what they expand to with the **ident** command as shown in the above session.

14.3.13 AFTER-WORK CLEANUP

Once you have installed changes to a module, you should release the working directory by using the **release** command. This command removes all the files in your working directory after checking that all your modifications have been committed. If any file was modified but not committed, CVS will inform you accordingly. A file modified but not committed has a marker M in front of it and a file unknown to CVS has a ? character in front of it. A file tagged with a ? character is usually a binary file (executable or core file) that you may have generated as you tested your modifications. The following session shows an example of this command where we release the sandbox for project1.

```
$ cd ..
$ ls
```

```
project1
$ cvs release project1
You have [0] altered files in this repository.
Are you sure you want to release directory 'project1': y
$
```

14.3.14 REMOTE REPOSITORIES AND ACCESSING THEM THROUGH A CLIENT

CVS allows you to maintain your sandbox and source repositories on different machines. Using CVS in this style is known as the client/server operation. The machine that mounts your sandbox is known as the client and the machine that mounts your source repository is known as the server. You need to use the following format for accessing a source repository maintained on a remote host.

```
:method:[[user-name][:password]@Hostname[:[port]]/source-repository
```

Here 'source-repository' is the absolute pathname of the source repository. If 'method' is not specified, and the repository name contains ':' then, depending on your platform, the default method is 'ext' or 'server'. If your user name is the same on both hosts, then you can omit 'user-name'. Suppose that your local machine is willamette.pdx.com and your user name on it is john. You want to access a module project1 in the source repository /home/share/projects on a remote host columbia.pdx.com. If your user name on the remote machine is also john, then you need to use the following command to check out the project1 module.

```
$ cvs -d columbia.pdx.com:/home/share/projects checkout projects1
...
$
```

If your user name on the remote host is dave (not john), then you need to use the following command to check out project1.

```
$ cvs -d dave@columbia.pdx.com:/home/share/projects checkout projects1
...
$
```

CVS uses the `rsh` command to perform remote operations, which means that your local host must be a trusted host and/or you must be a trusted user on the remote host. Thus the remote host's /etc/hosts.equiv file must have an entry like the following for you (user name john) to be able to access the remote source repository.

```
willamette.pdx.com john
```

If such an entry does not exit in the /etc/hosts.equiv file on the remote host then the remote user's (dave's in our case) ~/.rhosts file must contain this entry.

14.3.15 USING CVS UNDER emacs

You can use the version control (**vc**) mode of the **emacs** editor to invoke **cvs** commands. As stated earlier, a **vc mode** command is **C-x v** followed by a single letter. Before starting **emacs**, you must set the *CVSROOT* environment variable correctly. The **C-x v v** command does the next right thing in most cases. For example, if a file is read-only, **C-x v v** will check it out for editing. If the file is an editable version, **C-x v v** will commit a modified file that has already been registered for version control. The **C-x v u** command unchecks out the current file and reverts to the previous version. The **C-x v l** command shows the CVS history (version log) of the file. The **C-x v ~** command prompts you for a revision number and retrieves the given version of the file in another window. The **C-x v s** command prompts you for a label name and gives that label to the version tree.

14.3.16 IMPORTANT ASPECTS OF CVS

The following are some important aspects of CVS that you should be aware of.

■ CVS does not have support for version control of directories.

■ Although it does have support for binary files, CVS is used mostly with text files.

■ CVS is not a "bug-tracking" or build system.

■ If you are working with remote repositories with a client, it is important to know that the **rsh** and **pserver** transmit data in plain text.

■ A local repository must have write permissions for developers, which leaves it open to hacking by a developer.

14.3.17 OBTAINING AND INSTALLING CVS

Installing CVS on your system is simple but you must log on as root. Before installing CVS on your system, you should first determine if it is already installed. You can do so by running any of the following commands: **cvs -v**, **whereis cvs**, or **find / -name cvs -print 2> /dev/null**. If CVS is not installed on your system then you need to perform the following steps for its installation.

1. Obtain a **tar** archive of the CVS version that you want to install from the primary CVS site ftp.cvshome.org or one of its mirror sites.

2. Unpack the **tar** archive in the directory where you want to install CVS by running the **tar** command.

3. Change directory to the cvs-version directory (where 'version' is the CVS version you are installing such as 1.11) and generate the CVS binary by running the **./configure** and **make** commands.

4. Install CVS by running the **make install** command.

In the following session, we show the installation of CVS version 1.11 in the /usr/local directory; the CVS source distribution is stored in the /usr/local/src/cvs-1.11 directory. The compressed (with **gzip**) **tar** archive of cvs-1.11 is stored at ftp.cvshome.org/pub/cvs-1.11/cvs-1.11.tar.gz. In the following session, we use the # prompt to indicate that you are logged on as root.

```
# cd /usr/local/src
# ftp ftp.cvshome.org
[ ... ]
ftp> cd pub/cvs-1.11
[ ... ]
ftp> bin
200 Type set to I.
ftp> get cvs-1.11.tar.gz
[ ... ]
ftp> quit
# tar xvzf cvs-1.11.tar.gz
[ ... ]
# cd cvs-1.11
# ./configure —prefix /usr/local
# make
[ ... ]
# make install
[ ... ]
#
```

You can install a more recent version of CVS if one is available. The latest version of CVS is available at **ftp.cvshome.org/pub/LATEST/**.

Once you have installed CVS, you will need to take additional steps to run it in the server mode. The additional steps may require obtaining and installing **rsh** or **ssh** (see www.ssh.com). After this has been done, you need to perform the following steps:

1. Add the following lines in the /etc/services file.

   ```
   cvspserver          2401/tcp
   cvspserver          2401/udp
   ```

2. Add the first line below in the /etc/inetd.conf file if you don't use tcpwrappers or the second line if you do use tcpwrappers.

   ```
   cvspserver stream tcp nowait root /usr/sbin/tcpd /usr/bin/cvs —allow-root=/usr/bin/cvsroot pserver
   ```

   ```
   cvspserver stream tcp nowait root /usr/bin/cvs cvs —allow-root=/usr/bin/cvsroot pserver
   ```

3. Restart the super-server daemon **inetd**.

14.4 WEB RESOURCES

Table 14.13 lists useful Web sites for RCS and CVS.

Table 14.3	Web Resources for RCS and CVS	
Reference	URL	Description
1	www.gnu.org/software/rcs/rcs.html	GNU page for RCS
2	www.cvshome.org	CVS information page: updates, latest versions, etc.
3	www.gnu.org/software/cvs	GNU page for CVS
4	www.loria.fr/~molli/cvs-index.html	For CVS updates and additional information
5	www.cs.utah.edu/dept/old/texinfo/cvs/FAQ.txt	Frequently asked questions about CVS
6	www.opensource.apple.com/tools/cvs/cederqvist/	Version management by Per Cederqvist et al. —an ultimate CVS manual
7	www.wincvs.org	A GUI front end for CVS
8	cvsbook.red-bean.com/	A free book on CVS
9	www.tldp.org/HOWTO/CVS-RCS-HOWTO-15.html	Configuration management tools, including RCS and CVS

14.5 SUMMARY

As you develop the source code for a software, you may need to undo changes made to it and go back to an earlier version of the software. Also, if you detect a bug in your software after it has been in use for a long time, you will want to be able to retrieve earlier versions of the software to determine the change that induced the bug. Moreover, if a team of programmers is working on a piece of software, each team member should be able to check out and check in editable (modifiable) versions of the software. LINUX and UNIX have has tools that support such features.

Version/revision control is the task of managing revisions to a software product. Typical software for revision control allows you to lock out other users from changing a file while one user is altering it (provide a check-out and check-in system of file access), create different versions of a file, help identify revisions to a file, store and retrieve different versions of a file, merge multiple versions of the same file to create a new "final" file, maintain a history of all versions of every file related to a product, access earlier versions of all the files of a product, and limit access to a file to a subset of users on the system.

Several LINUX/UNIX tools allow you to control versions of your files and almost all of them use the Revision Control System (RCS) as their engine. In this chapter we discussed many features of the Revision Control System and Concurrent Version System (CVS) with examples.

14.6 QUESTIONS AND PROBLEMS

1. What is revision control? What are the names of the two of the most popular LINUX/UNIX tools that you can use for revision control of your software? Give the full names and the acronyms.

2. What tasks does a revision control software allow you to perform?

3. What are the main differences between RCS and CVS?

4. Can you remove versions 1.1 and 1.2 from the version tree shown in Figure 14.1? Why or why not?

5. Create version 2.1 of the s.input.c file after creating versions 1.1, 1.2, 1.3, and 1.2.1.1. What command did you use? Show the command with its output.

6. What is a source repository? Write down the sequence of commands needed to import the files to be versioned (assume some file names). Place these files in the module myproject. Assume that the source repository is ~/cvsroot.

7. Suppose that the input.c file has versions 1.1 through 1.6 and that you need to delete version 1.3. How can you accomplish this task if the file is managed under

   `RCS (RCS/input.c,v)`

   `$CVSROOT/project1/input.c,v`

8. Under CVS and RCS, you have checked out the latest version of the input.c file. What would happen if you tried to check out the same file again? Why?

9. Give the command line that restricts access of the RCS log file RCS/input.c,v so that only users **dale** and **kent** can edit any version of this file. What is the command line for taking editing rights away from users **ahmed** and **tomn**?

10. Suppose that you have a CVS module $CVSROOT/EMBAproject. Write down the command(s) needed to display the log of all the files in this module.

11. What are remote repositories in CVS? How does the client/server model work under CVS? Explain your answer with an example.

12. What are some of the security risks with using CVS?

13. Write down the sequence of steps needed to install CVS on your system. What is the most recent version of CVS available for installation? How did you obtain your answer?

14. Write down the sequence of steps (with LINUX/UNIX commands) needed to install the CVS server for access via a client.

15. If you own a LINUX/UNIX machine or have administrative access to one, use the steps outlined in section 14.3.17 to install CVS on your system.

Appendix A:
Editing Text Files with vi and pico

THE VI OR VIM EDITOR

Vi is a popular UNIX text editor. The LINUX version of vi is vim. Although there are differences between **vi** and **vim**, we use these terms interchangably. You can use the **vi** (or **vim**) command to invoke the vim editor. In the following session, we use the **vi** command to edit a file called vi_demo. Figure A.1 shows the initial vi screen for the new file vi_demo. As the message at the bottom left of the screen indicates, vi_demo is a brand-new file. If vi_demo already exists, it is pulled into the vi screen, otherwise a new file called vi_demo is created.

$ vi vi_demo

While you use a text editor, the contents of your file and any changes made to it are stored in an area in the memory called the **editor buffer.** In order to commit changes to the file, you must explicitly save the editor buffer in the disk file.

```
~
~
~
~
~
~                      VIM — Vi IMproved
~
~                        version 5.8.7
~                    by Bram Moolenaar et al.
~
~                 Vim is freely distributable
~        type    :help uganda<Enter>       if you like Vim
~
~        type    :q<Enter>                  to exit
~        type    :help<Enter> or <F1>       for on-line help
~        type    :help version5<Enter>      for version info
~
~
~
~
~
"vi_demo" [New File]
```

Figure A.1 The initial vi screen for the new file `vi_demo`

The vi editor operates in two modes: **command mode** and **insert mode.** In the command mode, you can use certain key presses and commands to instruct the editor to take certain action such as deleting text, moving text, copying text, saving changes made to the text, entering the insert mode, and quitting. In the insert mode, you can insert text into the editor buffer for the file being edited. Figure A.2 shows how you can enter and exit the insert mode, execute commands in the command mode, save changes made to a document, and exit the editor. You exit the insert mode by pressing <Esc>.

Vi has a rich and powerful set of features for text editing. Many of these features are available in the command mode. Here, we discuss only a small subset of these features, sufficient for creating and editing text files with ease. In the descriptions of commands, < and > are used to enclose key presses and are not actually typed as part of the command.

COMMITTING CHANGES AND QUITTING VI

You can commit changes made to the file being edited with the `:w` command (*w* stands for write). If you do not execute this command, the changes are made only to the editor buffer and the disk copy of the file remains unchanged. After making the final changes, you can use the `:wq` command to write and quit. This command commits changes and quits `vi`. If the file is read-only, then use the `:wq!` command. We highly recommend that you use `:w` often during your editing session, otherwise you may lose changes if the system crashes or you are logged out for some reason. For many exceptions (e.g., your modem line hanging up when you are logged on a remote machine via modem), `vi` saves its editor buffer and sends you an e-mail message informing you how to recover it.

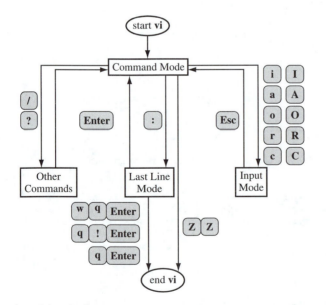

Figure A.2 Operating modes of the **vi** editor

Browsing the File

You can browse the file being edited in many ways in the command mode. At a micro level, you can use the `<j>` (next line), `<k>` (previous line), `<h>` (previous column), and `<l>` (next column) key presses to move the cursor by one column or line. At a macro level, you can use the `<Ctrl-F>` and `<Ctrl-B>` key presses to display the next or previous screen/page, respectively. You can display the next half screen with `<Ctrl-D>`.

Deleting Text

You can delete text from the file being edited in many ways. To delete a character, move the cursor under the letter to be deleted and hit `<x>`. To delete a word, move the cursor under the first letter of the word and hit `<d><w>` (i.e., hit `<d>`, then hit `<w>`). To delete a line, move the cursor to anywhere on the line and hit `<d><d>`. To delete a range of line, specify the range and hit `<d><d>`, as in `23,46<d><d>` for deleting line 23 through 46. To delete the rest of the line, hit `<D>`.

Copying and Cutting and Pasting Text

You can cut N lines of text starting with the current line by pressing `<N><d><d>`. For example, you can delete 18 lines starting with the current line by pressing `<1><8><d><d>`. You can paste these lines somewhere else in your document by moving the cursor to the desired line and pressing `<p>` to paste the deleted lines after the current line. For pasting the lines before the current line, press `<P>`. Commit changes made in the file with the `:w` command.

If you want to copy N lines of text starting with the current line, press `<N><y><y>` (for yanking N lines) as in `<1><8><y><y>`. You can paste the yanked lines anywhere in your document with the `<p>` (or `<P>`) command. Again, commit changes made in the file with the `:w` command.

String Search

You can forward search the file being edited for a string with the `/string-to-be-searched` command. For example, to forward search your file for the string Linus, type `/Linus` and hit `<Enter>`. The search stops at the first line containing the string with the cursor pointing at the beginning of the string. You can continue the search by pressing / and hitting `<Enter>`. For backward search, use `?` instead of `/`. If the string is not found, an error is reported at the bottom left of the screen.

Determining File Size

In vi, `$` stands for the last line. You can determine the line count in a file by typing `:$=` and hitting `<Enter>`.

Determining the Current Line Number

In vi, dot (`.`) stands for the current line. You can determine the line number of the current line (i.e., where the cursor is currently located) by typing `:.=` and hitting `<Enter>`.

MOVING THE CURSOR TO A LINE

You can move the cursor to a line by typing : line-number and hitting <Enter>. For example, :25 moves the cursor to line 25 and :$ moves the cursor to the last line of the file being edited.

DISPLAYING LINES

You can display a range of lines in the file being edited by typing :[m,n] and hitting <Enter>, where m is the starting line number and n is the ending line number. For example, :25,45 displays lines 25 through 45, :45,$ displays all the lines in the file starting with line 45, and :.,$ displays all the lines in the file starting with the current line.

REPLACING A STRING

You can replace a string with another string by using the following command syntax.

:[line-range]s/existing-string/new-string/gp

Without g, only the first occurrence of 'existing-string' in a line is replaced with 'new-string.' Without 'line-range,' the current line is used. With g (for global), all occurrences of 'existing-string' in a line (in the given line range) are replaced with 'new-string.' With p, the lines where replacement occurred are also displayed. For example, the :1,$s/Windows/LINUX/g command replaces every occurrence of the string Windows with LINUX in the whole file.

READING A FILE

You can read a file and place its contents at the current cursor position in the editor buffer with the :r file-name command. For example, if your cursor is at line 10, the :r data1 command will put text in the data1 file after line 10 in the editor buffer.

EXECUTING A SHELL COMMAND

You can run any shell command in the command mode by preceding the command with !. For example, in order to run the ls command, type !ls and hit <Enter>. After executing the command and displaying its output, vi goes back to the command mode.

REDRAWING THE SCREEN/WINDOW

You can redraw your vi screen (or window) with <Ctrl-R>. This removes any garbage from your screen and displays the vi window before it was garbled, perhaps due to a talk (chat) request, a message from the system administrator, or the output of a shell command.

SETTING UP THE vi ENVIRONMENT

You can customize the behavior of vi by setting any of the several environment options. These options include specifying automatic wrapping of the cursor to the next line, displaying the mode vi is currently in, and displaying line numbers. You can set these variables for the current vi session with the :set command in the command mode, as in :set wm=5 to set the wrap margin to five characters from the end of the line. The default line length is 25 characters. In order to permanently set the various options, place these settings in the ~/.exrc file with one or more set commands. For example, the

~/.exrc file shown below sets the wrap margin to five characters from the end of the line (**wm=5**), informs vi to show mode at the bottom right of the screen (**showmode**), display line numbers (**nu**), and ignore case (**ic**) while searching with the **/** or **?** commands.

```
$ cat ~/.exrc
set wm=5 showmode nu ic
$
```

THE PICO EDITOR

If you conclude after using the **vi** editor that it is not for you, you can use a non-native LINUX/UNIX text editor called pico. Pico is a simple window-based text editing tool. It is also used by a non-native LINUX/UNIX e-mail software, called pine. You can invoke pico with the **pico** command as shown below. Figure A.3 shows the pico interface when you edit a brand-new file, pico_demo in our case. If pico_demo is an existing file, it is pulled into the pico window, otherwise a new file called pico_demo is created.

```
$ pico pico_demo
```

A bar at the top of the window contains the version number of pico and the name of the file being edited. The bottom of the window contains the various editing commands and prompts when certain commands are executed. Editing with pico is quite simple because, unlike with vi, there aren't multiple modes of operation and most of the commands are listed at the bottom of the window. We discuss a few editing features supported by pico.

INSERTING TEXT

In order to insert text in the editor buffer of the file being edited, move the cursor to the desired cursor position with the arrow keys up ($\uparrow$), down ($\downarrow$), left ($\leftarrow$), and right ($\rightarrow$), and type the text to be entered. The text automatically wraps around.

```
 UW PICO (tm) 4.0              File: pico_demo




















 ^G Get Help    ^O WriteOut   ^R Read File  ^Y Prev Pg   ^K Cut Text    ^C Cur Pos
 ^X Exit        ^J Justify     ^W Where is   ^V Next Pg   ^U UnCut Text  ^T To Spell
```

Figure A.3 The pico interface for the new file `pico_demo`

Deleting Text

You can delete a character by placing the cursor after the character and pressing `<Backspace>`. For deleting multiple characters, press `<Backspace>` multiple times. To delete a line, move the cursor to the line and press `<Ctrl-K>`.

Committing Changes

You can commit changes made to the editor buffer with the `<Ctrl-O>` command. This command prompts you for the file name at the bottom left of a new window, as shown below. You can change the name of the file if you like and press `<Enter>` to commit changes to the file. You can use the `<Ctrl-C>` command to cancel this commit or hit `<Enter>` to commit changes. The screen shot in Figure A.4 demonstrates this point. After committing the changes, pico redisplays the main window.

Browsing the File

You can browse the file being edited with the arrow keys. You can move to (and display) the next page with `<Ctrl-V>` and the previous page with `<Ctrl-Y>`.

Cutting and Pasting

You can cut a block of text from the file being edited by moving the cursor to the desired starting position, pressing `<Ctrl-Shift-6>`, moving the cursor to one character beyond the desired ending position, and pressing `<Ctrl-K>`. To paste, move the cursor to the position where the text is to be pasted and press `<Ctrl-U>`.

Quitting pico

You can quit your pico session with the `<Ctrl-X>` command. If you did not commit any changes made to the file before quitting, pico will prompt you to do so.

```
UW PICO(tm) 4.0                   File: pico_demo

Inserting Text  In order to insert text in the editor buffer of the file
being edited, move the cursor to the desired cursor position with the
arrow keys and type the text to be entered. The text automatically wraps
around.

Committing Changes  You can commit changes made to the editor buffer with
the <Ctrl-O> command. This command prompts you for the file name at the
bottom left of the screen, as shown below. You can change the name of the
file if you like and hit <Enter> to commit changes to the file. After committing
the changes, pico redisplays the main window. You can use the <Ctrl-C>
command to cancel this commit or hit <Enter> to commit changes.
The following screen shot demonstrates this point.

File Name to write : pico_demo
^G Get Help   ^T To Files
^C Cancel     TAB Complete
```

Figure A.4 pico screen shot when the `<Ctrl-O>` command is executed for committing changes to the pico_demo file

Appendix B: Electronic Mail

LINUX and UNIX have several native and non-native tools for e-mailing, including mail and pine. We discuss briefly mail and pine here as they are the most commonly used. Whereas mail, perhaps the oldest UNIX e-mailing tool, is used mostly in shell scripts today, pine is a popular general e-mailing tool used by the LINUX community. The scope of our discussion here is limited to the basic use of the mail and pine commands for sending and receiving e-messages and e-files.

THE MAIL COMMAND

SENDING MAIL

You can send an e-mail message with the **mail** command by passing the e-mail addresses of the recipients as command-line arguments. In the following session, we use this command to send e-mail to johndoe@cold-mail.com. The **mail e-mailaddress** command prompts you for the subject of the mail message. After you type the subject and hit **<Enter>**, you are ready to type the message body. When you are done typing the message, type dot (**.**) and hit **<Enter>** on a new line to inform mail that it is the message body. You are prompted with **Cc:** so you could copy this message to someone else. To copy the message to someone, type his or her e-mail address and hit **<Enter>**. In our case, we send a copy of the message to sarwar@teachers.org. You can enter an address list by separating the addresses with commas. If you don't want to copy your message to anyone, just hit **<Enter>**.

```
$ mail johndoe@cold-mail.com
Subject: Greetings!
This is a test e-mail message composed and sent using the LINUX
mail utility.

Best,
Mansoor
.
Cc: sarwar@teachers.org
$
```

SENDING A FILE

If you have a prepared message in a text file, you can send it by using the < operator (see Chapter 3 for I/O redirection). The contents of the file become the message body. Sending non-text files may cause problems. In order to send non-text files in the message body, you should first uuencode them (with the LINUX/UNIX **uuencode** command). You can specify the subject header in the command line by using the **–s** option, as shown below. In the following session, we send the message in the ~/personal/johndoe1 file to johndoe@cold-mail.com with the subject header "Greetings from Lahore."

```
$ mail —s"Greetings from Lahore" johndoe@cold-mail.com < ~/personal/johndoe1
$
```

SENDING MAIL TO MULTIPLE USERS

You can use multiple send-to addresses in the command line by separating them with commas as in `mail jain@cold-mail.com, john@hot-mail.org < message1`. You can also make mail groups by using the `alias` command and putting the addresses in the ~/.mailrc file. The following session shows a sample ~/.mailrc file with two mail goups, MyPals and MyGroup1.

```
$ cat ~/.mailrc
alias MyPals jim@yahoo-oohay.com, jhon@cold-mail.com, jenny
alias MyGroup davis, jane@cold-mail.com, johndoe@mailspot.org
$
```

THE PINE COMMAND

STARTING PINE

Pine has a nice, intuitive interface that allows you to use it without much reading. You can invoke the pine software with the pine command, which puts you in the main window for pine, as shown in Figure B.1. You can move around this and any other pine window with the arrow keys and use single-character commands to perform various tasks. For example, pressing <i> takes you to the window that allows you to read, respond to, or forward your e-mail messages. Pressing <c> allows you to compose an e-mail message.

COMPOSING A MESSAGE

You can compose a message in pine by pressing <c> in the basic interface window. This puts you in a window as shown in Figure B.2. You can attach a file (of any type—text, picture, audio, etc.) by typing its pathname after `Attchmnt:`. In our case, we typed ~/papers/OOPSLA02 and it expanded to the absolute pathname of the file as shown in the window. You can move around in the window with arrow keys and make corrections just like you would in the pico editor. You can send the e-mail with <Ctrl-X>. This command will raise a prompt at the bottom left of the window asking whether you want to send the e-mail. Press <y> to send and <n> to return to the previous window. If you want to cancel the composing session, press <Ctrl-C> and you will be prompted for confirmation. If you press <y>, you will be returned to the previous window (the main window in our case).

SENDING A BLIND COPY OF YOUR E-MAIL

You can send a blind copy of your e-mail to someone by pressing <r> (to get the rich header) while you are in the header part of the screen and typing the e-mail address of the recipient at the `Bcc:` prompt in the window.

```
              MAIN MENU                    Folder: INBOX  2 Messages


      ?     HELP                  — Get help using Pine
      C     COMPOSE MESSAGE       — Compose and send a message
      I     MESSAGE INDEX         — View messages in current folder
      L     FOLDER LIST           — Select a folder to view
      A     ADDRESS BOOK          — Update address book
      S     SETUP                 — Configure Pine Options
      Q     QUIT                  — Leave the Pine program


   Copyright 1989—2001. PINE is a trademark of the University of Washington.



               [Folder "INBOX" opened with 2 messages]

O OTHER CMDS  > [ListFldrs]   N NextCmd          K KBLock
```

Figure B.1 The basic pine interface

READING, REPLYING, AND FORWARDING E-MAIL

You can press <i> to view your mailbox. This command takes you into a window that displays the headers for all your messages, as shown in Figure B.3. You can move around this window with the up and down arrow keys. The highlighted message is the current message.

```
To        : pohm@great-profs.org, jimdavis@great-advisors.org

Cc        : sarwar@teachers.org
Attchmnt: 1. home/faculty/msarwar/papers/OOPSLA02 (103.0 KB) ""
Subject : Greetings from Lahore
-----Message Text-----
Hello!

I hope that this message finds you in the best of health and spirits. I write
this to just say hello from the hot and dusty city of Lahore. I've attached the
final version of the paper draft for your review. Please get back to me ASAP.
Thanks!

Take care,
Mansoor



^G Get Help   ^X Send      ^R Read file   ^Y Prev Pg   ^K Cut Text    ^O Postpone
^C Cancel     ^J Justify   ^W Where is    ^V Next Pg   ^U UnCut Text  ^T To Spell
```

Figure B.2 Composing a message in pine

```
PINE 4.33   MESSAGE INDEX              Folder: INBOX        Message 2 of 2 NEW

+N  1 May  6 To: msarwar@reslab        (536) Test Message
+N  2 May  6 To: msarwar@reslab        (885) Greetings from Portland






                        [Export message cancelled]
? Help          < FldrList    P PrevMsg     - PrevPage    D Delete    R Reply
O OTHER CMDS    > [ViewMsg]   N NextMsg   Spc NextPage    U Undelete  F Forward
```

Figure B.3 Viewing mail in pine

You can view the current message by hitting **<Enter>**. Figure B.4 shows the screen that pine uses to display your messages. Note that the mail header informs you of the sender and the time of message arrival. You can display the next page of the message by pressing **<Spacebar>** and the previous page by hitting **<->**. You can forward a message by pressing **<f>**, reply by pressing **<r>**, and delete by pressing **<d>**. To read the previous message and next messages, press **<p>** and **<n>**, respectively.

```
PINE 4.33   MESSAGE INDEX              Folder: INBOX         Message 2
Date: Mon, 6 May 2002 14:23:18 +0500(PKT)
From: bobk@egr.up.edu
To: msarwar@reslab2.lums.edu.pk
Subject: Greetings from Portland

Hello Mansoor!

I hope that your stay in Pakistan is going well and that the kids have
adjusted in the new environment. How are they doing in School? We are
all doing well here but we do miss you. Yesterday was the Commencement
Day here and many of your students have graduated.

OK, I'll close now. Do write when you have a few moments.

Take care,
Bob



? Help          < MsgIndex    P PrevMsg     - PrevPage    D Delete    R Reply
O OTHER CMDS    > ViewAttch    N NextMsg   Spc NextPage    U Undelete  F Forward
```

Figure B.4 Viewing a message in pine

DEALING WITH ATTACHMENTS

If you want to read or save an attachment, press <v>. This will put you in a window that allows you to view or save attachments.

PRINTING AN E-MAIL MESSAGE

You can print an e-mail message while reading it by pressing <%>. You will be prompted to approve printing.

QUITTING PINE

You can press <q> to quit pine. Pine will prompt you to ask whether you really want to quit.

Glossary

ADT See Abstract Data Type.

Absolute Pathname A pathname that starts with the root directory. See Pathname.

Access Permissions See Access Rights.

Access Privileges See Access Rights.

Access Rights The type of operations that a user can perform on a file. In LINUX, access rights for a file can be read, write, and execute. The execute permission for a directory means permission to search the directory. The owner of a file dictates who can and who cannot access the file for various types of file operations.

Abstract Data Type A mathematical model for representing data along with operations on it. Some of the famous ADTs are stack, queue, linked list, hash table, and tree.

Activation Record See Stack Frame.

Archive A collection of files contained in a single file in a certain format.

Assembler A program that takes a program in assembly language as input and translates it into object code.

Assembly Language A low-level programming language.

Background Process When a process executes in such a way that it does not relinquish the control of the keyboard, it is said to execute in the background. The shell prompt is returned to the user before a background process starts execution, thus allowing the user to use the system (i.e., run commands) while the background processes execute.

Bi-state Devices The devices, such as transistors, that operate in "on" or "off" mode.

Bit Mask A sequence of bits (usually a byte or multiple bytes) used to retain values of certain bits in another byte (or multiple bytes), or to set them to 0s.

Black Box Testing During black box testing, the software is tested against its requirements. The test cases are, therefore, drawn up based on the requirements document.

Block-Oriented Devices A device, such as a disk drive, that performs I/O in terms of blocks of data (e.g., in 512-byte chunks). Also see Cluster.

Block Special Files The LINUX files that correspond to block-oriented devices. (See Block-Oriented Devices.) These files are located in the /dev directory.

Break Point A program statement where the execution of the program stops while using a symbolic debugger such as gdb.

Bss A UNIX term used for the uninitialized segment of a process.

Build The step used to create the executable file for software.

Build Directory The directory that contains the software source code and the associated makefile.

Build-and-Fix Model A software engineering life cycle that involves no planning or design (e.g., a software life cycle used by many students for coursework related programming exercises).

CVS See Concurrent Versions System.

Call Graph A graph (profile information) that shows the relationships between the caller and called functions and the frequency of execution of every function.

Character-Oriented Devices The devices, such as a keyboard, that perform I/O in terms of one byte at a time.

Character Special Files The LINUX files that correspond to character-oriented devices. These files are located in the /dev directory.

Class A feature in object-oriented languages that allows you to implement abstract data types. An instantiation of a class is called an object.

Code Coverage During white box testing, test inputs are chosen to invoke as many program statements as possible. The percentage of program statements that can be invoked during this phase of testing is called code coverage.

Code Generation Phase A software engineering life cycle phase during which the source and executable codes are created.

Code Inspection Describing the program source, line by line, to a software quality assurance group with the intention of identifying interface faults between functions and between modules.

Command Interpreter A computer program that starts execution when the computer system is turned on, or a user logs on. Its purpose is to capture user commands and execute them. In LINUX, the command is also known as a shell.

Command Mode A mode of operating for the vi editor under which it accepts editor commands.

Compiled Languages Programs written in a compiled language must be translated into machine code before they can be executed. See Machine Language.

Compiler A program that takes a program written in a high-level language and translates it into an assembly language program. Almost all C and C++ compilers also perform the tasks of pre-processing, assembly, and linking by default.

Concurrent Versions System A popular front end for RCS that has many features that RCS does not have, such as concurrent file checkouts without locking the file.

Conflict Resolution CVS allows multiple users to check out a file for editing and ensures that when users check in their versions, the final version will be the result of proper merging of the files checked out by the different users.

CPU Scheduling A mechanism that is used to multiplex a CPU in a computer system among several processes. This results in all processes making progress in an equal manner and increases utilization of hardware resources in the system.

Current Directory See Present Working Directory.

Current Job The job (process) that is presently being executed by the CPU.

Daemon A system process executing in the background to provide a service such as Web browsing. In a typical LINUX system, the `lpd` daemon provides the printing service, the `httpd` daemon provides the Web browsing service, and `fingerd` provides the finger service.

Data-Oriented Programming Paradigm A programming paradigm in which the focus is on objects that contain data and operations (i.e., methods) associated with data.

Debugger A software tool that allows you to debug software. See Debugging.

Debugging Identifying the causes of problems in a program as it runs.

Direct Metrics Metrics that can be measured directly such as lines of code (LOC), size of the executable in bytes, time taken for testing, number of defects, time taken by the programmer to complete a module or product, and running time for a program.

Directory A container that allows you to store any type of file, including directories, under them. Directories are also known as folders.

Directory Entry The file name and inode number in a directory in a LINUX/UNIX system. The inode number allows access to an operating system kernel data structure that contains the file's attributes, including its location on disk. See Inode.

Dot File See Hidden File.

Dotted Decimal Notation (DDN) The notation in which the 32-bit IPv4 addresses are, for example, 192.140.30.10.

Dynamic Analysis The analysis of a software as it executes. The analysis comprises debugging, tracing, and performance monitoring of the software, including testing it against product requirements.

Dynamic Linking With dynamic linking, every library call is replaced by a small piece of code, called a stub, whose execution causes the control to transfer to the code for the library call.

Most contemporary operating systems such as LINUX, UNIX, and Windows use dynamic linking.

Editor Buffer   While you edit a file, the part of the file that is displayed on the screen is stored in an area in the main memory called the editor buffer. The changes you make to the file are stored in this buffer and saved in the file (on disk) only when you use the editor command to do so.

End-of-File (EOF) Marker   A marker of one or more characters that every operating system puts at the end of a file.

Environment Variables   The shell variables (see Shell Variables) whose values control your environment while you use the system. For example, a variable dictates what shell process starts running and what directory you are put into when you log on.

FIFO   First-in-first-out order. See Named Pipe. File Descriptor A small, positive integer associated with every open file in LINUX. The kernel to access the inode for an open file and determine its attributes, such as the file's location on the disk that uses it.

File Descriptor Table   A per-process table maintained by the LINUX system that is indexed by using a file descriptor to access the file's inode.

File System Standard   Every LINUX system contains a set of specific files and directories organized according to a standard proposed in 1994, known as the File System Standard (FSSTND).

Filter   A LINUX term for a command that reads input from a standard input, processes it in some fashion, and sends it to standard output. Examples of LINUX filters are sort, pr, and tr.

First-Come, First-Serve (FCFS) Mechanism   A scheme that allows the print requests (or any other requests) to activate on the basis of their arrival time, serving the first request first.

First-Come, First-Serve (FCFS) Scheduling Algorithm   A method of prioritizing value. In this method, the process that enters the system first is assigned the highest priority and gets to use the CPU first.

Flat Profile   A profile of a program run that shows the amount of time spent in each function and the number of times each function is called. See Call Graph.

Foreground Process   A process that keeps control of the keyboard when it executes (i.e., the process whose standard input is attached to the keyboard). Only one foreground process can run on a system at a given time.

Fully Qualified Domain Name (FQDN)   The name of a host that includes the host name and the network domain on which it is connected. For example, www.up.edu is FQDN for the host whose name is www.

Function Call Graph   Shows how much time was spent in each function and its descendents.

Functional Programming Languages   In functional programming languages, computations are done by passing parameters to functions. Functional languages have no concept of variables, assignment statement, and iteration; making recursive calls to functions carries out repetitions. Some popular functional programming languages are LIST and ML.

Getty Process   At system boot up, LINUX starts running a process on each working terminal attached to the system. This process runs in the superuser mode and sets terminal attributes, such as baud rate, as specified in the /etc/ termcap file. Finally, it displays the login: prompt and waits for a user to log on. The process name is mingetty on LINUX and getty in UNIX.

Hidden Files   Files that are not listed when you display the contents of a directory by using the `ls` command. Since the names of hidden files start with the dot (.) character, they are also called dot files. Some commonly used hidden files are .bashrc (start-up file for Bash), .cshrc (start up file for C shell), and .profile (executed when you log on). All of these files reside in your home directory. Some applications and tools use hidden files as well.

History Expansion A feature in Bash and TC shells that allows you to take words from the history list (a list of previously executed commands under the shell) and insert them into the current command line. It makes it easier for you to repeat previously executed commands and or make changes in them and re-execute them.

Home Directory See Login Directory.

Huffman Coding A coding scheme that works based on the frequency of occurrence of every character in the input data and assigns the smallest code values to the most frequently occurring characters.

Hypertext Markup Language (HTML) A language that allows you to specify the appearance of your Web pages.

Imperative Programming Language Programs written in imperative programming languages use variables to store data, assignment statements to change data, and iterative repetition (although most imperative languages do allow recursive repetition). Some popular imperative programming languages are C, C++, Java, and FORTRAN.

Incremental Backup A backup of new files and files that were changed since the last backup.

Incremental Recompilation Recompiling only those source modules that have been updated since the last executable code was generated.

Indirect Metrics Software metrics that are derived, such as programmer productivity, module defect density, effort, and complexity of source code.

Information Hiding A key feature of object-oriented programming languages that allows you to hide the implementation details. The language feature that supports information hiding is class.

Init Process The first user process that is created when you boot up the LINUX system. It is the granddaddy of all user processes.

Inode An element of an array on disk (called an I-list) allocated to every unique file at the time it is created. It contains file attributes such as file size (in bytes). When a file is opened for an operation (e.g., read), the file's inode is copied from disk to a slot in a table kept in the main memory, called the inode table, so that the file's attributes can be assessed quickly.

Inode Number A 4-byte index value for the i-list used to access the inode for a file.

Inode Table A table (array) of inodes in the main memory that keeps inodes for all open files. The inode number for a file is used to index this array in order to access the attributes of an open file.

Insert Mode A mode in the `vi` and `vim` editors under which text can be inserted in the file being edited.

Instantiation Constructing an object of the class.

Interpreted Language A language whose programs are executed one statement or command at a time by a program called an interpreter. See Interpreted Program and Interpreter. **Interpreted Program** A program that is executed one statement or command at a time by an interpreter.

Interpreter See Language Interpreter.

IP Address A 32-bit positive integer (in IPv4) to uniquely identify a host on the Internet. In IPv6, it is a 128-bit positive integer.

Iteration A single execution of the piece of code in a loop. See Loop.

Java Bytecode A Java program translated into a form that can be understood by a Java Virtual Machine (the interpreter for the Java Bytecode). See Java Virtual Machine.

Java Virtual Machine The interpreter for Java Bytecode.

Job A job is a print request or a process running in the background.

Job ID A number assigned to a print job. On some systems, it is preceded by the name of the printer.

Job Number   An integer number assigned to a background process. When you run a process in background, the shell returns the job number in square brackets with the process ID (PID) next to it, as in [1] 39823 where 1 is job number and 39823 is PID.

Language Interpreter   A language interpreter is a program that executes statements (or commands) in a program, written in an interpreted language, one by one. An example of an interpreter is a LINUX shell that reads commands from a keyboard or a shell script and executes them one by one.

Language Libraries   A set of pre-written and pre-tested functions for various languages that can be used by application programmers instead of having to write their own.

Lazy Locking   In version control systems that allow multiple users to check out a file for editing, lazy locking does not lock the file until the file contents are changes by a user. The Concurrent Versions System (CVS) uses this file locking scheme.

Lempel-Ziv Coding   A coding technique used by the `gzip` and `gunzip` (and other related) commands for compressing and decompressing files.

Librarian   A nickname used for a LINUX utility that allows you to archive your object files into a single library file and manipulate the archive file in various ways.

Library   A set of pre-written and pre-tested functions in various languages (e.g., C, C++, Java) available to programmers for use with the software they are developing.

Linker   Also known as the linkage editor, the linker performs the task of linking (connecting) multiple object files to create an executable (binary) code.

Logic Programming Languages   Also known as rule-based programming languages, computations in logic programming languages are performed by specifying rules and letting the language implementation execute these rules in order to perform the desired computation. A famous logic programming language is Prolog.

Login Directory   The directory that you are placed in when you log on.

Login Process   A process created by the getty process (mingetty) that accepts your password, checks its validity, and allows you to log on by running your login shell process.

Login Shell   The shell process that starts execution when you log on.

Lpd   The line printer daemon. See Printer Daemon.

Machine Codes   See Machine Programs.

Machine Language   The instruction set of a CPU denoted in the form of 0s and 1s.

Machine Programs   The programs written in a CPU's machine language.

Macro   A feature of the preprocessor for C/CH languages that allows the definition of a word/token to be an arbitrary sequence of characters and the substitution of subsequent occurrences of the token by the string. The word/token is called a macro and the #define directive is used to define it.

Make Rules   The rules that are used by the LINUX make utility to compile and link multiple modules of a software product.

Makefile   A file consisting of make rules.

Marking Language   A language used to specify the general appearance of a document, usually to be displayed as a Web page. The most famous marking language is Hypertext Markup Language (HTML).

Method Invocation   Initiating the execution of a method of a class.

Method   A member function of a class.

Mode Control Word   See Symbolic Mode.

Module   A directory hierarchy of source code is called a module in CVS jargon. A file is also known as a module, such as a source module or a binary module.

Mount The LINUX and UNIX operating systems allow you to "connect" your hard drives, floppy drives, and partitions on drives to the file system structure. This is known as mounting the drives (or partitions). The directories where the drives are mounted are known as mount points. This allows you to access these drives as directories in the file system structure and not as A:, B:, C:, etc., as you have to do in some of the other operating systems.

Named Pipe Also known as a FIFO, a named pipe is a communication channel that can be used by unrelated LINUX processes on the same computer to communicate with each other. The LINUX system call mkfifo (mknod in older systems) is used to create a named pipe.

NIS Database A centralized repository of various pieces of systemwide information in a network environment.

Object An instantiation of a class.

Object-Oriented Programming Languages Object-oriented programming languages provide support for abstract data type in terms of classes. See Abstract Data Types.

Object-Oriented Programming Paradigm In the object-oriented programming paradigm, the focus is on objects that contain data and operations (i.e., methods) associated with the data packaged together.

Ordinary Files Files including text, graphics, executable, video, music, and postscript files.

Object Code A program generated by the assembler program. It is in the machine language of the CPU in the computer but is not executable.

Open Software System Software whose source code is freely available to the community of users so they can modify it as they wish. An example of such a system is the LINUX operating system.

Operating System Software that manages the resources in a computer system and provides an interface for users to use application software.

Pathname The specification of the location of a file (or a directory) in a system with a hierarchical file system.

Pipe An interprocess communication channel in LINUX/UNIX that allows two related processes (i.e., process with parent-child, grandparent-grandchild, or sibling relationship) on the same computers to communicate with each other. At the command line, the "|" operator can be used to make two commands communicate with each other, as in ls –l | less.

Pipeline A sequence of commands interconnected via a number of pipes.

Present Working Directory The directory you are in at a given time while using a computer system, also known as your current directory. In LINUX, the pwd command can be used to display the absolute pathname of your current directory.

Print Job A print request for a printer.

Print Queue A queue associated with every printer where incoming print requests are lined up if the printer is busy printing. It then sends each request one by one as the printer becomes available.

Printer Daemon See Printer Spooler.

Printer Spooler A system process running in the background that receives print requests and sends them to the appropriate printer for printing. If the printer is busy, its request is put in the printer's print queue.

Procedural Programming Paradigm In the procedural programming paradigm, data are passed to subprograms (functions or procedures) that process data to produce the desired results. Some of the popular programming languages that are designed around this paradigm are C, FORTRAN, BASIC, and Perl. C++ also supports the procedural programming paradigm.

Process An executing program.

Process Address Space The main memory space allocated to a process for its execution. When a process tries to access any location outside its address space, the operating system takes over the control, terminates the process, and displays an error message that informs the user of the problem.

Process Identifier (PID) An integer number assigned to a process when the process is created.

Processor Scheduler A piece of code in an operating system that implements a CPU scheduling algorithm.

Program Generation Phase A phase of a software life cycle used to create the source code and generate the executable code for the source code.

Program Generation Tools Software tools and utilities that can be used by application programmers to generate program and executable files. Examples of such tools are editors, compilers, and the make utility.

Redirection See I/O Redirection.

Redirection Operator An operator used in a LINUX shell for attaching standard input, standard output, and standard error of a process to a desired file. (See Standard Files.)

Regular Expression A set of rules that can be used to specify one or more items in a single character string (sequence of characters). Many LINUX tools such as awk, egrep, fgrep, grep, sed, and vi support regular expressions.

RCS See Revision Control System.

Revision Control System A LINUX tool for revision control.

Root The login name of the superuser in a LINUX system.

Root Directory The directory under which all files and directories hang in a computer system with a hierarchical file system. Thus, it is the granddaddy of all the files and directories.

Sandbox The "working directory" while using the CVS system. This directory contains the files that you check out.

Script A sequence of commands to be interpreted by an interpreter.

Scripting Languages The scripting languages allow you to place a list of commands, known as a script, in a file. The language interpreter executes the command in the script, one by one. Some of the popular scripting languages are awk, tcl, tk, bash, Perl, and Javascript.

Search Path A list of directories that your shell searches to find the location of the executable file (binary or shell script) to be executed when you type an external command at the shell prompt and hit the **<Enter>** key.

Session The execution of a shell process.

Session Leader The login shell process.

Set-Group-ID (SGID) Bit A special file protection bit that, when set for an executable file, allows you to execute the file on the behalf of the file's group. Thus you execute the file with group privileges.

Set-User-ID (SUID) Bit A special file protection bit that, when set for an executable file, allows you to execute the file on the behalf of the file's owner. Thus you execute the file with the owner's privileges.

Shell A computer program that starts execution when the computer system is turned on, or the user logs on. Its purpose is to capture user commands and execute them.

Shell Environment Variables Shell variables used to customize the environment in which your shell runs and for proper execution of shell commands.

Shell Metacharacters Most of the characters other than letters and digits have special meaning to a shell, and are known as shell metacharacters. They are treated specially and therefore cannot be used in shell commands as literal characters without specifying them in a particular way.

Shell Prompt A character or character string displayed by a shell process to inform you that it is ready to accept your command. The default shell prompt for Bash is $ and for TC shell is %. You can change the prompt for your shell to any character or character string.

Shell Script A program consisting of shell commands.

Shell Variable A memory location that is given a name, which can then be used to read or write the memory location.

Signal See Software Interrupt.

Single Stepping A feature in symbolic debuggers that allows you to stop program execution after every instruction execution. The next instruction is executed by using a command. This is sometimes called tracing program execution.

Software Cost Models Empirical formulae that allow you to use direct metrics and estimate the cost of a software system in terms of its duration and effort.

Software Interrupt An interrupt (event) sent to a process is known as a software interrupt, also known as a signal in LINUX/UNIX jargon.

Software Life Cycle A sequence of phases that are to be followed to develop a software product. Some popular software life cycles are the waterfall model and the spiral model.

Software Metrics Software metrics are usually meant to determine software product properties such as the number of lines of code (LOC), size in bytes of the executable, software structure, time taken for testing, total number of defects found in the product, number of defects found per hour, the number of function points (FPs) or object points (OPs) for your software, and the running time of the program. Some of the metrics can be measured directly (direct metrics) and some are derived (indirect metrics). See Direct Metrics and Indirect Metrics.

Software Profiling Determining certain parameters of your program when it executes. These parameters include the most time-consuming segment of the program, the execution frequency of each line (or function), and the function call graph. (See Function Call Graph.) The purpose of software profiling is to identify the segments in a program where the program spends most of its time when it executes. Such information allows you to enhance the perfor-

mance of your program by optimizing the code that executes frequently.

Source Repository The directory that contains the source code for a project that you want to manage by using a revision control software such as CVS.

Special Targets Predefined targets in the make utility that are treated by it in a special way. For example, the special target .PHONY allows you to specify a target that is not a file. This target allows you to instruct **make** to invoke a sequence of commands from the makefile even if a file with the name of the target file exists in your build directory.

Special/Device File A special file represents a device such as a keyboard. These files are divided into two types: character special files and block special files. See Character Special Files and Block Special Files.

Spiral Model A software engineering life cycle typically used for an organization's internal, large projects.

Stack Frame When a function call is made, many items such as actual parameters, local variables, and return address, are pushed on the stack for proper execution of the function and return from it. These items comprise the stack frame (also known as activation record) for the function call.

Standard Dependency The capability of the make utility to recognize that the name of an object file is usually the name of the source file.

Standard Error See Standard Files.

Standard Files The files where the input of a process comes from, and where its output and error messages go to. The standard file where a process reads its input is called standard input. The process output goes to standard output, and the error messages generated by a process go to standard error. By default, the standard input comes from your keyboard, and standard output and standard error are sent to the display screen.

Standard Input   See Standard Files
Standard Output   See Standard Files
Static Analysis   The static analysis of software involves analyzing its structure and properties without executing it.
Static Analysis Phase   The phase of a software life cycle model under which static analysis is carried out.
Sticky Bit   When an executable file with sticky bit is executed, the LINUX kernel keeps it in the memory for as long as it can so that the time taken to load it from the disk can be saved when the file is executed the next time. When such a file has to be taken out of the main memory, it is saved on the swap space, thus resulting in less time to load it into memory again.
Suffix Rules   The predefined make rules that allow the make utility to perform many tasks automatically. See Standard Dependency.
Superuser   There is a special user in every LINUX system that can access any file or directory on the system. This user is the system administrator, commonly known as the superuser on the system.
Sure Kill   Sending signal number 9 to a process is known as the sure kill as this signal cannot be intercepted by the process, and therefore the process is definitively terminated.
Swap Space   An area set aside on the disk at system boot up where processes can be saved temporarily in order to be reloaded into the memory at a later time. The activity of saving processes on the swap space is called swap out, and of bringing them back into the main memory is known as swap in. The time taken to load a process from the swap space into main memory is less than the time taken to load a file from the disk when it is stored in the normal fashion.
Swapper Process   A process that swaps in a process from the swap space into the main memory, or swaps out a process from the main memory to the swap space. See Swap Space.
Symbolic Debugger   A software tool such as GNU gdb that allows you to debug your program by performing tasks such as setting break points, single stepping, listing source code, editing source code, accessing and modifying program variables, and tracing program execution.
Symbolic Link   When a symbolic link to a shared file is created in a directory, a link file is created that contains a pathname of the shared file. The link therefore "points to" the shared file. The ln -s command is used to create a symbolic link.
Symbolic Mode   Used with the `chmod` command, it allows specifications of file privileges by using letters such as u (for user) and w (for write privilege), as in `chmod ug+x lab3.c` for adding the execute permission to the lab3.c file for the owner of the file and the users in owner's group.

Tar   A LINUX/UNIX utility that allows you to pack (archive) and unpack directory hierarchies. It was originally designed to create tape backups of file systems but is also used now for distributing software packs and for copying directory hierarchies and for creating their disk backups.
Testing   A phase in a software engineering life cycle in which you work with a "working" program and run it against a set of input data (expected and unexpected) to ensure that it produces expected output. The goal of testing is to fail the software.
Time-Sharing System   A multi-user, multi-process, and interactive operating system. UNIX and LINUX are prime examples of the time-sharing system.

User-Defined Macros   Macros defined by a user or programmer.

Waterfall Model   A popular software engineering life cycle that involves the following phases: requirements, specifications, planning, designing, coding and integration, testing, installation, and maintenance.
Web Browser   An Internet application that allows you to surf the Web by allowing users to, among other things, view Web pages.

White Box Testing A testing technique whose goal is to identify interface faults by testing the software against well-thought-out test inputs, which are drawn up based on the structure of the code. Testers choose input data to invoke as many program statements in the software as possible.

X Window System A graphical intermediary between the user and the LINUX operating system. It was developed at MIT in 1983 as part of the Athena Project and is the defacto LINUX GUI.

Xterm An X application that allows you to pull up a window that provides you with a command-line interface of the LINUX/UNIX system.

Zombie A dying LINUX process is known as a zombie process. A process that exits, becomes a zombie process and it remains this state until its status is communicated to its parent so that it can be gracefuly. Zombie processes whose parents terminate before them, are owned by the graddady "init" processSuch processes have finished their work but still have some system resources allocated to them, thus resulting is wastage of system resources.

Index